THE
VICTORIAN
HOUSE
CATALOGUE

FOREWORD BY
PETER HOWELL
CHAIRMAN OF
THE VICTORIAN SOCIETY

 Sterling Publishing Co., Inc.   New York

Sidgwick & Jackson gratefully acknowledge Charles Brooking, owner of The Brooking Collection, who introduced Young & Marten's Catalogue to them and recommended that it should be published.

Library of Congress Cataloging-in-Publication Data

The Victorian house catalogue / Young & Marten ; edited by
  Anne Smith ; foreword by Peter Howell.
       p.   cm.
  ISBN 0-8069-8614-X
  1. Building fittings—Catalogs. 2. Architecture,
Victorian—Catalogs. 3. Young & Marten (Firm)—
Catalogs. I. Smith Anne. II. Young & Marten.
TH2055.V53   1992
690′.29′442—dc20   91–39270
                                            CIP

10 9 8 7 6 5 4 3 2

First published in the United States in 1992
by Sterling Publishing Company, Inc.
387 Park Avenue South, New York, N.Y. 10016
Originally published in Great Britain and
© 1990 by Sidgwick & Jackson Limited
1 Tavistock Chambers, Bloomsbury Way, London WC1A 2SG
Distributed in Canada by Sterling Publishing
% Canadian Manda Group, P.O. Box 920, Station U
Toronto, Ontario, Canada M8Z 5P9
Manufactured in the United States of America
All rights reserved

Sterling ISBN 0-8069-8614-X

CONTENTS

FOREWORD

EVERYONE WILL ENJOY LOOKING AT THIS BOOK, WHETHER FOR THE SHEER VISUAL PLEASURE OF MARBLED ROMAN-SHAPE BATHS AND FLORAL W. C. PEDESTALS, OR FOR THE FASCINATING INSIGHTS IT PROVIDES INTO VANISHED WAYS OF LIFE. BUT IT WILL ALSO HAVE PRACTICAL USES. MANY OF US LIVE IN VICTORIAN HOUSES, AND DELIGHT IN THEIR ELABORATE DECORATIVE DETAIL. FORTUNATELY THE DAYS ARE PAST WHEN ORNAMENT WAS THOUGHT TO BE A CRIME, AND IT WAS FASHIONABLE TO STRIP AWAY AS MUCH AS POSSIBLE. THE WHEEL HAS TURNED FULL CIRCLE, AND NOT ONLY IS SURVIVING DETAIL TREASURED AND RESTORED WITH LOVING CARE, BUT THERE IS A WIDESPREAD DESIRE TO REPLACE WHAT IS MISSING.

FOR THOSE IN THIS POSITION, THIS PUBLICATION OF A SELECTION FROM YOUNG AND MARTEN'S CATALOGUES WILL BE AN IMMENSELY USEFUL SOURCE-BOOK. THEIR ONE GREAT FRUSTRATION WILL BE THAT IT IS NO LONGER POSSIBLE SIMPLY TO ORDER THE GOODS ADVERTISED. HOWEVER, IF A DEMAND IS STIMULATED WHICH PROMPTS MANUFACTURERS TO SUPPLY IT, SO MUCH THE BETTER. ONE EXAMPLE OF HOW THIS IS ALREADY HAPPENING IS PROVIDED BY THE FACT THAT THE TERRACOTTA MANUFACTURERS ARE BEGINNING TO TURN OUT ORNAMENTAL DETAILS ONCE AGAIN.

IT IS TO BE HOPED THAT THOSE RESTORING VICTORIAN HOUSES WILL RESPECT THE SOCIAL HIERARCHY. A BASTARD STATUARY CHIMNEYPIECE THAT COST 225/– WOULD CLEARLY BE OUT OF PLACE IN A HOUSE WHICH COULD ONLY HAVE RUN TO ENAMELLED SLATE AT 30/9. THOSE LIVING IN MR POOTER'S MODEST HOME SHOULD NOT ASPIRE TO THE GREATER LUXURY OF THE HOUSES DECORATED BY ROBERT TRESSELL'S 'RAGGED TROUSERED PHILANTHROPISTS'. THE VERY FACT THAT THESE HIERARCHIES ARE DEMONSTRATED IN SUCH MANIFEST WAYS IS ONE OF THE MANY FASCINATIONS OF THIS BOOK.

PETER HOWELL
CHAIRMAN OF THE VICTORIAN SOCIETY

YOUNG & MARTEN

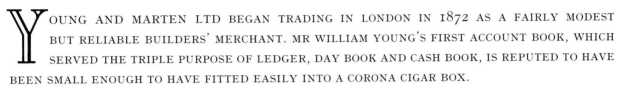

Young and Marten Ltd began trading in London in 1872 as a fairly modest but reliable builders' merchant. Mr William Young's first account book, which served the triple purpose of ledger, day book and cash book, is reputed to have been small enough to have fitted easily into a Corona cigar box.

Yet, some twenty years later, it would apparently have taken a whole day to inspect the showroom and warehouses 'even in the most cursory manner'. The main warehouses in Stratford, East London, then occupied a lineal floor space of about half a mile, while the company's unloading dock and shunting spur were reckoned to have capacity for forty full-sized goods wagons. By the 1890s, Young and Marten also had branches in Walthamstow, Leytonstone, Southend-on-Sea and Brentford and was well known throughout Britain, Europe and the outer reaches of the colonies.

Its phenomenal success was largely due to the intense building activity and to technical advances which took place during the Victorian era. The confident dignity of the Latin tag 'Supremus' (highest, uppermost), which was later adopted by the firm as its motto, was an underlying characteristic at all times.

In 1883 William Young died prematurely at the age of forty-two. Three years earlier, he had set up a fruitful partnership with Mr Harry Holdich Marten, a far-sighted man who had hitherto traded as a lead merchant. Mr Marten brought a new strength of purpose to this thriving enterprise and was initially responsible for much of the expansion which was to follow.

Another significant guiding spirit appears to have been Mr E. Montague Edwards, who joined Mr Young as an inexperienced assistant when he first opened for business. In 1880, he was elevated to the post of general manager and he remained with Young and Marten until his death nearly sixty years later. An employee paid tribute to him during the company's sixtieth anniversary celebrations: 'Throughout all the long history of the concern, the business skill, the genius and the initiative and resource of Mr E. Montague Edwards have been outstanding contributories to success.' Mr Edwards was an energetic and single minded man with an abundance of self-esteem, but he also had a talent for commanding respect and loyalty from employees at all levels. Even after he became managing director in 1899, he liked to be regarded as a father figure, and as a local J.P., he became well versed in handling people. He also understood the importance of material rewards in coaxing the best performance out of the work force – hence the introduction of a universal prosperity-sharing scheme.

MANY CURRENT OWNERS OF VICTORIAN AND EDWARDIAN HOMES, WHETHER HUMBLE TERRACES OR GRANDER DETACHED VILLAS, STILL RETAIN YOUNG AND MARTEN PRODUCTS TO THIS DAY. IT IS PROOF OF THEIR ENDURING QUALITY AND OF THE MARKETING SKILLS OF MR EDWARDS, WHO RECOGNISED THE BENEFITS OF PUBLISHING A COMPREHENSIVE CATALOGUE WITH DETAILED DRAWINGS. THE CATALOGUE MADE ITS DEBUT IN 1895 WITH 846 PAGES, PRINTED IN TWO VOLUMES, FOLLOWING A CHANCE MEETING WITH MR J. T. EMERY, WHO WAS THEN RATHER DESPERATE TO FIND WORK AS AN ASSISTANT WITH YOUNG AND MARTEN. MR EMERY HAD RECENTLY BEEN MADE REDUNDANT AFTER THE CLOSURE OF A LONG-ESTABLISHED LONDON IRONMONGERS. ATTEMPTING TO IMPRESS HIS CREDENTIALS ON MR EDWARDS, HE SHOWED HIM AN EXTENSIVE CATALOGUE WHICH HE HAD COMPILED FOR HIS PREVIOUS EMPLOYERS. MR EDWARDS SPOTTED A GOOD OPPORTUNITY TO GET AHEAD OF HIS RIVALS; THUS THE CATALOGUE WAS BORN AND MR EMERY WAS GIVEN A JOB.

BY THIS TIME, THE COMPANY WAS ABOUT THREE HUNDRED TIMES LARGER THAN MR YOUNG'S ORIGINAL BUSINESS. IT OFFERED EVERY CONCEIVABLE ITEM FOR PRIVATE HOMES, SHOPS, OFFICES, SCHOOLS AND OTHER PUBLIC BUILDINGS – FROM FINE TESSELATED PAVEMENTS TO GULLIES, TACKS AND TOMBSTONE RAILS. EACH CATALOGUE BORE THE PROUD BOAST 'STERLING QUALITY, NOMINAL PRICES AND PROMPT DELIVERY'. 'MODERN DESIGN' WAS LATER ADDED TO THIS LIST OF CLAIMS. THESE MERITS, KNOWN AS THE COMPANY'S 'TRADE ENSIGN', AND THE BENEFITS OF A HUGE STOCK WERE IMPRESSED UPON POTENTIAL CUSTOMERS. 'THERE WAS A TIME WHEN THE RANGE OF DESIGNS IN ALL CLASSES OF BUILDING MATERIALS WAS VERY LIMITED AND VOID OF AN ORNATE CHARACTER, BUT TODAY, WITH THE PREDOMINANCE OF MORE ARTISTIC TASTES AND A MUCH INCREASED DEMAND, THE PATTERNS, SIZES AND FINISHES OF SUCH GOODS HAVE BEEN SO MULTIPLIED THAT IT IS PRACTICALLY IMPOSSIBLE FOR ANY CUSTOMER TO STOCK IN SUFFICIENT QUANTITIES EVEN ITEMS WHICH HAVE NOW BECOME EVERYDAY NECESSITIES IN HIS BUSINESS ROUTINE.'

THE SHOWROOMS WERE OPEN FROM 8 A.M. UNTIL 7 P.M. EACH WEEKDAY, AND CUSTOMERS FLOCKED FROM ALL OVER THE UNITED KINGDOM AND ABROAD. ALL WERE GIVEN THE CHOICE OF BEING MET BY A YOUNG AND MARTEN REPRESENTATIVE 'AT ANY LONDON TERMINUS, FREE OF CHARGE' IN ORDER TO BE CONVEYED TO THE SHOWROOMS. BY 1914, WITH TYPICAL UP-TO-THE-MINUTE EFFICIENCY, THE COMPANY OFFERED ITS OWN PRIVATE MOTOR CAR TO MEET ITS LONG-DISTANCE CLIENTS. THERE WAS A FREE, AND OFTEN DAILY, DELIVERY SERVICE WITHIN THE LONDON AREA BY THE COMPANY'S VAST FLEET OF VANS. REGULAR SHIPMENTS WERE ALSO MADE TO THE CONTINENT AND TO 'IMPORTANT COMMERCIAL CENTRES OF THE COLONIES', INCLUDING PARTS OF WEST AFRICA AND GIBRALTAR. SUCH WAS THE HUGE SUCCESS OF THE CATALOGUE THAT OTHER FIRMS TRIED TO MATCH IT. THE COMPILER REGISTERS A MILD PROTEST: 'WE ARE OBLIGED BY THE COMPLIMENT PAID US BY COMPETING HOUSES IN COPYING OUR PREVIOUS ISSUE OF CATALOGUES. WE, HOWEVER, TRUST THAT FOR THE FUTURE THEY MAY STRICTLY ADHERE TO THE LINES OF THEIR OWN ORIGINALITY.'

ADDITIONAL FINANCIAL BACKING CAME FROM MR JAMES CLARK DURING THE LATTER PART OF THE VICTORIAN PERIOD. HE JOINED THE COMPANY IN 1885 AS A 'SLEEPING PARTNER' AND WAS SUCCEEDED ON HIS DEATH, IN 1913, BY HIS TWO SONS AND EVENTUALLY A GRANDSON.

MR EDWARDS PROSPERED WITH THE COMPANY, CELEBRATING THE JUBILEE OF HIS SERVICE IN 1922 WITH A SPECIAL STAFF GATHERING. TOGETHER, THEY ALL LISTENED TO SPEECHES AND MUSICAL INTERLUDES PLAYED BY THE FIRM'S OWN 'SUPREMUS' ORCHESTRA, BEGINNING WITH NOWOWIESKI'S 'UNDER FREEDOM'S FLAG'.

HARRY MARTEN HAD DIED IN MARSEILLES DURING THE PREVIOUS YEAR. HIS GREAT GRAND-SON, MR DAVID HESKETH, CONTINUES THE FAMILY TRADITION AND IS NOW MANAGING DIRECTOR OF YOUNG AND MARTEN. IT IS VERY MUCH A TRIBUTE TO THE EARLY ENTREPRENEURIAL SPIRIT OF THE COMPANY THAT IT SURVIVES TODAY. THIS RE-ISSUED CATALOGUE IS PART OF ITS HISTORY AND A SOURCE OF KNOWLEDGE AND PLEASURE. IT HAS 'EVERY REQUISITE A BUILDER, DECORATOR, GASFITTER, PLUMBER AND, INDEED, ANY INDIVIDUAL INTERESTED IN EITHER OF THE MULTI-FARIOUS SECTIONS OF THE BUILDING TRADE COULD POSSIBLY REQUIRE'.

PLAN

SHOWING THE RAPID RISE AND PROGRESS

OF

YOUNG & MARTEN'S BUSINESS

— EXPLANATION —

THIS Diagram shows the relative superficial area of floor space of our Warehouses and Showrooms from 1872 to 1897 inclusive, with the additions which have been made year by year. The figures given indicate the aggregate total at the dates named. The initial portion, acquired in 1872, shown by the diminutive column on left hand, represents one floor, 80×14 feet $= 1120$ superficial square feet, yet sufficiently capacious for the purpose at the time. This is still in our occupation, but with the enormous additions represented by the series of progressive columns, till to-day our Premises occupy an area of

OVER 200 TIMES

that with which the business was commenced.

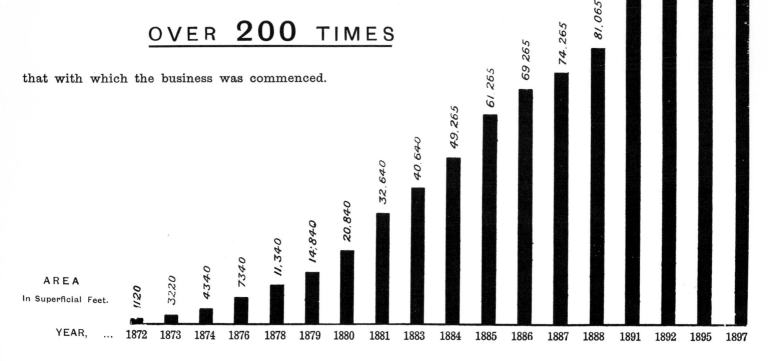

AREA
In Superficial Feet.

YEAR, ...	1872	1873	1874	1876	1878	1879	1880	1881	1883	1884	1885	1886	1887	1888	1891	1892	1895	1897
	1120	3220	4340	7340	11,340	14,840	20,840	32,640	40,640	49,265	61,265	69,265	74,265	81,065	111,465	131,715	206,060	266,193

STRATFORD, E., WALTHAMSTOW, N.E., AND LEYTONSTONE, E., LONDON

HEAD ESTABLISHMENT

IN THE BROADWAY

STRATFORD, LONDON, E.

In it are located SHOWROOMS in conjunction with

1. PAPERHANGINGS DEPARTMENT
2. GASFITTINGS DEPARTMENT
3. BUILDERS' IRONMONGERY DEPARTMENT
4. KITCHEN RANGE, STOVES, AND CHIMNEY-PIECE DEPARTMENT
5. BUILDERS' CASTINGS, HEATING APPARATUS, AND STABLE FITTINGS DEPARTMENT
6. GENERAL MANAGER'S AND CORRESPONDENCE DEPARTMENT
7. FORWARDING DEPARTMENT
8. COUNTING HOUSE DEPARTMENT

NEW PREMISES, SHOWROOMS, AND WAREHOUSES

— AT THE —

JUNCTION OF ROMFORD ROAD AND THE GROVE, STRATFORD

And quite close to the Head Establishment described on preceding page.

In this Building are located the SHOWROOMS and STORES, in conjunction with—

1. PLUMBERS' GOODS AND SANITARY ENGINEERS' APPLIANCE DEPARTMENT
2. METALS (LEAD AND ZINC) DEPARTMENT
3. WHITE LEAD, OILS, COLORS, AND VARNISHES DEPARTMENT
4. ARTISTS' MATERIAL DEPARTMENT

And near to the foregoing are—

5. JOINERY AND TIMBER DEPARTMENT
6. PLATE AND SHEET WINDOW GLASS DEPARTMENT
7. LEADED CATHEDRAL LIGHT AND STAINED GLASS MANUFACTORY

At Wharf Road, Burford Road, Stratford Market, on the Channelsea River, in direct communication with the Thames, is situated

OUR WHARF

As shown by the following Drawing.

At this Department orders are executed for

LIME, CEMENT, PLASTER. SLATES, ROOFING AND PAVING TILES, DRAIN PIPES,
LATHS, FELT, SINKS, CHIMNEY POTS, AND BLUE BRICKS

FULL TRUCK LOADS, BY ARRANGEMENT, SENT CARRIAGE PAID TO ANY STATION

The phenomenal increase in our business necessitated the erection of WAREHOUSES, with Railway Siding, at which to keep a much increased stock, against demand to file large and urgent orders; and although already the largest in the trade, and have been in operation only one year, **OUR STORES** have been found quite inadequate in area for the purpose designed. We have found it necessary to increase these by four times their original stocking capacity.

THE ABOVE DRAWING SHOWS—

1.—Railway Siding, 600 feet long, capable of accommodating 40 goods trucks at one time, and with the addition of the shunting space 55 goods trucks can be provided for.

2.—Warehouses and Stores, three floors, each 430 feet long × 60 feet wide, with railway loading bank whole length.

3.—Joinery and Wood-working Mill, 70 × 40 feet.

4.—Loading Banks and Lay-by for Vans, 196 × 28 feet. Stables, 196 × 28 feet. Chaff Cutting and Forage Store, 196 × 28 feet, on south side.

Sanitary Goods Showroom.   From a photograph.

Export Glass-cutting Floor.   From a photograph.

Wharf Department, Stratford Market. From a photograph.

Interior of Store, 220 × 40 feet. From a photograph.

YOUNG & MARTEN, Ltd., Merchants and Manufacturers,

WOOD BALUSTERS AND NEWELS.

For Square Turned Newels and Balusters, see pages 386 and 387.

——— WOOD BALUSTERS. ———

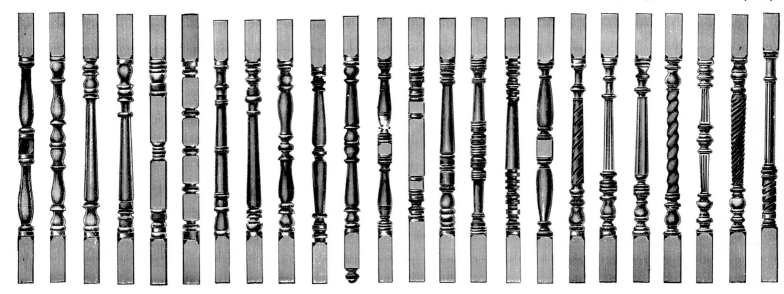

WB30 WB32 WB33 WB34 WB35 WB36 WB37 WB40 WB41 WB42 WB43 WB44 WB45 WB46 WB47 WB48 WB49 WB53 WB54 WB55 WB61 WB62 WB67 WB70

3 feet long. *For Prices see next page.*

——— WOOD NEWELS. ———

WN21 WN22 WN23 WN24 WN25 WN26 WN27 WN28 WN29 WN30 WN31 WN33 WN36 WN40 WN41

4 feet 6 inches long. *For Prices see next page.*

ESTIMATES GIVEN FOR SQUARE OR SPECIAL TURNING, CARVING, &c., OF ALL DESCRIPTIONS.

STRATFORD, Walthamstow, Leytonstone, Millwall, & Brentford.

SQUARE-TURNED WOOD NEWELS.

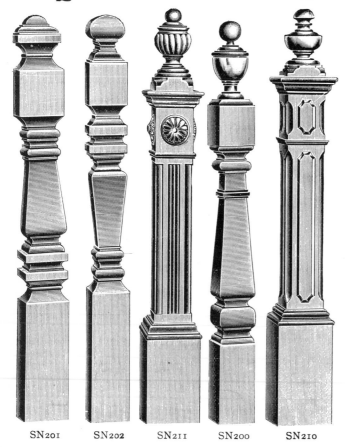

SN201   SN202   SN211   SN200   SN210

N E W E L S.

4 ft. 6 ins. long.

Pattern No.	Size.			Price, each.				
				Deal.	P. Pine.	Mahogany.	Oak.	Walnut.
	4 ins. × 4 ins.			10/6	12/-	13/9	15/-	17/-
SN200 Round Top.	4½ ,, × 4½ ,,			—	14/6	17/6	18/9	21/3
	5 ,, × 5 ,,			—	17/-	20/-	21/3	23/9
	6 ,, × 6 ,,			—	22/6	27/6	31/3	33/9
	4 ,, × 4 ,,			13/-	15/6	18/-	19/6	20/6
SN201 or SN202	4½ ,, × 4½ ,,			—	18/-	21/3	23/9	25/-
	5 ,, × 5 ,,			—	20/6	26/3	28/9	30/-
	6 ,, × 6 ,,			—	30/-	35/-	37/6	40/-

SN212   SN209   SN214   SN204   SN213

SQUARE BUILT-UP NEWELS.

Solid Centre.   4 ft. 6 ins. long.

Pattern No.	Size.		Price, each.			
			P. Pine.	Oak or Mahogany.	Walnut.	French Polishing extra.
SN204	5 ins. × 5 ins.		38/9	42/6	45/-	6/3
	6 ,, × 6 ,,		50/-	55/-	60/-	8/9
SN209	8 ,, × 8 ,,		31/3	41/3	43/9	6/3
	10 ,, × 10 ,,		52/6	67/6	72/6	11/3
SN210	7 ,, × 7 ,,		40/-	47/6	50/-	6/3
	8 ,, × 8 ,,		42/6	52/6	55/-	7/6
	10 ,, × 10 ,,		80/-	90/-	92/6	12/6
SN211 and SN212	7 ,, × 7 ,,		52/6	60/-	62/6	7/6
	8 ,, × 8 ,,		60/-	67/6	70/-	10/-
	10 ,, × 10 ,,		92/6	100/-	102/6	12/6
SN213	7 ,, × 7 ,,		57/6	63/9	67/6	7/6
	8 ,, × 8 ,,		65/-	72/6	75/-	10/-
	10 ,, × 10 ,,		150/-	157/6	160/-	15/-
SN214	7 ,, × 7 ,,		72/6	77/6	80/-	10/6

Estimates given for Square or Special Turning, Carving, &c., of all Descriptions.

STRATFORD, Walthamstow, Leytonstone, Millwall, & Brentford.

YOUNG & MARTEN, Ltd., Merchants and Manufacturers,

No. B1575.
Zinc, 10¾ in. square, 2/6 ea.
No. B1576.
Paper, 10¾ in. square, 1/3 ea.

No. B1577.
Zinc, 10¼ in. square, 2/6 ea.
No. B1578.
Paper, 10¼ in. square 1/3 ea.

No. B1579.
Zinc, 1/- ea.
No. B1580.
Paper, 6d. ea.
Size 11 × 2¾ in.

No. B1581.
Zinc, 1/- ea
No. B1582.
Paper, 6d. ea.
Size 8 × 4¼ in.

No. B1583.
Zinc, 1/- ea.
No. B1585.
Paper, 6d. ea.
Size 10½ × 5¼ in.

No. B1586.
Zinc, 8¼ in. square, 1/6 ea.
No. B1587.
Paper, 8¼ in. square, 9d. ea.

No. B1588.
Zinc, 10¾ in. square, 2/6 ea.
No. B1589.
Paper, 10¾ in. square, 1/3 ea.

No. B1650.
Zinc, 8 × 5¾ in., 1/- ea.
No. B1651.
Paper, 8 × 5¾ in. 6d. ea.

No. B1652.
Zinc, 1/- ea.
No. B1653.
Paper, 6d. ea.
Size 16 × 3½ in.

No. B1654
Zinc, 17½ × 5¾ in., 2 ea.
No. B1655.
Paper, 17½ × 5¾ in., 1/- ea.

No. B1706.   Zinc, 16 × 16 in., 4/- ea.
No. B1707.   Paper   „   2/- ea.

No. B1708.
Zinc, 17¾ × 8¼ in., 4/- ea.
No. B1709.
Paper, 17¾ × 8¼ in., 2/- ea.

No. B1712.
Zinc, 9d. ea.
No. B1713.
Paper, 5d. ea.
Size 6½ × 5¼ in.

No. B1710.
Zinc, 1/- ea.
No. B1711.
Paper, 6d. ea.
Size 13 × 2½ in.

No. B1716.
Zinc, 11½ in. square, 2/6 ea.
No. B1717.
Paper, 11½ in. square, 1/3 ea.

No. B1714.
Zinc, 10 in. square, 2/6 ea.
No B1715.
Paper, 10 in. square, 1/3 ea.

No. B1724.   Zinc, 9½ × 20 in., 3/6 ea.
No. B1725.   Paper   „   „   1/9 ea.

No. B1722.   Zinc, 18¼ in. square, 6/6 ea.
No. B1723.   Paper   „   „   3/3 ea.

No. B1720.   Zinc, 12 × 24 in., 3/6 ea.
No. B1721.   Paper   „   „   1/9 ea.

No. B1718.   Zinc, 19½ in. square, 6/6 ea.
No. B1719.   Paper   „   „   3/3 ea.

ABOVE SELECTION OF STENCILS ARE FROM A GREAT VARIETY OF EVERY DESCRIPTION ALWAYS IN STOCK.
Architects' Sketches, Panels, Borders, Friezes, Signs, Trade Marks, etc., cut to order in one day in Paper, Zinc, or Copper.
For orders of 3 dozen assorted Stencils an allowance of 25 per cent. is made.   When ordering please quote Number.

STRATFORD, Walthamstow, Leytonstone, Millwall, & Brentford.

YOUNG & MARTEN, Ltd., Merchants and Manufacturers,

DECORATORS' STENCILS.

No. B333. Zinc, 2½ in., 1/6 each.
Nc. B335. Paper, ,, 9d. ,,

No. B345. Zinc, 3 in., 1/6 each.
No. B353 Paper, ,, 9d. ,,

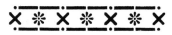

No. B325. Zinc, 2 in., 1/3 each.
No. B326. Paper, ,, 7½d. ,,

No. B329. Zinc, 2¼ in., 1/3 each.
No. B330. Paper, ,, 7½d. ,,

No. B843. Zinc, 3 in., 1/6 each.
No. B844. Paper, ,, 9d. ,,

No. B336. Zinc, 2½ in., 1/3 each.
No. B337. Paper, ,, 7½d. ,,

No. B338 Zinc, 3 in., 1/6 each.
No. B339. Paper, ,, 9d. ,,

No. B340. Zinc, 2¼ in., 1/3 each.
No. B344. Paper, ,, 7½d. ,,

No. B855. Zinc, 3 in., 1/6 each.
No. B854. Paper, ,, 9d. ,,

No. B354 Zinc, 3 in., 1/6 each.
No. B355. Paper, ,, 9d. .

No. B848. Zinc, 4½ in., 1/6 each.
No. B849. Paper, ,, 9d. ,,

No. B639. Zinc, 3 in., 1/6 each.
No. B842. Paper, ,, 9d. ,,

No. B925. Zinc, 4½ in., 1/6 each.
No. B933. Paper, ,, 9d. ,,

No. B858. Zinc, 4 in., 1/6 each.
No. B859. Paper, ,, 9d. ,,

No. B860. Zinc, 4 in., 1/6 each.
No. B861. Paper, ,, 9d. ,,

No. B862. Zinc, 3½ in., 1/6 each.
No. B924. Paper, ,, 9d. ,,

No. B946. Zinc, 4¼ in., 1/6 each.
No B947. Paper, ,, 9d. ,,

No. B949. Zinc, 4¾ in., 1/3 each.
No B950. Paper, ,, 7½d. ,,

No B951. Zinc, 5 in., 1/6 each.
No. B953. Paper, ,, 9d. ,,

No. B954. Zinc, 4½ in., 1/6 each.
No. B957. Paper, ,, 9d. ,,

No. B958. Zinc, 4½ in., 1/6 each.
No B959. Paper, ,, 9d. ,,

No. B960. Zinc, 4¾ in., 1/6 each.
No. B961. Paper, ,, 9d. ,,

No. B970. Zinc, 4½ in., 1/6 each.
No. B971. Paper, ,, 9d. ,,

No. B964. Zinc, 4½ in., 1/6 each.
No. B965. Paper, ,, 9d. ,,

No. B966. Zinc, 5¼ in., 1/6 each.
No. B967. Paper, ,, 9d. ,,

No. B982. Zinc, 5½ in., 1/6 each.
No. B983. Paper, ,, 9d. ,,

No. B984. Zinc, 4½ in., 1/6 each.
No. B985. Paper, ,, 9d. ,,

No. B972. Zinc, 4½ in., 1/6 each.
No. B978. Paper, ,, 9d. ,,

No. B979. Zinc, 5½ in., 1/6 each.
No. B980. Paper, ,, 9d. ,,

No. B992. Zinc, 5¼ in., 1/6 each.
No. B993. Paper, ,, 9d. ,,

No. B994. Zinc, 5½ in., 1/6 each.
No. B995. Paper, ,, 9d. ,,

No. B987. Zinc, 5¼ in., 1/6 each.
No. B988. Paper, ,, 9d. ,,

No. B1553. Zinc, 7¼ in., 2/6 each.
No. B1554. Paper, ,, 1/3 ,,

No. B989. Zinc, 5¼ in., 1/6 each.
No. B990. Paper, ,, 9d. ,,

No. B1555. Zinc, 6½ in., 2/6 each.
No. B1556. Paper, ,, 1/3 ,,

No. B1557. Zinc, 7¾ in., 2/6 each.
No. B1560. Paper, ,, 1/3 ,,

Above selection of Stencils are from a great variety always in Stock.
ARCHITECTS' SKETCHES, PANELS, BORDERS, FRIEZES, SIGNS, TRADE MARKS, &c., CUT TO ORDER IN ONE DAY, IN PAPER, ZINC, OR COPPER.
For orders of three dozen assorted Stencils, an allowance of 25 per cent. is made.   When ordering, please quote numbers.

STRATFORD, Walthamstow, Leytonstone, Millwall, & Brentford.

YOUNG & MARTEN, Merchants and Manufacturers,

PAPER-STUCCO OVERDOORS AND PANELS.

Paper-Stucco being made of compressed paper by the aid of very powerful machinery, is not only a capital substitute for the ordinary plasterwork and carved woodwork, but is preferred on account of its **lightness, elegant appearance, correct and excellent execution, artistic design,** and saving of time in fixing.—These decorations can be affixed with **common screws or thin wire nails** by any builder, carpenter or painter, and can be decorated with any material.

On account of its extreme lightness it puts no strain on walls or ceilings.

These can be easily cut and altered to suit any size door, window, overmantel, pier glass, etc., etc.

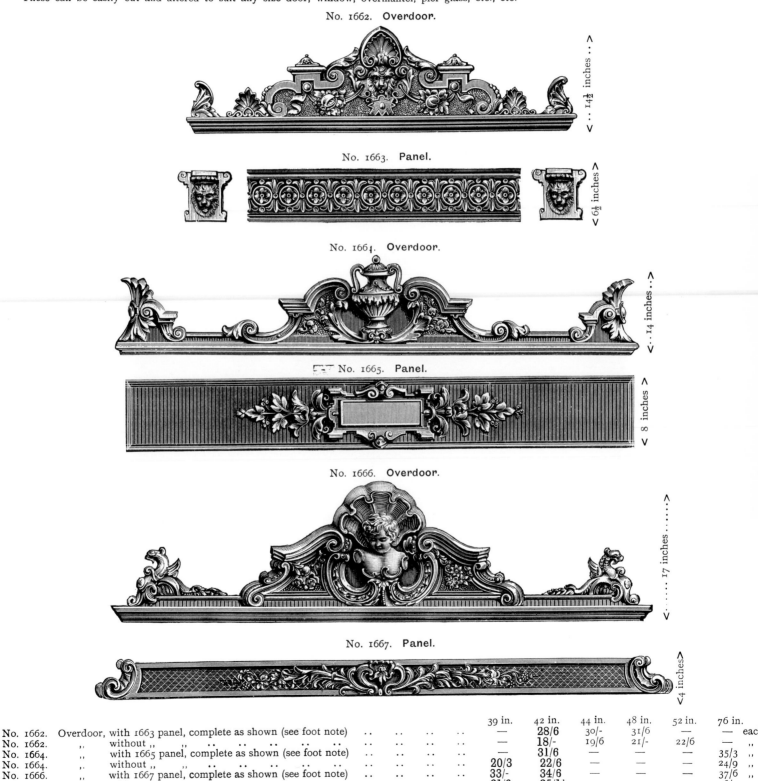

No. 1662. Overdoor.

No. 1663. Panel.

No. 1664. Overdoor.

No. 1665. Panel.

No. 1666. Overdoor.

No. 1667. Panel.

			39 in.	42 in.	44 in.	48 in.	52 in.	76 in.	
No. 1662.	Overdoor, with 1663 panel, complete as shown (see foot note)		—	28/6	30/-	31/6	—	—	each
No. 1662.	,, without ,, ,,		—	18/-	19/6	21/-	22/6	—	,,
No. 1664.	,, with 1665 panel, complete as shown (see foot note)		—	31/6	—	—	—	35/3	,,
No. 1664.	,, without ,, ,,		20/3	22/6	—	—	—	24/9	,,
No. 1666.	,, with 1667 panel, complete as shown (see foot note)		33/-	34/6	—	—	—	37/6	,,
No. 1666.	,, without ,, ,,		21/9	25/1½	—	—	—	26/3	,,

Overdoors from 39 inches to 48 inches wide have no end ornaments.

STRATFORD, Walthamstow and Leytonstone.

YOUNG & MARTEN, Merchants and Manufacturers,

PAPER-STUCCO OVERDOORS, CORNICES, FRIEZES AND MOULDINGS, AND GLAZIERS' DIAMONDS.

These Decorations, which are made in lengths of about 10 feet with wood Bead top and bottom, being very light, put no strain whatever upon ceilings, &c., but rather help to support them and prevent the usual unsightly cracks caused by the use of heavy materials.

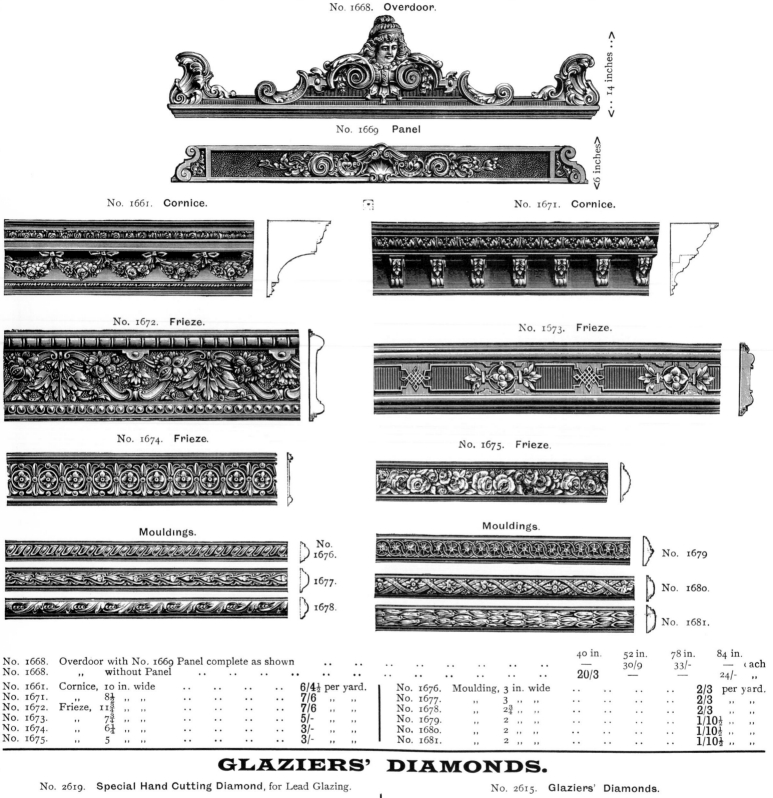

No. 1668. Overdoor.

No. 1669 Panel

No. 1661. Cornice.

No. 1671. Cornice.

No. 1672. Frieze.

No. 1673. Frieze.

No. 1674. Frieze.

No. 1675. Frieze.

Mouldings.

Mouldings.

No. 1676.
1677.
1678.

No. 1679
No. 1680.
No. 1681.

		40 in.	52 in.	78 in.	84 in.	
No. 1668.	Overdoor with No. 1669 Panel complete as shown	—	30/9	33/-	—	each
No. 1668.	,, without Panel	20/3	—	—	24/-	,,

					No. 1676.	Moulding, 3 in. wide				2/3	per yard.
No. 1661.	Cornice, 10 in. wide			6/4½ per yard.	No. 1677.	,, 3 ,, ,,				2/3	,, ,,
No. 1671.	,, 8½ ,, ,,			7/6 ,, ,,	No. 1678.	,, 2¾ ,, ,,				2/3	,, ,,
No. 1672.	Frieze, 11½ ,, ,,			7/6 ,, ,,	No. 1679.	,, 2 ,, ,,				1/10½	,, ,,
No. 1673.	,, 7¼ ,, ,,			5/- ,, ,,	No. 1680.	,, 2 ,, ,,				1/10½	,, ,,
No. 1674.	,, 6¼ ,, ,,			3/- ,, ,,	No. 1681.	,, 2 ,, ,,				1/10½	,, ,,
No. 1675.	,, 5 ,, ,,			3/- ,, ,,							

GLAZIERS' DIAMONDS.

No. 2619. Special Hand Cutting Diamond, for Lead Glazing.

Price 31/6 each. These are specially manufactured for cutting glass with an uneven surface, viz.; Cathedral, Muffled, &c.

No. 2615. Glaziers' Diamonds.

Quality				C	B	A	S	Plate.
				15/9	18/9	23/3	31/6	52/6 each.

STRATFORD, Walthamstow and Leytonstone.

YOUNG & MARTEN, Merchants and Manufacturers,

PAPER STUCCO CENTRE PIECES FOR CEILINGS.

EXTREME LIGHTNESS.—A 36-in. Stucco Centre Piece only weighs 2 lbs. 14 ozs.

EXTREME CHEAPNESS.—Will compare favourably with prices of heavier material for time in fixing.

EXCELLENT DESIGNS.—The designs are elegant and appreciable.

Design Nos.	1558	1552	1666	1559	1584	1604	1643	1670
Diameter ..	19	22¾	29	36	36¾	36	46½	49 in.
Price	3/-	5/1½	7/6	17/7½	20/7½	23/7½	28/1½	32/7½ each

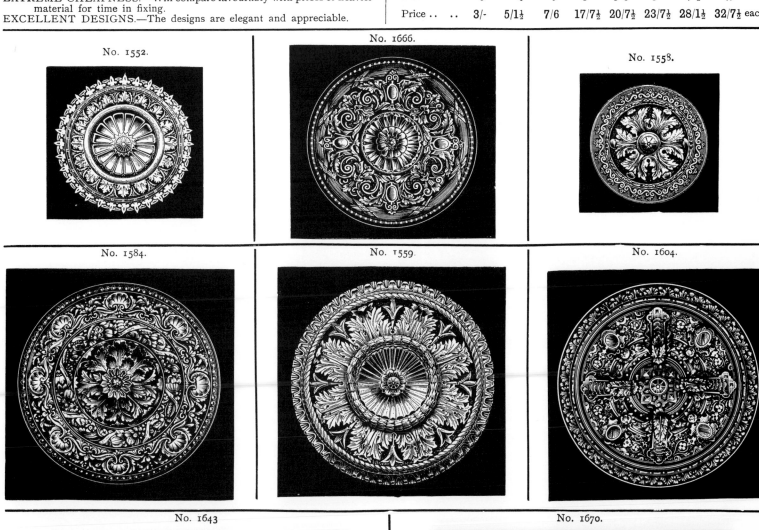

No. 1552.

No. 1666.

No. 1558.

No. 1584.

No. 1559.

No. 1604.

No. 1643

No. 1670.

Various Designs in PLASTER in Stock, Plain or Perforated for Ventilation.

	12	16	20	24	27	30 inches diameter
	1/6	1/10½	2/3	3/-	3/9	4/6 each.

STRATFORD, Walthamstow and Leytonstone.

YOUNG & MARTEN, Ltd., Merchants and Manufacturers,

PAPER STUCCO PANELS for CEILING DECORATIONS.

No. B4009.   24 in. by 24 in., **2/6** each.

No. B4010.   24 in. by 24 in., **2/6** each.

No B4011.   24 in. by 24 in.   **2/6** each.

No. B4012.   24 in. by 24 in., **2/6** each.

No. B4013.   24 in. by 24 in., **2/6** each.

No. B4014.   24 in. by 24 in., **2/6** each.

These Panels, when used in conjunction with Paper Stucco Mouldings and Corners, form an attractive ceiling, in bold relief, and can be decorated with any material.

Complete Catalogues of Paper Stucco Decorations can be obtained at 5/- each, which amount is refunded upon return of the book in good condition, or credited on orders of £5 nett value.

CARTON PIERRE MOULDINGS & CENTRE FLOWERS.

No. B4015.   Moulding, ¾ in. wide, **6d.** per ft. run.

No. B4016.   Moulding, 1½ in. wide, **10½d.** per ft. run.

No. B4017.   Moulding, 1 in. wide, **6d.** per ft. run.

No. B4018. Moulding, 1¾ in. wide, **10½d.** per ft. run.

No. B4019.   Moulding, 1¼ in. wide, **7½d.** per ft. run.

No. B4020.   Moulding, 2¼ in. wide, **1/-** per ft. run.

No. B4021.   Moulding, 2⅝ in. wide, **1/6** per ft. run.

No. B4022.   Moulding, 2 in. wide, **1/3** per ft. run.

No. B4023.   Moulding, 3½ in. wide, **1/9** per ft. run.

OTHER DESIGNS IN STOCK AND MADE TO ORDER.

No. B4024
Centre Flower 24 in. diam., **9/6** each.

No. B4025.
Centre Flower, 30 in. diam., **15/-** each.

No. B4026.
Centre Flower, 36 in. diam., **21/-** each.

STRATFORD, Walthamstow and Leytonstone.

PLASTER & FIBROUS PLASTER CEILING CENTRES.

No. B3801. Plaster, 22 in. diam.   **3/-** each
No. B3802. Fibrous, 22 in.   ,,   **3/9** ,,

No. B3748. Plaster, 19½ in. diam. **2/6** each
No. B3804. Fibrous, 19½ in.   ,,   **3/4½** ,,

No. B3749. Plaster, 24 in. diam.   **3/-** each
No. B3803. Fibrous, 24 in.   ,,   **3/9** ,,

No. B3903. Plaster, 26½ in. diam. **3/9** each
No. B3904. Fibrous, 26½ in.   ,,   **4/6** ,,

No. B3809. Plaster, 25 in. diam. **3/-** each
No. B3900. Fibrous, 25 in.   ,,   **3/9** ,,

No. B3807. Plaster, 41 in. diam. ..   ..**15/9** each
No. B3808. Fibrous, 41 in   ,, ...**18/-** ,,

No. B3901. Plaster, 32 in. diam.   **6/-** each
No. B3902. Fibrous, 32 in.   ,,   **6/9** ,,

No. B3805. Plaster, 28 in. diam. **3/9** each
No. B3806. Fibrous, 28 in.   ,,   **4/6** ,,
OTHER DESIGNS STOCKED OR MADE
TO ORDER.

No. B3905. Plaster, 30 in. diam. **4/6** each
No. B3906. Fibrous, 30 in.   ,,   **5/3** ,,

STRATFORD, Walthamstow and Leytonstone.

YOUNG & MARTEN, Ltd., Merchants and Manufacturers,

PLASTER & FIBROUS PLASTER TRUSSES & CEMENT CAPS.

 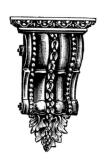  

Width of Cap	...	17 inches
Height over all	...	19½ ,,
No. B3759 Plaster	...	3/9 each
,, B3984 Fibrous	...	4/6 ,,

Width of Cap	...	10½ inches
Height over all	...	17 ,,
No. B3756 Plaster	...	1/10½ each
,, B3985 Fibrous...		2/3 ,,

Width of Cap...	...	7½ inches
Height over all	...	13 ,,
No. B3982 Plaster	...	1/10½ each
,, B3983 Fibrous...		2/3 ,,

Width of Cap	...	12¾ inches
Height over all	...	18 ,,
No. B3758 Plaster	...	2/3 each
,, B3987 Fibrous...		3/- ,,

No. B4006 Cement.
28 in. high × 7 in. wide
10/6 each.

No. B4005 Cement.
24 in. high × 6 in. wide
Without cap.
7/6 each.
No. B4005 Cement.
36 in. high × 6 in. wide
With cap as shown.
10/6 each.

W. of Cap, 5 in.
Height ... 6 ,,
No. B3751 Plaster.
9d each.
No. B3994 Fibrous.
1/1½ each.

Width of Cap ...	...	13 inches
Height over all	...	12 ,,
No. B3988 Plaster	...	2/3 each
,, B3989 Fibrous	...	3/- ,,

Width of Cap	...	10½ inches
Height over all	...	12½ ,,
No. B3755 Plaster	...	1/6 each
,, B3990 Fibrous...		1/10½ ,,

Width of Cap	...	9 inches
Height over all	...	14 ,,
No. B3753 Plaster	...	1/6 each
,, B3991 Fibrous...		1/10½ ,,

Width of Cap...	...	12 inches
Height over all	...	14 ,,
No. B3757 Plaster	...	2/3 each
,, B3995 Fibrous	...	3/- ,,

PLASTER BLOCKS & PATERAS.

Size of Block ...	4½ × 3	3½ × 3½	4 × 3¾	4 × 4	5½ × 4	4 × 4	inches.
N.s. ...	B3768	B3764	B3765	B3766	B3767	B3769	
Price ...	4/6	4/6	4/6	6/-	6/-	6/-	per dozen pairs.

PLASTER & FIBROUS PLASTER CAPS.

<— 22 inches —>

18 inches

36 inches

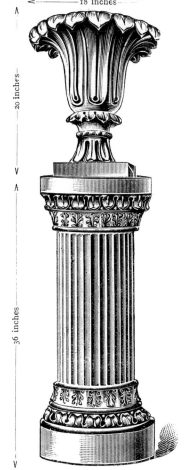

No. B3597 Cement Vase ... 15/- each
,, B3999 Cement Pedestal... 10/6 ,,

Width of Base ...	...	...	8½ inches
Height over all ...		...	12 ,,
No. B3760 Plaster	...	...	10/6 each
,, B4001 Fibrous	...	...	12/- ,,

Width of Base ...	...	...	12 inches
Height over all ...		...	17 ,,
No. B3761 Plaster	...	...	10/6 each
,, B4002 Fibrous	...	...	12/- ,,

Width of Base ...	...	...	9 inches
Height over all ...		...	12 ,,
No. B3763 Plaster for round cols.			17/6 each
,, B4004 Fibrous	,,	,,	19/6 ,,

Width of Base ...	...	...	6 inches
Height over all ...		...	9 ,,
No. B3762 Plaster	...	...	12/- each
B4003 Fibrous	...	...	13/6 ,,

<— 18 inches —>

20 inches

36 inches

No B3998 Cement Vase ... 15/- each
,, B3999 Cement Pedestal 10/6 ,,

STRATFORD, Walthamstow and Leytonstone.

YOUNG & MARTEN, Ltd., Merchants and Manufacturers,

PLASTER AND FIBROUS PLASTER CEILING LINES, BEDMOULDS AND SOFFITS.

PLASTER CEILING LINES.

No. B3964 Plaster, 1½ in. wide, 1½d. per foot
„ B3965 Fibrous „ 3d. „

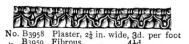

No. B3972 Plaster, 1⅝ in. wide, 1½d. per foot
„ B4008 Fibrous „ 3d. „

No. B3770 Plaster, 1½ in. wide, 1½d. per foot
„ B3963 Fibrous „ 3d. „

No. B3772 Plaster, 2 in. wide, 3d. per foot
„ B3951 Fibrous „ 4½d. „

No. B3771 Plaster, 1½ in. wide, 1½d. per foot
„ B3938 Fibrous „ 3d. „

No. B3773 Plaster, 3 in. wide, 3d. per foot
„ B3936 Fibrous „ 5¼d. „

No. B3971 Plaster, 1⅝ in. wide, 3d. per foot
„ B4007 Fibrous „ 4½d. „

No. B3946 Plaster, 4 in. wide, 3d. per foot
„ B3947 Fibrous „ 5¼d. „

BEDMOULDS.

No. B3958 Plaster, 2¼ in. wide, 3d. per foot
„ B3959 Fibrous „ 4½d. „

No. B3774 Plaster, 2 in. wide, 3d. per foot
„ B3935 Fibrous „ 4½d. „

No. B3775 Plaster, 1¾ in. wide, 3d. per foot
„ B3960 Fibrous „ 4½d. „

No. B3942 Plaster, 2½ in. wide, 3d. per foot
„ B3943 Fibrous „ 5¼d. „

SOFFITS.

No. B3932 Plaster, 4 in. wide, 3d. per foot
„ B3933 Fibrous „ 5¼d. „

No. B3920 Plaster, 4 in. wide, 3d. per foot
„ B3921 Fibrous „ 5¼d. „

No. B3922 Plaster, 4 in. wide, 3d. per foot
„ B3923 Fibrous „ 5¼d. „

No. B3788 Plaster, 6 in. wide, 3¾d. per foot
„ B3950 Fibrous „ 6d. „

No. B3778 Plaster, 3½ in. wide, 3d. per foot
„ B3956 Fibrous „ 5¼d. „

No. B3782 Plaster, 4 in. wide, 3d. per foot
„ B3966 Fibrous „ 5¼d. „

No. B3784 Plaster, 4½ in. wide, 3d. per foot
„ B3937 Fibrous „ 5¼d. „

No. B3779 Plaster, 3¾ in. wide, 3d. per foot
„ B3941 Fibrous „ 5¼d. „

No. B3783 Plaster, 4 in. wide, 3d. per foot
„ B3953 Fibrous „ 5¼d. „

No. B3790 Plaster, 4½ in. wide, 3d. per foot
„ B3957 Fibrous „ 5¼d. „

No. B3787 Plaster, 5 in. wide, 3¾d. per foot
„ B3952 Fibrous „ 6d. „

No. B3954 Plaster, 4 in. wide, 3d. per foot
„ B3955 Fibrous „ 5¼d. „

No. B3948 Plaster, 4 in. wide, 3d. per foot
„ B3949 Fibrous „ 5¼d. „

No. B3928 Plaster, 5 in. wide, 3¾d. per foot
„ B3929 Fibrous „ 6d. „

No. B3789 Plaster, 6 in. wide, 3¾d. per foot
„ B3934 Fibrous „ 6d. „

No. B3786 Plaster, 5½ in. wide, 3¾d. per foot
„ B3940 Fibrous „ 6d. „

PLASTER AND FIBROUS PLASTER OVERDOORS.

No. B3909 Plaster, 33½ in. × 13½ in., 3/6 each
„ B3910 Fibrous „ „ 4/6 „

No. 3907 Plaster, 40 in. × 13 in., 4/6 each
„ 3908 Fibrous „ „ 6/- „

No. B3914 Plaster, 36 in. × 14½ in., 3/6 each
„ B3915 Fibrous „ „ 4/6 „

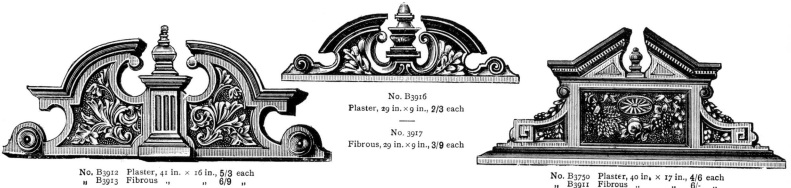

No. B3912 Plaster, 41 in. × 16 in., 5/3 each
„ B3913 Fibrous „ „ 6/9 „

No. B3916
Plaster, 29 in. × 9 in., 2/3 each

No. 3917
Fibrous, 29 in. × 9 in., 3/9 each

No. B3750 Plaster, 40 in. × 17 in., 4/6 each
„ B3911 Fibrous „ „ 6/- „

STRATFORD, Walthamstow and Leytonstone.

HARP AND HALL PENDANTS

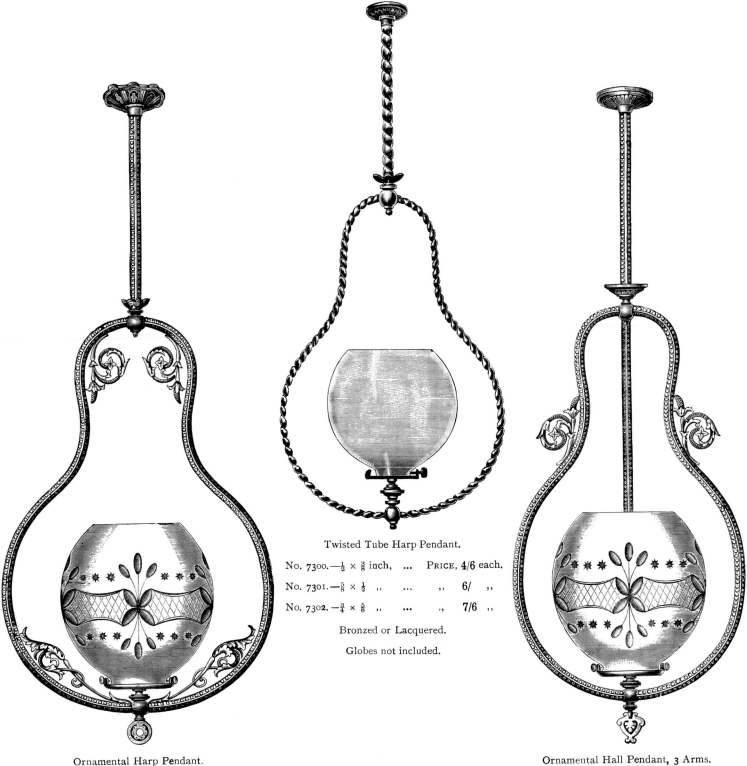

Twisted Tube Harp Pendant.

No. 7300.—$\frac{1}{2} \times \frac{3}{8}$ inch, ... PRICE, **4/6** each.

No. 7301.—$\frac{5}{8} \times \frac{1}{2}$,, ... ,, **6/** ,,

No. 7302.—$\frac{3}{4} \times \frac{5}{8}$,, ... ,, **7/6** ,,

Bronzed or Lacquered.

Globes not included.

Ornamental Harp Pendant.

No. 7305.—$\frac{1}{2} \times \frac{7}{16}$ inch, ... PRICE, **8/3** each.

No. 7306.—With Ball Joint, $\frac{5}{8} \times \frac{1}{2}$ inch, ,, **12/** ,,

Bronzed or Lacquered.

Ornamental Hall Pendant, 3 Arms.

No. 7308.—$\frac{1}{2} \times \frac{3}{8}$ inch, ... PRICE, **12/** each.

No. 7309. - Plain Pattern, $\frac{1}{2} \times \frac{3}{8}$ inch, ,, **9/** ,,

Bronzed or Lacquered.

Scale—Nos. 7305 and 7308, One-fifth; No. 7300, One-sixth.

STRATFORD, E., WALTHAMSTOW, N.E., AND LEYTONSTONE, E. LONDON

HALL LIGHTS

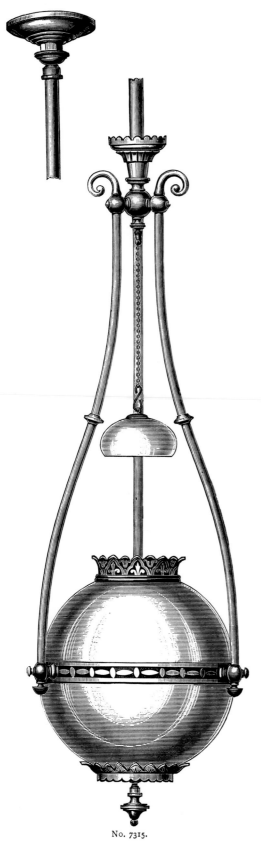

No. 7315.

PRICE, Bronzed or Lacquered,... ... 37/6 each.
,, Polished, ... 42/ ,,
Complete, with Opal Globe and Consumer.

No. 7316.

PRICE, Bronzed or Lacquered, ... 51/ each.
,, Polished, ... 57/ ,,
Complete, with 12-in. Opal Globe and Consumer.

Scale—One-fifth.

STRATFORD, E., WALTHAMSTOW, N.E., AND LEYTONSTONE, E., LONDON

HALL LAMPS

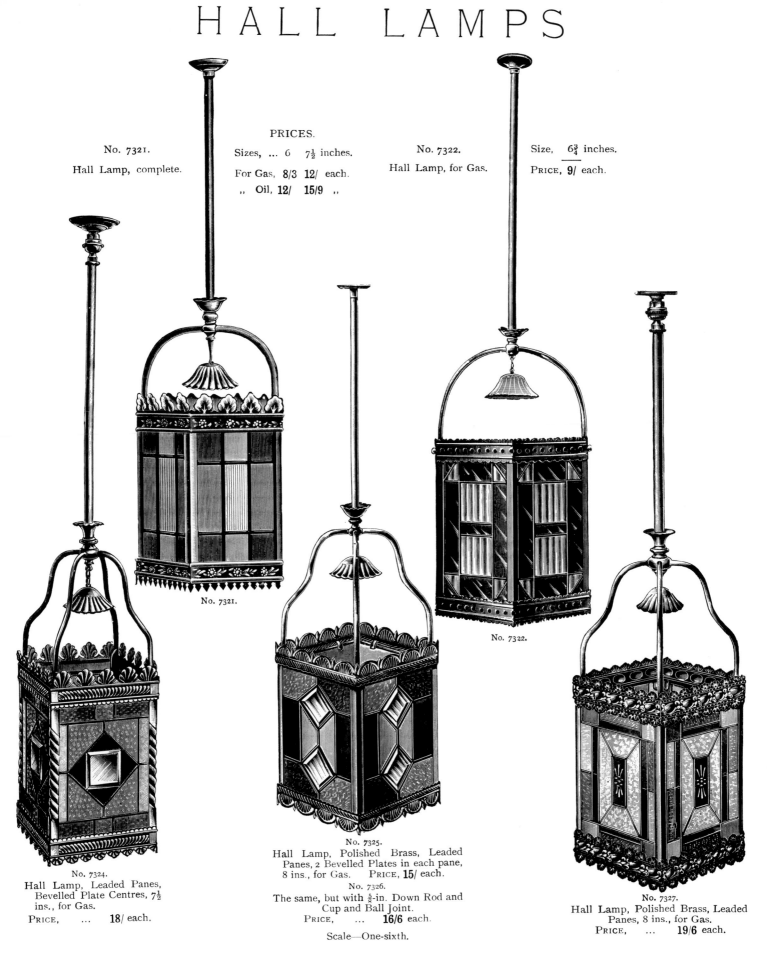

No. 7321.

Hall Lamp, complete.

PRICES.

Sizes, ... 6   7½ inches.

For Gas, **8/3 12/** each.

,, Oil, **12/ 15/9** ,,

No. 7322.

Hall Lamp, for Gas.

Size,   6¾ inches.

PRICE, **9/** each.

No. 7321.

No. 7322.

No. 7324.

Hall Lamp, Leaded Panes, Bevelled Plate Centres, 7½ ins., for Gas.

PRICE,   ... **18/** each.

No. 7325.

Hall Lamp, Polished Brass, Leaded Panes, 2 Bevelled Plates in each pane, 8 ins., for Gas.   PRICE, **15/** each.

No. 7326.

The same, but with ⅝-in. Down Rod and Cup and Ball Joint.

PRICE,   ... **16/6** each.

Scale—One-sixth.

No. 7327.

Hall Lamp, Polished Brass, Leaded Panes, 8 ins., for Gas.

PRICE,   ... **19/6** each.

HALL LAMPS

No. 7340.

Hexagon Hall Lamp, Polished Brass, Leaded Panes, Tinted Glass, Bevelled Plate Centres.

PRICE, ... **30**/ each.

No. 7341.

Hall Lamp, Polished Brass, Leaded Tinted Panes, Bevelled Plate Centres.

PRICE, 8 inches, ... **21**/ each.
,, 9 ,, ... **25/6** ,,

Scale—One-sixth.

No. 7342.

Hexagon Hall Lamp, Polished Brass, Leaded Tinted Panes, Bevelled Plate Centres.

PRICE, ... **33**/ each.

HALL LAMPS

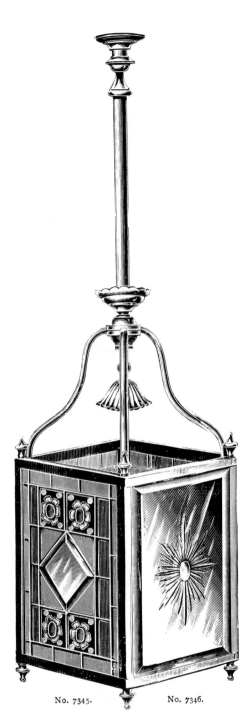

No. 7345.   No. 7346.

No. 7345—Hall Lamp, Polished Brass, Handsome Leaded Panes, Hand-painted Decoration and Bevelled Plate Centres, 10 inches.

PRICE, for Gas, ... **30/** each.
,, for Oil, with Duplex Burner, **34/6** ,,

No. 7346.—Hall Lamp, with Bevelled Brilliant Cut Plate Panes.

PRICE, for Gas, ... **37/6** each.
,, for Oil, with Duplex Burner, **42/** ,,

No. 7347.

Hall Lamp, Polished Brass, Handsome Leaded Tinted Panes.

PRICE, ... **57/** each.

No. 7349.

Hexagon Hall Lamp, Polished Brass, Leaded Tinted Panes.

PRICE, ... **36/** each.

Scale—One-sixth.

STRATFORD, E. WALTHAMSTOW, N.E. AND LEYTONSTONE, E. LONDON

HALL LAMPS

REGISTERED DESIGNS

No. 7378.—Hall Lamp, Polished Brass, Richly Etched Glass with Rose Tinted Decoration, **36/** each.

No. 7382.—Hall Lamp, Polished Brass, with Ruby Shaded Glass and Smoke Bell, **23/3** each.

No. 7384.—Hall Lamp, Bright Brass, with Amber Glass, **16/9** each.
No. 7385.—Hall Lamp, Bright Brass, with Ruby Glass, **19/6** each.

No. 7383.—Hall Lamp, Polished Brass, with New Aurora Tinted Glass, **25/6** each.

Scale—One-sixth.

HALL LAMPS

REGISTERED DESIGNS

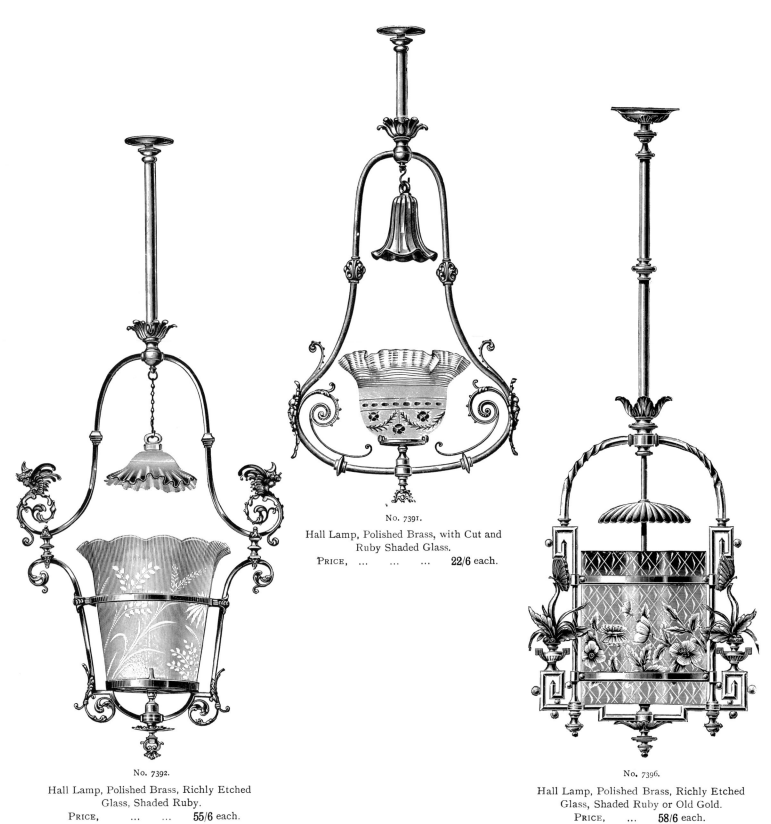

No. 7391.

Hall Lamp, Polished Brass, with Cut and
Ruby Shaded Glass.

PRICE, ... 22/6 each.

No. 7392.

Hall Lamp, Polished Brass, Richly Etched
Glass, Shaded Ruby.

PRICE, ... 55/6 each.

No. 7396.

Hall Lamp, Polished Brass, Richly Etched
Glass, Shaded Ruby or Old Gold.

PRICE, ... 58/6 each.

Scale—One-sixth.

HALL LAMPS

No. 7371.

Hall Lamp, Polished Brass, Handsome Leaded Panes, Hand-painted Decoration, Bevelled Plate Centres and Jewels.

PRICE, ... 45/ each.

Scale—One-sixth.

No. 7370.

Hall Lamp, Polished Brass, Leaded Panes, Hand-painted Decoration, Bevelled Plate Centres and Jewels.

PRICE, ... 72/ each.

No. 7372

Hall Lamp, Cast Polished Brass, Leaded Panes, Hand-painted Decoration, Bevelled Plate Centres.

PRICE, ... 88/6 each.

STRATFORD, E., WALTHAMSTOW, N.E., AND LEYTONSTONE, E., LONDON

"CYLINDER" HALL LAMPS

Superior Quality.

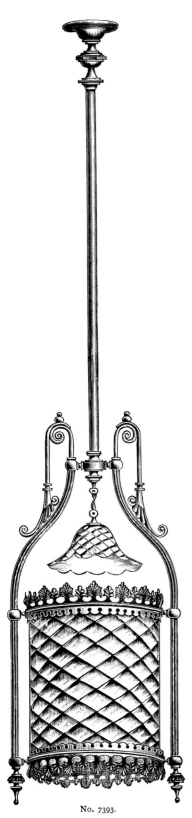

No. 7393.

Polished Brass, Opalescent Tinted
Glass.

PRICE, ... **42**/ each.

No. 7394.

Polished Brass, Iced Glass, Shaded
Rose Tint.

PRICE, ... **60**/ each.

Scale—One-sixth.

No. 7395.

Polished Brass, Opalescent Shaded Glass.

PRICE, .. **63**/ each.

"CYLINDER" HALL LAMPS

REGISTERED DESIGNS

No. 7387.

Polished Brass Hall Lamp (Renaissance), Glass Cylinder, either Flint Ruby Shaded, or Citron and Ruby, or all Citron.

PRICE, ... **46/6** each.

No. 7386.

Polished Brass Hall Lamp (Louis XIV.), Glass Cylinder, either Flint Ruby Shaded, or Ruby and Citron, or all Citron.

PRICE, ... **63/** each.

Scale—One-eighth.

No. 7388.

Polished Brass Hall Lamp (Louis XIV.), Glass Cylinder, either Flint Ruby Shaded, or Ruby and Citron, or all Citron.

PRICE, ... **72/** each.

STRATFORD, E., WALTHAMSTOW, N.E., AND LEYTONSTONE, E., LONDON

HALL LAMPS

Superior Quality.

No. 7421.

Hall Lamp, Polished Brass, Iced Glass, Old Gold
Tinted, Plaques Shade and Consumer to match.

PRICE, ... **96**/ each.

Length over all, 4 feet.

No. 7420.

Hall Lamp, Polished Brass, Rich Murano Glass.
Rose-tinted Decoration.

PRICE, ... **93**/ each.

Length over all, 4 feet.

Scale—One-sixth.

HALL LAMPS

Superior Quality.

No. 7422.

Hall Lamp, Cast Polished Brass, Brilliant Cut and Bevelled Plate Glass.

PRICE, ... **144/** each.

Length over all, 5 feet.

No. 7426.

Hall Lamp, Cast Polished Brass, Bevelled and Brilliant Cut Plate Panes.

PRICE, ... **117/** each.

Scale—One-sixth.

No. 7423.

Hall Lamp, Cast Polished Brass, Brilliant Cut and Bevelled Plate Glass.

PRICE, ... **165/** each.

Length over all, 5 feet.

BRASS GAS BRACKETS

No. 7817.—Swing Bracket.
PRICE, Polished, ... **30/** each.
Shaped Walnut Block, ... **4/** ,,

No. 7814.—Swing Bracket.
PRICE, Polished or Steel Bronzed, **16/6** each.
Shaped Walnut Block, ... **2/** ,,

No. 7816.—Swing Bracket and Consumer Suspender.
PRICE, Polished or Steel Bronzed, **42/** each.
Glass not included.

Scale—One-fourth.

No. 7815.—Swing Bracket.
PRICE, Polished or Steel Bronzed, **25/6** each.

STRATFORD, E., WALTHAMSTOW, N.E., AND LEYTONSTONE, E., LONDON

BRASS GAS BRACKETS

Stiff Bracket.

No. 7885.—PRICE, 7 inches long, ... **18/** each.

,, 7886.— ,, 9 ,, ,, ... **34/6** ,,

No. 7888.

Treble Swing Bracket.

PRICE, Polished, 31 inches long, ... **24/9** each.

Shaped Walnut Block, ... **3/6** ,,

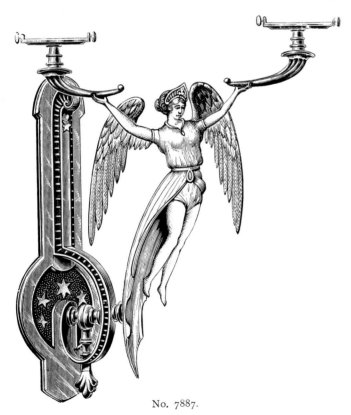

No. 7887.

Two-light Bracket, Stiff.

PRICE, Polished, ... **69/** each.

No. 7889.

Swing Bracket.

PRICE, Polished, ... **25/6** each.

Scale—One-fourth.

BRASS GAS BRACKETS

No. 7896.—Two-light Bracket, to Swing.   PRICE, Polished, ...   **27/** each.

No. 7897.—Two-light Bracket, to Swing.   PRICE, Polished, **45/** each ; Shaped Walnut Block, **3/6** each.

No. 7898.—Two-light Bracket, to Swing.   PRICE, Polished, **67/6** each ; Shaped Walnut Block, **4/6** each.
Scale—One-fourth.

STRATFORD, E., WALTHAMSTOW, N.E., AND LEYTONSTONE, E., LONDON

No. F9111.
$\frac{5}{8} \times \frac{3}{8}$ in. complete with 14 in. Opal Shade, **12/-.**

No. F9112.
$\frac{1}{2} \times \frac{5}{16}$ in. complete with 12 in. Opal Shade, **8/4.**

Burners not included.

No. F9116.
$\frac{5}{8}$ in. × $\frac{3}{8}$ in. Polished Brass with 16 in. Crimped Opal Shade,

1 Light **16/-**
2 ,, ... **17/-**
With Plain Opal Shade, **6**d. less.

No. F9137.
Polished Brass, 3 lights complete with 12 in. Opal Shades, Holders, and Eye Screens, **56/-.**

No. F9118.
Polished, complete with 16 in. Opal Shade,

2 Lights **16/8**
3 ,, ... **17/6**

Crimped Opal Shade, **8**d. extra.

No. F9114.
$\frac{1}{2}$ in. × $\frac{5}{16}$ in. Polished Brass, with 14 in. Crimped Opal Shade, **13/-.**

No. F9113.
With Plain Opal Shade, **12/6.**

Scale, about one-eighth.

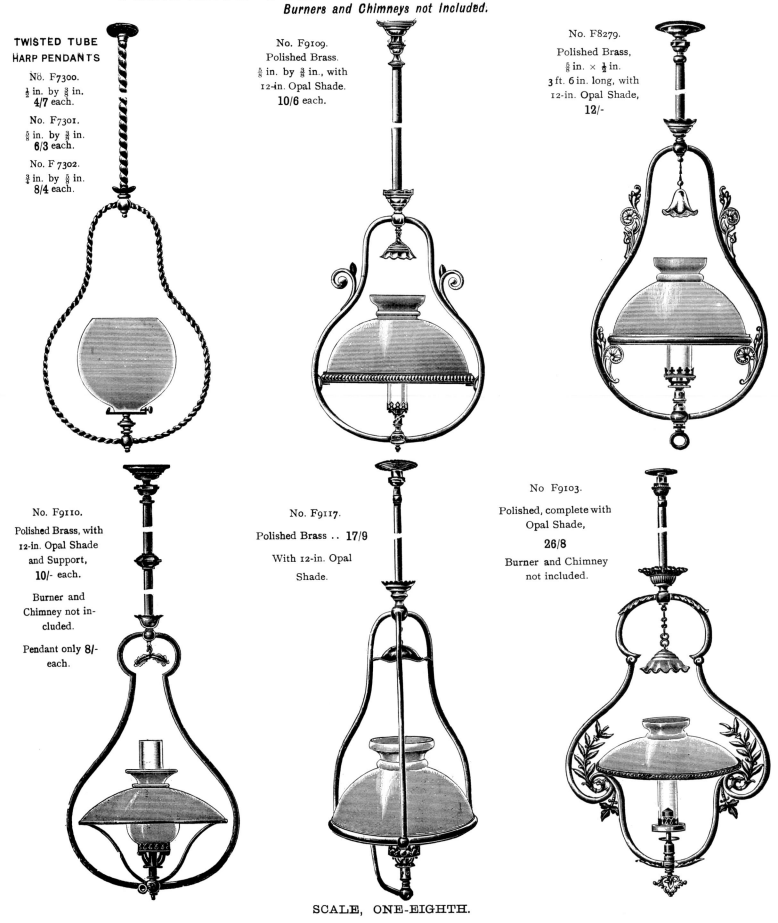

TWISTED TUBE HARP PENDANTS

No. F7300.
½ in. by ⅜ in.
4/7 each.

No. F7301.
⅝ in. by ⅜ in.
6/3 each.

No. F7302.
¾ in. by ⅝ in.
8/4 each.

No. F9109.
Polished Brass.
⅝ in. by ⅜ in., with
12-in. Opal Shade.
10/6 each.

No. F8279.
Polished Brass,
⅝ in. × ½ in.
3 ft. 6 in. long, with
12-in. Opal Shade,
12/-

No. F9110.
Polished Brass, with
12-in. Opal Shade
and Support,
10/- each.

Burner and
Chimney not in-
cluded.

Pendant only 8/-
each.

No. F9117.
Polished Brass .. 17/9

With 12-in. Opal
Shade.

No F9103.
Polished, complete with
Opal Shade,
26/8
Burner and Chimney
not included.

SCALE, ONE-EIGHTH.

STRATFORD, Walthamstow and Leytonstone.

YOUNG & MARTEN, Ltd., Merchants and Manufacturers,
PENDANTS FOR INCANDESCENT GAS BURNERS.

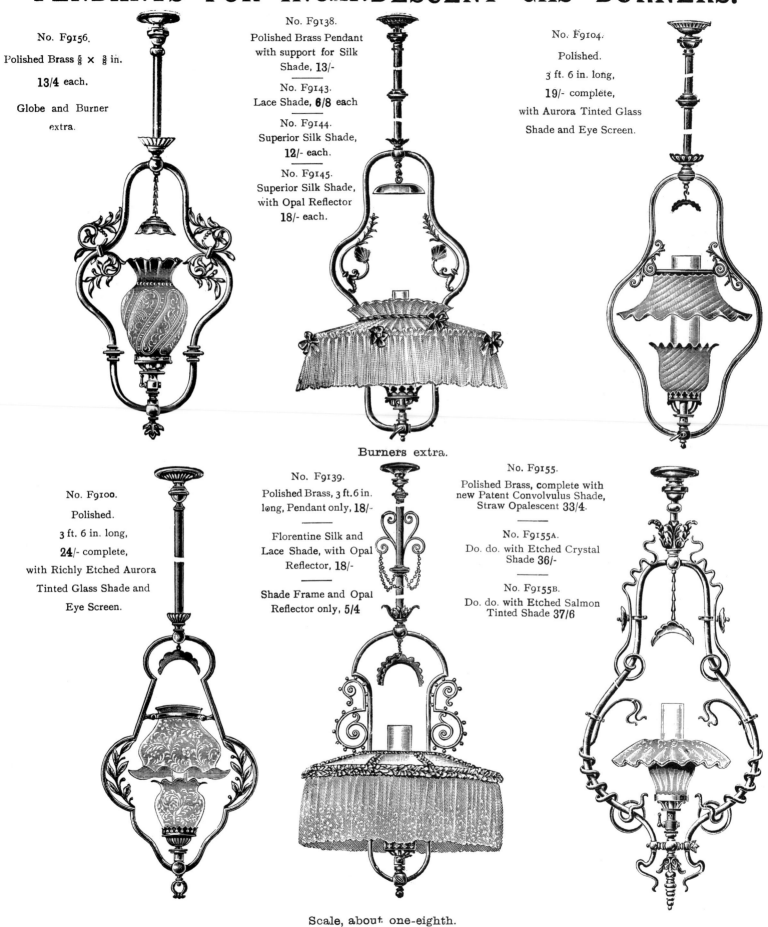

No. F9156.

Polished Brass ⅝ × ⅜ in.

13/4 each.

Globe and Burner extra.

No. F9138.
Polished Brass Pendant with support for Silk Shade, **13/-**

No. F9143.
Lace Shade, **6/8** each

No. F9144.
Superior Silk Shade, **12/-** each.

No. F9145.
Superior Silk Shade, with Opal Reflector **18/-** each.

No. F9104.

Polished.

3 ft. 6 in. long,

19/- complete,

with Aurora Tinted Glass Shade and Eye Screen.

Burners extra.

No. F9100.

Polished.

3 ft. 6 in. long,

24/- complete,

with Richly Etched Aurora Tinted Glass Shade and Eye Screen.

No. F9139.
Polished Brass, 3 ft. 6 in. long, Pendant only, **18/-**

Florentine Silk and Lace Shade, with Opal Reflector, **18/-**

Shade Frame and Opal Reflector only, **5/4**

No. F9155.
Polished Brass, complete with new Patent Convolvulus Shade, Straw Opalescent **33/4**.

No. F9155A.
Do. do. with Etched Crystal Shade **36/-**

No. F9155B.
Do. do. with Etched Salmon Tinted Shade **37/6**

Scale, about one-eighth.

STRATFORD, Walthamstow and Leytonstone.

YOUNG & MARTEN, Ltd., Merchants and Manufacturers,

WROUGHT-IRON AND COPPER
PENDANTS FOR THE INCANDESCENT GAS BURNER.

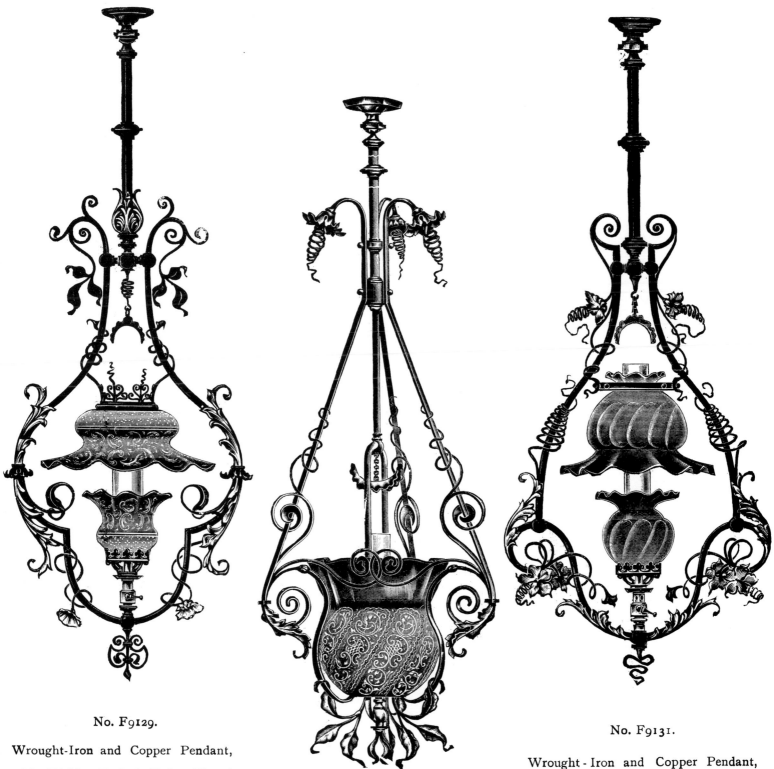

No. F9129.

Wrought-Iron and Copper Pendant, with Richly Etched Ruby Tinted Glass Shade and Eye Screen, **54/-**.

No. F9130.

Wrought-Iron and Copper Hall Lamp, with Rose Shaded Glass, 4 ft. 6 in. long, **54/-**.

SCALE—ONE-SIXTH.

No. F9131.

Wrought-Iron and Copper Pendant, with Aurora Tinted Glass Shade and Eye Screen, **51/-**.

STRATFORD, Walthamstow and Leytonstone.

YOUNG & MARTEN, Ltd., Merchants and Manufacturers,

FANCY TINTED GAS GLOBES.

No. 3419   Ruby Shaded
Comet fitting, **18/-** per dozen
2⅝-inch   ,,   **16/6**   ,,

No. 3420   Ruby Shaded
Comet fitting, **19/6** per dozen
2⅝-inch   ,,   **18/-**   ,,

No 3421   Optic Fluted, Ruby, Aurora,
or Yellow Shaded
Comet fitting, **21/-** per dozen
2⅝-inch   .,   **19/6**   ,,

No. 3422   Ruby or Aurora Shaded
2⅝-inch fitting, **21/9** per dozen

No. 3426   Optic Fluted, Aurora,
Ruby, or Yellow Shaded
Comet fitting, **23/3** per dozen
2⅝-inch   ,,   **21/9**   ,,

No. 3424   Optic Fluted, Ruby,
Aurora, or Yellow Shaded
2⅝-inch fitting, **24/-** per dozen

No. 3423   Ruby, Aurora, Yellow, or
Green Shaded
Comet fitting, **23/3** per dozen,
2⅝-inch   ,,   **21/9**   ,,

No. 3425   Optic Fluted, Ruby, Aurora,
or Yellow Shaded
Comet fitting, **25/6** per dozen

No. 3405   Ruby or Turquoise Threaded,
21/- per dozen

No. 3406   Cut, Ruby or Turquoise
Threaded, **21/-** per dozen
Comet fitting, **24/9** per dozen

No 3407   Engraved, Ruby or Turquoise
Threaded, **22/6** per dozen

No. 3412   Engraved, Ruby or Turquoise
Threaded, **21/-** per dozen
Comet fitting, **24/9** per dozen

No. 3410   Etched, Ruby, Aurora, or
Peacock Green Shaded
30/- per dozen

No. 3409   Etched, Ruby, Aurora, or
Peacock Green Shaded
30/- per dozen

No. 3413   Richly Cut, Ruby, or
Turquoise Threaded
30/- per dozen

No. 3411   Richly Cut, Ruby Shaded
Comet fitting, **51/-** per dozen

STRATFORD, Walthamstow, Leytonstone, Millwall, & Brentford.

47

No. E.L. 5055.

6 in. × 4 in. Opal Langham.
PRICE, 4/8 per doz.

No. E.L. 5047.

Manography Aurora Tinted.
PRICE, 12/- per doz.

No. E.L. 5086.

PRICE, 12/6 per doz.
Opalescent.

No. E.L. 5092.

PRICE, 16/- per doz.
Etched Ruby or Aurora.

No. E.L. 5052.

Clear Flint. PRICE, 19/8 doz.
Aurora   „   26/8 „

No. E.L. 5040.

PRICE, 6/- per doz.
Clear Optic.

No. E.L. 5054.

Opal Irene.
PRICE, 4/8 per doz.

No. E.L. 5049.

Brilliant Cut, Clear.
PRICE, 14/4 per doz.

No. E.L. 5048.

Twisted Satin Opalescent.
PRICE, 12/- per doz.

No. E.L. 5046.

Green Opalescent.
PRICE, 8/- per doz.

No. E.L. 5050.

Brilliant Cut, Rose Tinted.
PRICE, 16/- per doz.

No. E.L. 5045.

Green Opalescent.
PRICE, 8/- per doz.

No. E.L. 5028. "THISTLE."

PRICE, 24/- per doz.
Yellow Opalescent.

No. E.L 5024.

Satin Finish, either Flint,
Citron, or Rose.
PRICE, 9/4 per doz.

No. E.L. 5017. "IRENE."

Clear Iced. PRICE, 6/8 doz.
Rose   „   „ 8/8 „

No. E.L. 5036.

Satin Finish, with Ruby, Citron,
Green, or Turquoise Edge.
PRICE, 13/4 per doz.
No. E.L. 5037.   Opalescent.
PRICE, 10/8 per doz.

No. E.L. 5051.

Clear etched, PRICE, 21/4 doz.
Ruby   „   „ 29/4 „

No. E.L. 5026. "LYDIA."

Best quality.
PRICE 13/4 per doz.
Citron, Salmon,
Turquoise, or Green edge.

No. E.L. 5093.

PRICE, 8/- per doz.
Plain Obscured.

No. E.L. 5020. "POPPY."

3½ × 3¾ × 1⅜. PRICE, 21/4 doz.
4½ × 5 × 1⅞.   „   29/4 „
Yellow Opalescent.
Satin Finish.

No. E.L. 5019.
SATIN "IRENE."

PRICE, 21/4 per doz.
No. E.L. 5031. Second quality.
PRICE, 10/8 per doz.

No. E.L. 5018.
Clear Etched "IRENE."

Ruby or Blue-threaded edge.
PRICE, 21/4 per doz.

No. E.L. 5087.

Satin Finish, Etched,
Ruby Shaded.
PRICE, 26/8 per doz.

No. E.L. 5090.

PRICE, 12/6 per doz.
Rose, Pink, or Citron.

No. E.L. 5061.

PRICE, 4/8 each.
Very richly-cut Crystal.

No. E.L. 5022.

PRICE 21/4 per doz.
Yellow Opalescent.
Satin Finish.

No. E.L. 5056.

ICED "IRENE."
Green, Rose, or Citron
Shaded.
PRICE, 10/8 per doz.

No. E.L. 5088.

PRICE, 10/8 per doz.
Iced Flint.

No. E.L. 5030.

PRICE, 4/6 each.
Very richly-cut Crystal.

No. E.L. 5058.

Green Opalescent.
PRICE, 12/- per doz.

No. E.L. 5060.

PRICE, 72/- per doz.
Satin Finish and Etched.

No. E.L. 5085.

Rose, Aurora, or Yellow
Etched.
PRICE, 21/4 per doz.

No. E.L. 5057.

Rose Beaded, Satin Finish.
PRICE, 32/- per doz.

No. E.L. 5062.

Etched and Satin Finish.
Price 9/4 each.

No. E.L. 5034.

Richly-cut Thistle.
PRICE, 4/6 each.

No. E.L. 5068.

PRICE, 44/6 per doz.
Yellow Opalescent.

No. E.L. 5001. Opal Conical Shades.

Size.	Price, per doz., from Stock.	Original cases to arrive, per doz.
6 ins.	3/8	3 4
8 ,,	4/4	3/7
9 ,,	4/8	3/11
10 ,,	5/-	4/-
12 ,,	9/-	7/8
15 ,,	16/-	13/4

No. E.L. 5002. Green and White Conical Shades.

Size.	Price, per doz., from Stock.
8 ins.	16/-
9 ,,	18/8
10 ,,	21/4
12 ,,	30/8
15 ,,	80/-

No. E.L. 5005. OPAL LANGHAM.

Size.	Price, per doz., from Stock.
6 ins.	4/-
9 ,,	5/8
12 ,,	10/8

No. E.L. 5006. OPALESCENT LANGHAM.

Size.	Price, per doz.
7½ ins.	14/-
10 ,,	16/8
12 ,,	28/-
15 ,,	40/-

DEEP CONIC.

No. E.L. 5010. Opal — 9-in. 10 in. 9/- doz.
No. E.L. 5011. Green Cased Opal, 18/8 21/4 ,,

No. E.L. 5012. FLUTED OPAL.

8 in., 5/9, 10 in., 6/4 per doz.

No. E.L. 5009. Enamelled Iron Saucer Shade.

10 in. diam., Price 6/8 per doz.
15 ,, ,, ,, 13/4 ,,

No. E.L. 5008. Enamelled Iron Shades

Size.	Price, per doz., from Stock.	Price, per original case to arrive.
8 ins.	4/8	
9 ,,	5/-	Quoted
10 ,,	5/4	on
12 ,,	9/-	Application.
15 ,,	14/-	

No. E.L. 5013. OPAL CONICAL SHADE.

10 ins. × 3¼ ins., Lip Fitting.
Price, 5/- per doz.

No. E.L. 5053. ETCHED & SATIN FINISHED LANGHAM.

White Opalescent Shaded,
Price, 28/- per doz.

No. E.L. 5123. GREEN CARDBOARD SHADES for Electric Billiards.

20 in. diameter. Price, 14/4 per doz.
Wire Frames to fit inside Collar at top to suit 3¼ in. fittings. Price, 7/4 per doz.
Other sizes and Colors to order.
½ in. or 1⅛ in. Brass Langham Galleries, No. 2006.
Price, 13/4 per doz.

No. E.L. 5122. GIMBAL SHADE.

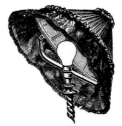

For Electric Table Standard, fitted with 1⅛-in. Swivel Fittings.
Florentine, Pleated, lined white

	6	8	9	10	12 inch.
	4/8	6/-	6/8	7/4	9/- each.
Sarsnet, ditto,	5/8	7/4	8/-	9/-	10/8 ,,

No. E.L. 5124. THE "FACILE" ELECTRIC SHADE REMOVER.

Price, 1/4 each.

Directions.

Place the ring on any flat surface, then press the Remover over the ring; put the Shade over all, and lift up to the Lampholder; screw up, and when the screw is home the Remover will come away easily, and thus avoid any breaking of Shade from overscrewing.

No. E.L. 5120. The "VANDYKE" DOME SILK SHADE.

In any Stock Color, with Lace to match, lined white Sarsnet,

16	18	20 ins
30/-	38/-	44/- ea.
22	24 ins.	
50/-	58/- each.	

State size of Gallery when ordering.

No. E.L. 5121. FLORENTINE, gathered Ruche top and bottom, lined white Lace to match.

16	18	20 ins.
14/-	19/-	22/- each.
22	24	27 ins.
25/-	27/-	33/- each

Sarsnet, ditto.

16	18	20 ins.
25/-	30/-	33/4 each.
22	24	27 ins.
37/-	42/-	50/- each.

State size of Gallery when ordering.

YOUNG & MARTEN, Ltd., Merchants and Manufacturers,

FANCY ELECTRIC BRASS, COPPER, AND WROUGHT-IRON BRACKETS.

Scale about one-sixth.

HANDSOME CAST AND POLISHED BRACKET.

No. E.L. 2199.   Price, **15/2** each.

FANCY POLISHED BRASS BRACKET

No. E.L. 2194.   Price, **10/8** each.

HANDSOME CAST AND POLISHED BRACKET.

No. E.L. 2200.   Price, **18/8** each.

WROT.-IRON AND POLISHED COPPER BRACKET.

No. E.L. 2190.   Price, **12/6** each.

WROT.-IRON AND POLISHED COPPER BRACKET

No. E.L. 2192.   Price, **13/4** each.

POLISHED AND LACQUERED BRASS BRACKET.

No. E.L. 2195.   Price, **13/10** each.

MASSIVE CAST AND POLISHED BRACKET.

No. E.L. 2202.   Price **28/-** each.

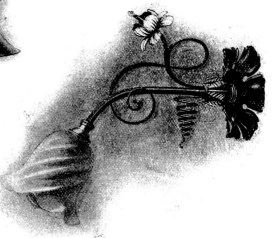

WROT.-IRON AND POLISHED COPPER BRACKET.

No. E.L. 2191.   Price, **8/-** each.

LAMPS, HOLDERS,
SHADES, and
WIRING EXTRA.
——
NIPPLES, ½-inch.

STRATFORD, Walthamstow, Leytonstone, Millwall, & Brentford.

YOUNG & MARTEN, Ltd., Merchants and Manufacturers,

PLAIN and FANCY BRASS ELECTRIC STANDARDS.

Polished or Bronzed.
Scale, one-sixth.
No. E.L. 2280.
Price, **4/6** each.

Polished.
9-in. to Nipple.
No. E.L. 2282.
Price, **5/-** each.

Polished and Copper.
6-in. to Nipple.
No. E.L. 2286.
Price, **5/-** each.

9-in. to Nipple.
No. E.L. 2287.
Price, **5/10** each.

Polished.
11-in. to Nipple.
No. E.L. 2283.
Price, **10/-** each.

Polished or Bronzed
13-in. to Nipple.
No. E.L. 2281.
Price, **5/4** each.

Polished.
11-in. to Nipple.
No. E.L. 2305.
Price, **5/4** each.

Gilt and Onyx Pillar.
Scale, one-sixth.
No. E.L. 2302.
Brazilian Onyx, **13/4** each.
Mexican Green Onyx, **11/2** each.
Mexican White, **10/8** each.

Polished. Ebony Pillar.
15½-in. to Nipple.
No. E.L. 2290.
Price, **15/2** each.

No. E.L. 2303.
Scale, one-sixth.
Brazilian Onyx, **17/9** each.
Mexican Green Onyx, **16/-** each.
Mexican White, **14/3** each.

Lamps, Holders, Shades, and Wiring extra.   Nipples, ½-inch.

STRATFORD, Walthamstow, Leytonstone, Millwall, & Brentford.

IRON OVERMANTELS

No. 3455 Overmantel.

No. 699 Overmantel.

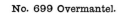

With Small Bracket and Bevelled-edge Mirror.

Width,	...	...	...	33 inches.
Height,	...	...	...	20½ ,,
Mirror,	...	...	...	18 × 6 ,,
Bracket Shelf,	...	...	4¼ ,,

PRICE, Fine Cast, ... **11/3 each.**

With Bevelled-edge Mirror.

Width,	...	...	24½	28½ inches.
Height,	...	...	25¼	27¼ ,,
Mirror,	...	...	9½ × 14	9½ × 14 ,,

PRICES, Fine Cast,... **10/6** **13/6 each.**

No. 700 Overmantel.

With Shelf above Bevelled-edge Mirror.

Width,	...	...	...	39 inches.
Height,	...	...	...	30 ,,
Mirror,	...	...	...	12 × 12 ,,
Single Shelf,	...	...	...	30 × 7 ,,

PRICE, Fine Cast, ... **22/6 each.**

No. 2431 Overmantel.

With Bevelled-edge Mirror.

Width,	...	...	35	39 inches.
Height,	...	...	36	36 ,,
Mirror,	...	...	13 × 13⅝	17 × 13⅝ ,,

PRICES, Fine Cast, **25/6** **27/ each.**

No. 755 Overmantel.

With Bevelled-edge Mirror.

Width,	...	...	22	25	30 inches.
Height,	...	...	21	23½	25 ,,
Mirror,	...	...	12 × 8	14 × 9	16 × 10 ,,

PRICES, Fine Cast, **10/6** **13/6** **16/6 each.**

No. 2413 Overmantel.

With Oval Bevelled-edge Mirror.

Width,	...	...	...	38 inches.
Height,	...	...	...	36 ,,
Mirror,	...	...	...	12¼ × 16 ,,

PRICE, Fine Cast, ... **39/ each.**

No. 2412 Overmantel.

With three Bevelled-edge Mirrors.

Width,	...	...	...	46 inches.
Height,	...	...	...	38 ,,
Centre Mirror,	...	...	14 × 19 ,,
Two Side Mirrors,	...	...	5 × 9 ,,

PRICE, Fine Cast, ... **56/3 each.**

No. 750 Overmantel.

With three Bevelled-edge Mirrors and two Balconettes.

Width,	...	...	...	...	41 inches.
Height,	...	...	...	...	35 ,,
Centre Mirror,	...	...	...	15¼ × 18 ,,
Two Side Mirrors,	...	...	3 × 7¼ ,,

PRICE, Fine Cast, ... **39/ each.**

No. 2414 Overmantel.

With large Bevelled-edge Mirror, and Shelf to same, and Alcoves.

Width,	...	...	...	48 inches.
Height,	...	...	...	41 ,,
Mirror,	...	...	...	19 × 23 ,,
Ledge Shelf,	...	...	...	20 × 3¼ ,,

PRICE, Fine Cast, ... **96/ each.**

STRATFORD, E., WALTHAMSTOW, N.E., AND LEYTONSTONE, E., LONDON

—— IRON OVERDOORS ——

No. 3320.

Width,								32 inches.
Height,								12 „
PRICE,								6/ each.

No. 3322.

Width,							35	39 inches.
Height,							12	12 „
PRICES,							7/	7/3 each.

No. 3319.

Width,				33	36	39	42 inches.
Height,				15½	15½	15½	15½ „
PRICES,				7/	7/3	7/6	7/9 each.

No. 3321.

Width,						33	36 inches.
Height,						14	14 „
PRICES,						9/	9/3 each.

No. 683.

Width,						27	33 inches.
Height,						19	22 „
PRICES,						4/6	5/3 each.

With Shelf 22½ × 4½ inches, **9d. each extra.**

No. 1340.

Width,						30	32 inches.
Height,						17	17 „
PRICES,						7/6	7/9 each.

With Shelf 22½ × 4½ inches, **9d. each extra.**

No. 3398.

Width,				32	36	40 inches.
Height,				18	18	18 „
PRICES,				9/9	10/6	11/3 each.

No. 3399.

Width,				32	36	40 inches.
Height,				13	13	13 „
PRICES,				9/9	10/6	11/3 each.

The above prices are for fine cast.   These can be decorated very easily and cheaply.

YOUNG & MARTEN, Ltd., Merchants and Manufacturers,

HAND-CARVED WOOD ORNAMENTS.
LONDON MADE. SUPERIOR FINISHED.
OVERDOORS.

No. CW533.

No. CW540.

No. CW539.

No. CW562.

No. CW552.

No. CW534.

No. CW554

No. CW578.

		American Whitewood.		Oak, Walnut, or Mahogany.			
Width	.. .. ..	29 or 34	40	29	34	40	inches.
No. CW533 or 552	.. ..	8/6	9/3	11/3	11/9	13/3	each.
,, CW540	.. .. ..	11/-	11/9	14/9	15/6	17/3	,,
,, CW534 or 539	.. .. ..	14/-	14/9	17/3	18/-	19/6	,,

		American Whitewood.		Oak, Walnut, or Mahogany.			
Width	.. ..	29 or 34	40	29	34	40	inches.
No. CW554	.. .. ..	14/9	15/6	18/9	19/6	21/-	each.
,, CW562 or 578	.. ..	17/3	18/-1	22/-	22/9	24/3	,,

10 per cent. reduction for dozen lots of one size and pattern.

CARVED BRACKETS.

No. CW1.   No. CW2.   No. CW3.   No. CW4.

PRICES each.

	Size.	Deal	P.Pine	Mahogany
No. CW 1 or 2	.. 9½×3×3 in.	-/10	1/1	1/4½
,, CW 1 or 2	.. 12 ×4×4 ,,	1/8	2/6	3/4
,, CW 3	.. 9½×3×3 ,,	1/3	1/8	2/-
,, CW 3	.. 12 ×4×4 ,,	2/-	2/9	3/6
,, CW 4	... 12 ×3×4 ,,	2/6	3/4	4/2
,, CW 4	.. 15 ×4×5 ,,	3/9	4/9	5/6

These patterns can be made to any size or length.

Price upon application.

FRET-CUT STAIR BRACKETS.
For 9 in. Treads.

No. T5.   No. T6.

No. T7.   No. T8.

PRICES per dozen.

		Deal.	P. Pine.	Oak, Mahogany, or Walnut.
No. 5	.. ..	3/6	4/9	6/3
,, 6 or 8	.. ..	5/7½	7/6	9/-
,, 7, Carved	..	26/3	27/6	37/6

FRET-CUT BALUSTERS.
Planed and cleaned up ready for fixing.

No. T76.   No. T77.   No. T78.   No. T79.

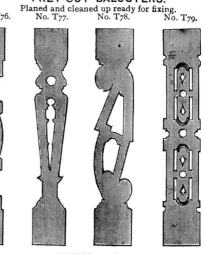

PRICES per dozen.

No.	Size.	Deal.	P. Pine	Mahogany	Oak.	Walnut
No. 76	3 ×⅞ in.	9/4½	12/6	19/6	20/-	20/9
,, 77, 78	3½×⅞ ,,	13/9	22/6	27/6	28/9	30/-
,, 77, 78	4½×⅞ ,,	14/4½	23/1½	30/-	31/3	32/6
,, 79	4½×⅞ ,,	25/-	31/3	41/3	42/6	43/9

STRATFORD, Walthamstow and Leytonstone.

MANTEL-PIECES

No. 2941 Iron Mantel-piece.

Jambs, ...	8	8	8	8	8	inches.
Projection, ...	$2\frac{1}{8}$	$2\frac{1}{8}$	$2\frac{1}{8}$	$2\frac{1}{8}$	$2\frac{1}{8}$	,,
Lintel, ...	10	10	10	10	10	,,
Openings { Width, ...	24, 26	28, 30, 32	34, 36	36	38	,,
Openings { Height, ...	36	36	36	38	38	,,
Single Shelf, ...	7	7	7	7	7	ins. wide.
PRICES, Fine Cast, ...	**16/6**	**18/**	**19/6**	**21/**	**22/6 each.**	

With Iron Towel Rail, 3/ each extra.

No. 2942 Iron Mantel-piece.

Jambs, ...	9	9	9	inches.
Projection, ...	$2\frac{3}{4}$	$2\frac{3}{4}$	$2\frac{3}{4}$	,,
Lintel, ...	$12\frac{1}{2}$	$12\frac{1}{2}$	$12\frac{1}{2}$	,,
Openings { Width, ...	30	36	36	,,
Openings { Height, ...	36	36	38	,,
Single Shelf, ...	55 × 8	61 × 10	61 × 10	,,
PRICES, Fine Cast, ...	**22/6**	**25/6**	**27/**	**each.**

Double Shelf, 6/ extra.

No. 2943 Iron Mantel-piece.

Jambs, ...	9	9	inches.
Projection, ...	$2\frac{3}{4}$	$2\frac{3}{4}$	,,
Lintel, ...	$12\frac{1}{2}$	$12\frac{1}{2}$	,,
Openings { Width, ...	36	36	,,
Openings { Height, ...	36	38	,,
Single Shelf, ...	61 × 10	61 × 10	,,
PRICES, Fine Cast, ...	**28/6**	**30/**	**each.**

Double Shelf, 6/ each extra.

No. 2944 Iron Mantel-piece.

Jambs, ...	$8\frac{1}{2}$	$8\frac{1}{2}$	$8\frac{1}{2}$	inches
Projection, ...	$1\frac{3}{4}$	$1\frac{3}{4}$	$1\frac{3}{4}$	,,
Lintel, ...	$14\frac{1}{2}$	$14\frac{1}{2}$	$14\frac{1}{2}$	,,
Openings { Width, ...	36	36	38	,,
Openings { Height, ...	36	38	38	,,
Double Shelf, ...	8	8	8	ins. wide
PRICES, Fine Cast, ...	**31/6**	**33/**	**34/6 each.**	

Also made with Deep Flanges, making Jambs project $4\frac{3}{4}$ inches,
and with 11-in. Double Shelf, **15/ extra.**

MANTEL-PIECES

No. 2344 Iron Mantel-piece.

Jambs, ...	5	5	5	5	ins.
Projection, ...	2½	2½	2½	2½	,,
Lintel, ...	14	14	14	14	,,
Openings { Width, ...	30	34	36	38	,,
{ Height, ...	36	36	38	38	,,
Double Shelf, ...	43 × 11	47 × 11	49 × 11	51 × 11	,,

PRICES, Fine Cast and Painted one coat,	36/	40/6 each.
,, Decorated in Oak, &c., or two Colors, ...	51/	55/6 ,,

No. 2345 Iron Mantel-piece.

In the " Adam " style.

Jambs, ...	5	5	5	5	ins.
Projection, ...	4	4	4	4	,,
Lintel, ...	11	11	11	11	,,
Openings { Width, ...	30	34	36	38	,,
{ Height, ...	36	36	38	38	,,
Double Shelf, ...	48 × 8½	52 × 8½	54 × 8½	56 × 8½	,,

PRICES, Fine Cast and Painted one coat,	33/	37/6	40/6	45/ each.
,, Decorated in Oak, &c., or two Colors, ...	48/	52/6	55/6	60/ ,,

No. 2346 Iron Mantel-piece.

Jambs, ...	11¼	11¼ ins.
Projection, ...	4¾	4¾ ,,
Lintel, ...	15	15 ,,
Openings { Width, ...	36	38 ,,
{ Height, ...	38	38 ,,
Double Shelf, ...	64½ × 9½	66½ × 9½ ,,

PRICE, Fine Cast, ...	57/ each.
,, Mantel in Imitation of Oak, Walnut, &c., or Marbles, ...	96/ ,,

No. 2347 Iron Mantel-piece.

Jambs, ...	8¼	8¼ ins.
Projection, ...	4¼	4¼ ,,
Lintel, ...	16¼	16¼ ,,
Openings { Width, ...	36	38 ,,
{ Height, ...	38	38 ,,
Double Shelf, ...	65¾ × 10	67¾ × 10 ,,

PRICE, Fine Cast, ...	57/ each.
,, Mantel in Imitation of Oak, Walnut, &c., or Marbles,	96/ ,,

MANTEL-PIECES

No. 2945 Iron Mantel-piece.

Iron Mantel-piece.

Jambs,	...	...	...	$5\frac{1}{2}$ ins.	
Projection,		...	...	$2\frac{3}{4}$,,	
Lintel,	...	...	...	$14\frac{1}{2}$,,	
Openings	Width, 36		38	,,	
	Height, 38		38	,,	
Width over Jambs, 46			48	,,	
Height to Shelf,	53		53	,,	
Double Shelf,	49×11	51×11	,,		

No. 2946 Iron Mantel-piece.

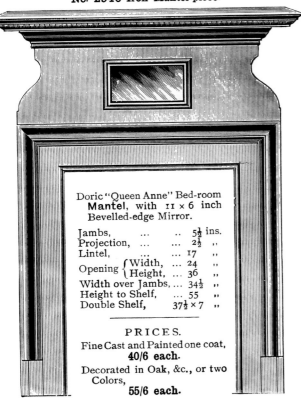

Doric "Queen Anne" Bed-room **Mantel**, with 11 × 6 inch Bevelled-edge Mirror.

Jambs,	...	...	..	$5\frac{1}{2}$ ins.
Projection,	...		...	$2\frac{1}{2}$,,
Lintel,		...	...	17 ,,
Opening	Width,	...	24	,,
	Height,	...	36	,,
Width over Jambs,		...	$34\frac{1}{2}$	,,
Height to Shelf,		...	55	,,
Double Shelf,		$37\frac{1}{2} \times 7$		,,

No. 2947 Iron Mantel-piece.

Doric "Queen Anne" Bed-room **Mantel**, with three Bevelled-edge Mirrors—one 11 × 6 ins., two 6 ins. diameter.

Jambs,	...	...	$5\frac{1}{2}$ ins.
Projection,	...	...	$2\frac{1}{2}$,,
Lintel,	...	...	17 ,,
Opening	Width,	... 30	,,
	Height,	... 36	,,
Width over Jambs,	...	$40\frac{1}{2}$	,,
Height to Shelf,	...	55	,,
Double Shelf,	$43\frac{1}{2} \times 7$		,,

MANTEL-PIECES

No. 550—The "Peace and Plenty" Iron Mantel-piece.

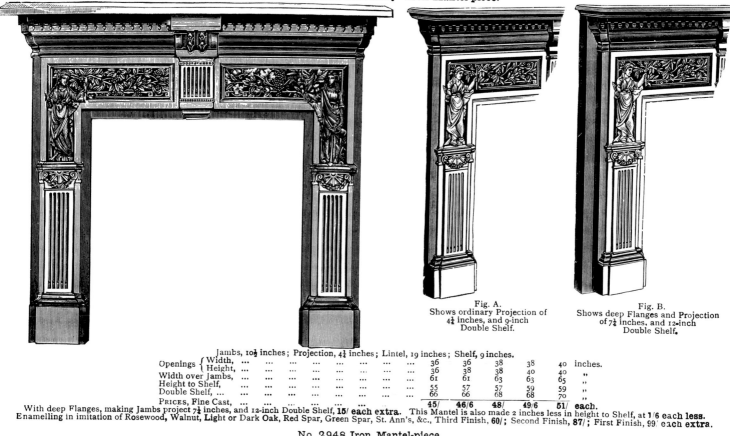

Fig. A.
Shows ordinary Projection of
4¼ inches, and 9-inch
Double Shelf.

Fig. B.
Shows deep Flanges and Projection
of 7¼ inches, and 12-inch
Double Shelf.

Jambs, 10½ inches; Projection, 4¼ inches; Lintel, 19 inches; Shelf, 9 inches.

Openings												
Width,	...	...	...	...	...	...	...	36	36	38	38	40 inches.
Height,	...	...	...	...	...	...	...	36	38	38	40	40 ,,
Width over Jambs,	...	...	...	...	...	...	...	61	61	63	63	65 ,,
Height to Shelf,	...	...	...	...	...	...	...	55	57	57	59	59 ,,
Double Shelf,	...	...	...	...	...	...	...	66	66	68	68	70 ,,
PRICES, Fine Cast,	...	...	...	...	...	...	...	45/	46/6	48/	49/6	51/ each.

With deep Flanges, making Jambs project 7¼ inches, and 12-inch Double Shelf, **15/ each extra.** This Mantel is also made 2 inches less in height to Shelf, at **1/6 each less.**
Enamelling in imitation of Rosewood, **Walnut, Light or Dark Oak,** Red Spar, Green Spar, St. Ann's, &c., Third Finish, **60/**; Second Finish, **87/**; First Finish, **99/ each extra.**

No. 2948 Iron Mantel-piece.

Jambs,	...	...	...	...	...	11 inches.
Projection,	...	...	...	...	5¾ ,,
Lintel,	...	...	...	...	14 ,,
Openings { Width,	...	38	40	,,
Openings { Height,	...	38	38	,,
Width over Jambs,	...	60½	62½	,,
Height to Shelf,	...	54	54	,,
Double Shelf,	...	69 × 14	71 × 14	,,

PRICES.

Fine Cast and Painted one coat,	...	**84/ each.**
Enamelled in two Colors—		
Special Finish,	... ...	**139/6 ,,**
Best Finish,	... ...	**180/ ,,**
Enamelled in Imitation of Oak, Walnut, Rosewood, Marbles, or Granite—		
Special Finish,	... ...	**155/ ,,**
Best Finish,	... ...	**204/ ,,**

STRATFORD, E., WALTHAMSTOW, N.E., AND LEYTONSTONE, E., LONDON

MANTEL-PIECES

No. 2949 Iron Mantel-piece.

IRON MANTEL-PIECE

Jambs,	...	...	...	...	...	$9\frac{3}{4}$ inches
Projection,	...	...	...	...	...	3 ,,
Lintel,	...	...	...	...	...	$10\frac{1}{2}$,,
Opening { Width,	...	...	...	...	36 ,,
Opening { Height,	...	...	...	...	38 ,,
Width over Jambs,	...	...	...	...	52 ,,
Height to Shelf,	...	...	...	...	$46\frac{1}{2}$,,
Single Shelf,	...	...	...	...	$57\frac{1}{4} \times 8$,,

PRICES.

Fine Cast,	...	...	...	...	...	25/6 **each**
Enamelled in two Colors—						
Special Finish,	...	...	...	48/	,,
Best Finish,	...	...	...	69/	,,
Double Shelf,	...	...	...	...	3/9 **extra**.

No. 2950 Iron Mantel-piece.

IRON MANTEL-PIECE

Jambs,	...	...	$7\frac{1}{2}$	$8\frac{3}{4}$	$8\frac{3}{4}$ inches.
Projection,	...	...	$3\frac{1}{2}$	4	4 ,,
Lintel,	...	...	10	11	11 ,,
Openings { Width,	...	30	36	38 ,,
Openings { Height,	...	36	38	38 ,,
Width over Jambs,	...	$43\frac{1}{2}$	52	54 ,,
Height to Shelf,	...	45	48	$48\frac{1}{2}$,,
Double Shelf,	...	51×8	60×9	62×9 ,,

PRICES.

Sizes,	...	...	...	30	36	38 inches.
Fine Cast and Painted one coat, ...	33/	40/6	42/ **each**.
Enamelled in two Colors—				
Special Finish,	...	55/6	67/6	69/ ,,
Best Finish,	...	75/	90/	91/6 ,,
Enamelled in Imitation Oak, Walnut, Rosewood, Marbles, etc.—				
Special Finish,	...	60/	72/	73/6 ,,
Best Finish,	...	84/	96/	97/6 ,,

MANTEL-PIECES

No. 2951 Iron Mantel-piece.

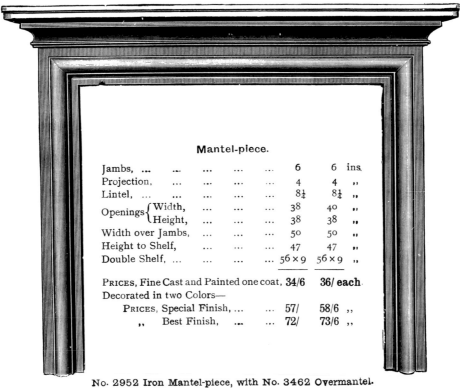

Mantel-piece.

Jambs,	...	...	...	...	6	6 ins.
Projection,	...	...	...	...	4	4 ,,
Lintel,	...	...	...	...	8¼	8¼ ,,
Openings { Width,	...	...	...	38	40 ,,
Height,	...	...	...	38	38 ,,
Width over Jambs,	...	...	...	50	50 ,,
Height to Shelf,	...	...	...	47	47 ,,
Double Shelf,	...	...	...	56 × 9	56 × 9 ,,

PRICES, Fine Cast and Painted one coat, **34/6 36/ each.**
Decorated in two Colors—

    PRICES, Special Finish, ... **57/ 58/6 ,,**
    ,,   Best Finish, ... **72/ 73/6 ,,**

No. 2952 Iron Mantel-piece, with No. 3462 Overmantel.

Overmantel.

Width,	...	...	54 ins.
Height,	...	...	16 ,,
Bevelled-edge Mirror,	...25 × 9 ,,
Serpentine Shelf,	...35 × 5 ,,

Mantel-piece, strong pattern, with extra deep return ends.

Jambs,	...	...	8 ins.
Projection,	...	...	7½ ,,
Lintel,	...	...	8½ ,,
Opening { Width,	...	38 ,,
Height,	...	38 ,,
Width over Jambs,	...	54 ,,
Height to Shelf,	...	46½ ,,
Double Shelf,	...	...58 × 10 ,,

PRICES.
—

Overmantel, with Mirror.

Fine Cast and Painted one coat,
36/ each.

Decorated in Oak, &c., or two Colors,
46/6 each.

PRICES.
—

Mantel-piece.

Fine Cast and Painted one coat,
51/ each.

Decorated in Oak, &c., or two Colors,
72/ each.

PRICES, COMPLETE.
—

No. 2952 **Iron Mantel-piece,** with No. 3462 **Overmantel.**

Fine Cast and Painted one coat,
87/ per set.

Decorated in Oak, &c., or two Colors,
118/6 per set.

MANTEL-PIECES, WITH OVERMANTELS

No. 2953 Mantel-piece, with No. 3463 Overmantel.

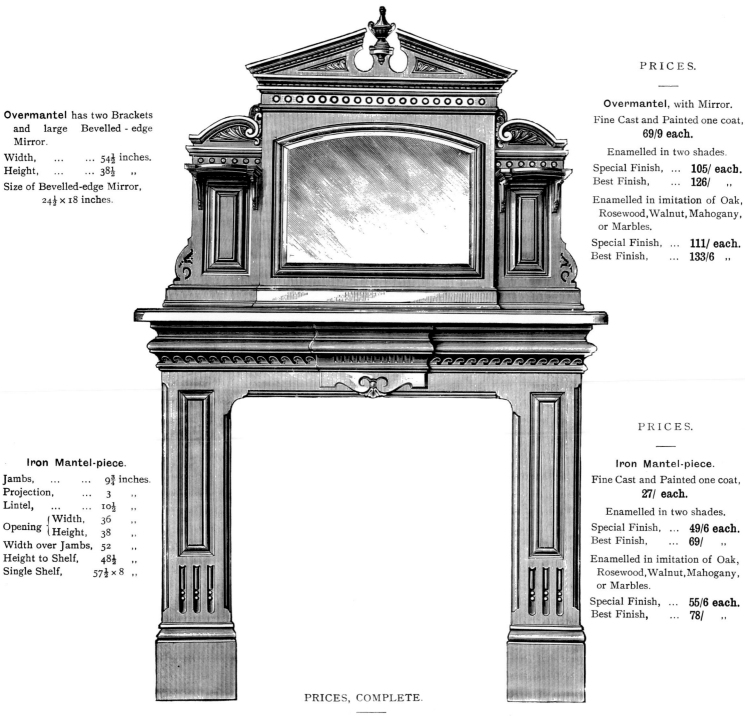

Overmantel has two Brackets and large Bevelled-edge Mirror.

Width,	... ...	54½ inches.
Height,	... ...	38½ ,,

Size of Bevelled-edge Mirror, 24½ × 18 inches.

PRICES.

Overmantel, with Mirror.

Fine Cast and Painted one coat,
69/9 each.

Enamelled in two shades.

Special Finish,	...	**105/ each.**
Best Finish,	...	**126/** ,,

Enamelled in imitation of Oak, Rosewood, Walnut, Mahogany, or Marbles.

Special Finish,	...	**111/ each.**
Best Finish,	...	**133/6** ,,

Iron Mantel-piece.

Jambs,	... ...	9¾ inches.
Projection,	...	3 ,,
Lintel,	...	10½ ,,
Opening { Width,	36	,,
{ Height,	38	,,
Width over Jambs,	52	,,
Height to Shelf,	48½	,,
Single Shelf,	57½ × 8	,,

PRICES.

Iron Mantel-piece.

Fine Cast and Painted one coat,
27/ each.

Enamelled in two shades.

Special Finish,	...	**49/6 each.**
Best Finish,	...	**69/** ,,

Enamelled in imitation of Oak, Rosewood, Walnut, Mahogany, or Marbles.

Special Finish,	...	**55/6 each.**
Best Finish,	...	**78/** ,,

PRICES, COMPLETE.

No. 2953 **Mantel-piece** and No. 3463 **Overmantel.**

Fine Cast and Painted one coat, ...	**96/9 per set.**	

Enamelled in two shades.

Special Finish, ...	**154/6 per set.**	
Best Finish, ...	**195/** ,,	

Enamelled in imitation of Oak, Rosewood, Walnut, Mahogany, or Marbles.

Special Finish, ...	**166/6 per set.**	
Best Finish, ...	**211/6** ,,	

Total height, 87 inches.

MANTEL-PIECES, WITH OVERMANTELS

No. 2954 Mantel-piece, with No. 3464 Overmantel.

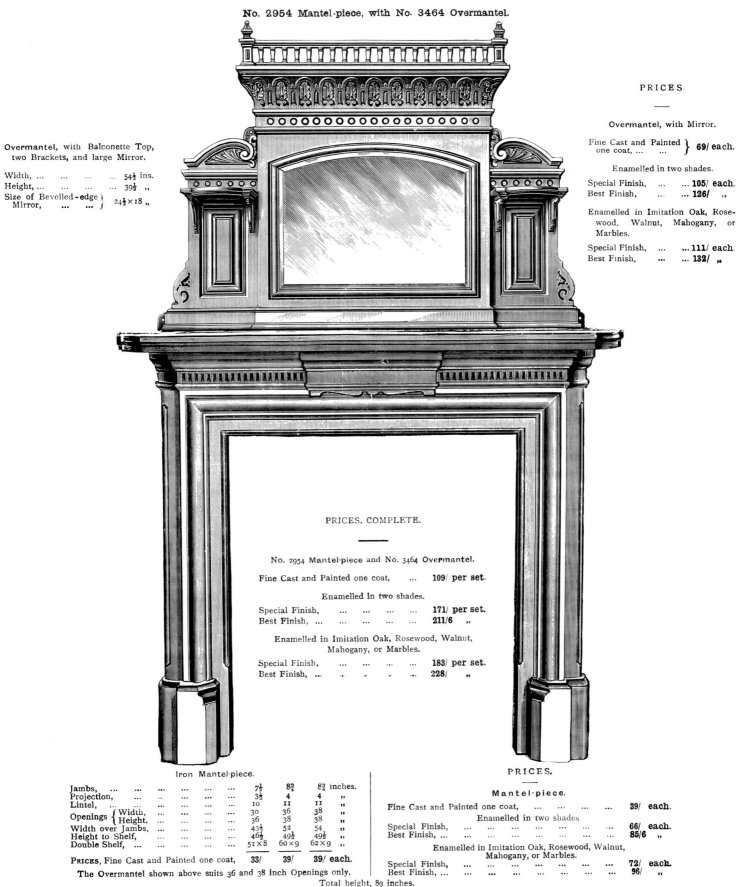

Overmantel, with Balconette Top, two Brackets, and large Mirror.

Width, ...	54½ ins.
Height, ...	39½ „
Size of Bevelled-edge Mirror, ...	24½ × 18 „

PRICES.

Overmantel, with Mirror.

Fine Cast and Painted one coat, ... } **69/ each.**

Enamelled in two shades.

Special Finish, ... **105/ each.**
Best Finish, ... **126/ „**

Enamelled in Imitation Oak, Rosewood, Walnut, Mahogany, or Marbles.

Special Finish, ... **111/ each.**
Best Finish, ... **132/ „**

PRICES, COMPLETE.

No. 2954 Mantel-piece and No. 3464 Overmantel.

Fine Cast and Painted one coat, ... **109/ per set.**

Enamelled in two shades.

Special Finish, ... **171/ per set.**
Best Finish, ... **211/6 „**

Enamelled in Imitation Oak, Rosewood, Walnut, Mahogany, or Marbles.

Special Finish, ... **183/ per set.**
Best Finish, ... **228/ „**

Iron Mantel-piece.

Jambs, ...	7½	8¾	8¾ inches.
Projection, ...	3½	4	4 „
Lintel, ...	10	11	11 „
Openings {Width, ...	30	36	38 „
Openings {Height, ...	36	38	38 „
Width over Jambs, ...	43½	52	54 „
Height to Shelf, ...	46½	49½	49½ „
Double Shelf, ...	51×8	60×9	62×9 „

PRICES, Fine Cast and Painted one coat, **33/ 39/ 39/ each.**

The Overmantel shown above suits 36 and 38 inch Openings only.

Total height, 89 inches.

PRICES.

Mantel-piece.

Fine Cast and Painted one coat, ... **39/ each.**
Enamelled in two shades.
Special Finish, ... **66/ each.**
Best Finish, ... **85/6 „**
Enamelled in Imitation Oak, Rosewood, Walnut, Mahogany, or Marbles.
Special Finish, ... **72/ each.**
Best Finish, ... **96/ „**

MANTEL-PIECES, WITH OVERMANTELS

No. 2967 Mantel-piece, with No. 3437 Overmantel

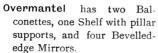

Overmantel has two Balconettes, one Shelf with pillar supports, and four Bevelled-edge Mirrors.

Width,	... ...	63 & 65 ins.
Height,	... ...	48 ,,
Large Centre Mirror,	36½ × 21 ,,
Small ,,	11 × 6 ,,
Top Side Mirrors,	9 × 6 ,,
Shelf,	... ...	42 × 6 ,,

PRICES.

Overmantel, with Mirrors.

Fine Cast and Painted one coat,
157/6 each.

Painted in two shades,
202/6 each.

Iron Mantel-piece.

Jambs, ...	11¼	11¼	11¼	11¼ ins.
Projection, ...	4¼	4¼	4¼	4¼ ,,
Lintel, ...	12	12	12	12 ,,
Openings { Width, ...	38	42	40	44 ,,
Openings { Height, ...	38	40	38	40 ,,
Width over Jambs, ...	59½	59½	61½	61½ ,,
Height to Shelf, ...	51½	51½	51½	51½ ,,
Double Shelf, ...	70 × 9	70 × 9	72 × 9	72 × 9 ,,

Total height, 99½ inches.

PRICES.

Mantel-piece.

Fine Cast and Painted one coat,	...	...	75/ each.
Painted in two Shades, ...	...	99/ ,,

PRICES, COMPLETE.

No. 2967 **Mantel-piece**, with No. 3437 **Overmantel.**

Fine Cast and Painted one coat,	...	232/6 per set.
Painted in two Shades, ...	...	301/6 ,,

MANTEL-PIECES, WITH OVERMANTELS

No. 2955 Mantel-piece, with No. 3465 Overmantel.

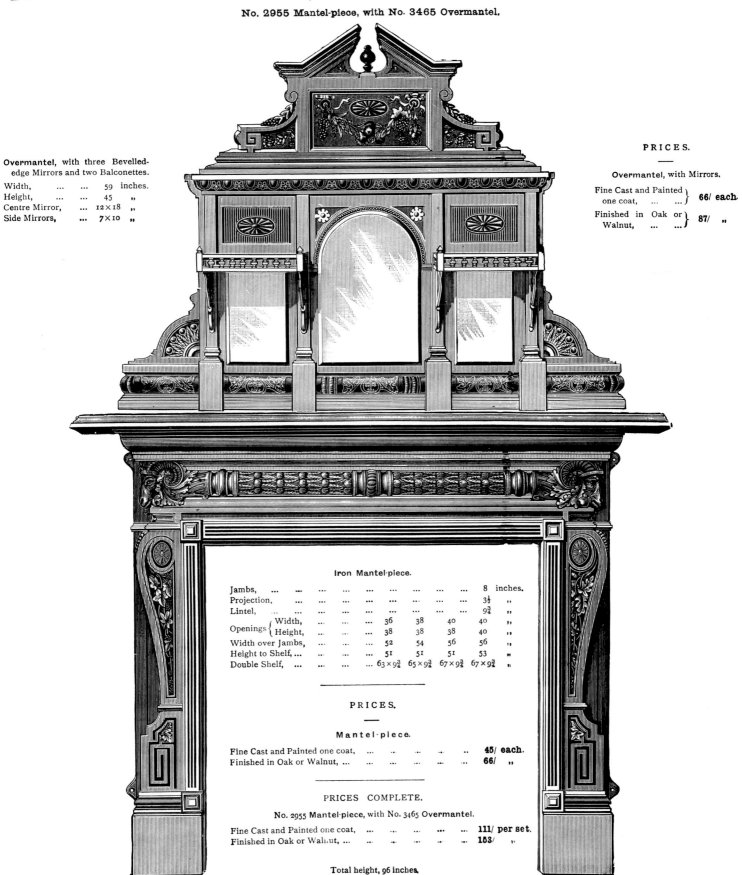

Overmantel, with three Bevelled-edge Mirrors and two Balconettes.

Width,	...	...	59 inches.
Height,	...	...	45 ,,
Centre Mirror,	...	12×18	,,
Side Mirrors,	...	7×10	,,

PRICES.

—

Overmantel, with Mirrors.

Fine Cast and Painted one coat, ... } 66/ **each**

Finished in Oak or Walnut, ... } 87/ ,,

Iron Mantel-piece.

Jambs,					8 inches.
Projection,					3½ ,,
Lintel,					9¾ ,,
Openings { Width,	36	38	40	40	,,
Openings { Height,	38	38	38	40	,,
Width over Jambs,	52	54	56	56	,,
Height to Shelf,	51	51	51	53	,,
Double Shelf,	63×9¾	65×9¾	67×9¾	67×9¾	,,

PRICES.

—

Mantel-piece.

Fine Cast and Painted one coat, ... 45/ **each.**

Finished in Oak or Walnut, ... 66/ ,,

PRICES COMPLETE.

No. 2955 Mantel-piece, with No. 3465 Overmantel.

Fine Cast and Painted one coat, ... 111/ **per set.**

Finished in Oak or Walnut, ... 153/ ,,

Total height, 96 inches.

STRATFORD, E., WALTHAMSTOW, N.E., AND LEYTONSTONE, E., LONDON

MANTEL-PIECES, WITH OVERMANTELS

No. 2957—The "Adam" Mantel-piece, with No. 3467 Overmantel.

Overmantel, with three
Bevelled-edge Mirrors.

Width,	...	...	52 inches.
Height,	...	...	36 ,,
Centre Mirror,	27 × 12½ ,,
Side Mirrors,	13½ × 3 ,,

PRICES.

——

Overmantel, with Mirrors.

Rubbed and Painted one coat,

69/ each.

Decorated in Oak, Walnut, &c.,
or two Colors,

93/ each.

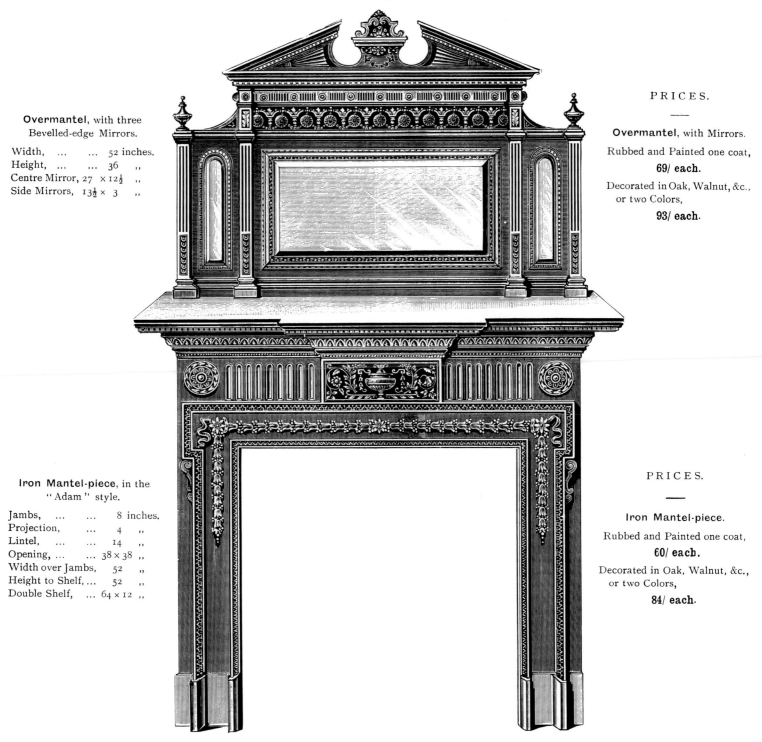

Iron Mantel-piece, in the
"Adam" style.

Jambs,	...	...	8 inches.
Projection,	...	4 ,,
Lintel,	...	...	14 ,,
Opening,	...	...	38 × 38 ,,
Width over Jambs,	52 ,,
Height to Shelf, ...	52 ,,
Double Shelf,	...	64 × 12 ,,

PRICES.

——

Iron Mantel-piece.

Rubbed and Painted one coat,

60/ each.

Decorated in Oak, Walnut, &c.,
or two Colors,

84/ each.

PRICES, COMPLETE.

——

No. 2957 **Mantel-piece**, with No. 3467 **Overmantel**.

Rubbed and Painted one coat, ... **129/** per set.
Decorated in Oak, Walnut, &c., or two Colors, ... **177/** ,,

Total Height, 86 inches.

MANTEL-PIECES, WITH OVERMANTELS

No. 2958 Mantel-piece, with No. 3468 Overmantel.

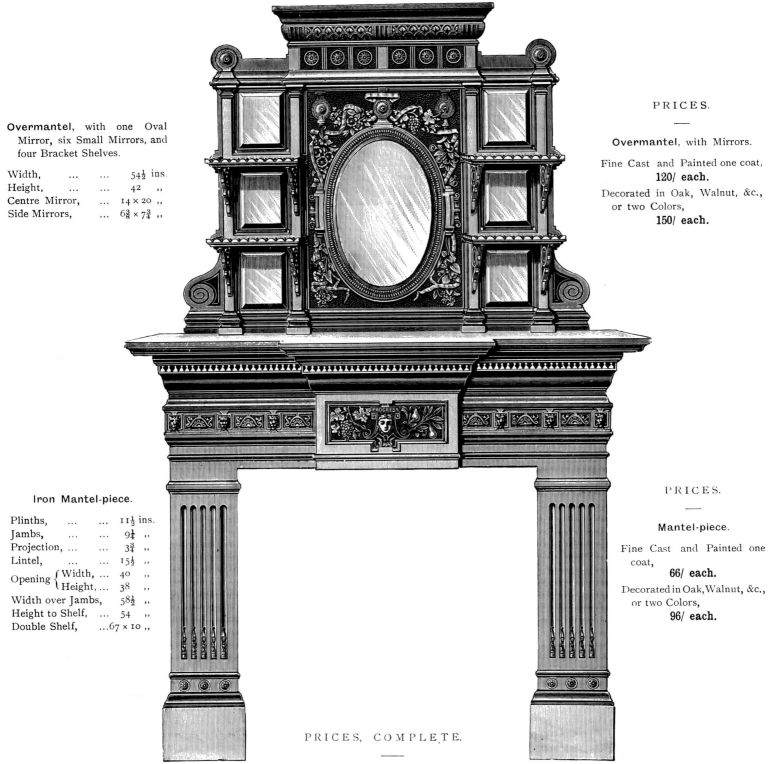

Overmantel, with one Oval Mirror, six Small Mirrors, and four Bracket Shelves.

Width,	... ...	54½ ins.
Height,	... ...	42 ,,
Centre Mirror,	...	14 × 20 ,,
Side Mirrors,	...	6⅜ × 7¾ ,,

PRICES.

—

Overmantel, with Mirrors.

Fine Cast and Painted one coat,
120/ each.

Decorated in Oak, Walnut, &c., or two Colors,
150/ each.

Iron Mantel-piece.

Plinths,	... ...	11½ ins.
Jambs,	... ...	9¼ ,,
Projection,	...	3¾ ,,
Lintel,	...	15½ ,,
Opening { Width, ...		40 ,,
{ Height, ...		38 ,,
Width over Jambs,		58½ ,,
Height to Shelf,	...	54 ,,
Double Shelf,	...67 × 10 ,,

PRICES.

—

Mantel-piece.

Fine Cast and Painted one coat,
66/ each.

Decorated in Oak, Walnut, &c., or two Colors,
96/ each.

PRICES, COMPLETE.

—

No. 2958 Mantel-piece, with No. 3468 Overmantel.

Fine Cast and Painted one coat, ... **186/ per set.**
Decorated in Oak, Walnut, &c., or two Colors, **246/ ,,**

Total Height, 96 inches.

CHIMNEY PIECES: WITH TILE GRATES.

DESIGN
No. 2330

ENAMELLED
SLATE.

BLACK AND
PORPHYRY SPAR
WITH
GILT LINES.

DESIGN
No. 2357

ENAMELLED
SLATE.

WAULSORT
WITH BLACK
MOUNTS.

No. T. P. 154
Tile Panel

No. 3388
THE "CHESTER"
TILE GRATE.

No. T. P. 155
Tile Panel

DESIGN
No. 2331

ENAMELLED
SLATE.

DOVE AND
RED LIMESTONE
WITH BLACK
MOUNTS.

DESIGN
No. 2301

ENAMELLED
SLATE.

GREEN SERPENTINE
AND SPANISH
BROCATELLA
WITH
GILT LINES.

No. T. P. 156
Tile Panel

No. 2454
THE "HEREFORD"
TILE GRATE.

No. T. P. 157
Tile Panel

LITHOGRAPHED BY ALLBUT & DANIEL, HANLEY.

No. P 131

No. P 132

No. P 133

No. P 134

No. P 135

No. P 136

ALLBUT & DANIEL.

SCALE ¾ INCH TO THE FOOT.

LITH? HANLEY.

YOUNG & MARTEN'S LATEST DESIGNS FOR TILE PANELS & TESSELATED TILE PAVEMENTS.

YOUNG & MARTEN, CALEDONIAN WORKS, STRATFORD, LONDON, E.

COMBINATION BATHS

No. P3165. THE "ROLLARGIO" ROMAN SHAPE BATH

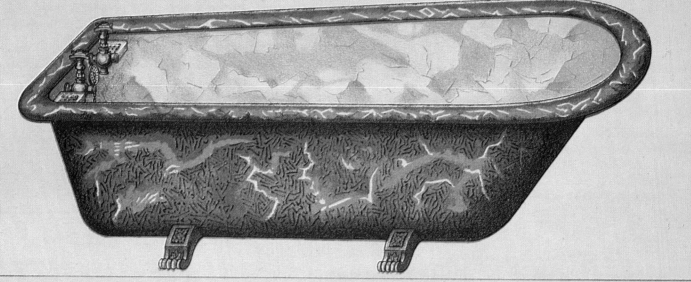

No. P1559. THE "CASCADIO" ROMAN SHAPE BATH

No. P4458. THE "VALORIO" ROMAN SHAPE BATH

STRATFORD, WALTHAMSTOW AND LEYTONSTONE.

PRICES OF THESE DESIGNS ARE GIVEN ON PAGE 16.

YOUNG & MARTEN, LTD.

DESIGNED IN YOUNG & MARTEN'S, LTD. STAINED GLASS STUDIOS,
Caledonian Works, STRATFORD, LONDON, E

17

YOUNG & MARTEN, LTD. LATEST DESIGNS FOR LEADED CATHEDRAL LIGHTS.

PRICES OF THESE DESIGNS ARE GIVEN ON PAGE 16.

YOUNG & MARTEN, LTD.

DESIGNED IN YOUNG & MARTEN'S, LTD. STAINED GLASS STUDIOS,
Caledonian Works, STRATFORD, LONDON, E

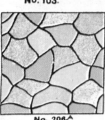

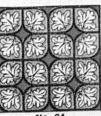

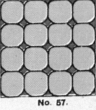

DURESCO

THE IMPROVED WATER PAINT.

TO HER MAJESTY'S WAR DEPARTMENT, ADMIRALTY, POST OFFICE, INDIA OFFICE, OFFICE OF WORKS, PRISONS, AND LONDON COUNTY COUNCIL.

For the treatment of Walls and Ceilings, either in Plain Work or Artistic Decoration.

DRIES PERFECTLY FLAT, AND IS NOT ABSORBENT LIKE COMMON DISTEMPER.

DURESCO is recommended for use in

HOSPITALS ASYLUMS	WORKHOUSES SCHOOLS	CHURCHES PUBLIC OFFICES	HOTELS HYDROPATHICS	BATHS & WASHHOUSES DWELLING HOUSES	OUTSIDE BUILDINGS STABLES

AND ALL PUBLIC BUILDINGS.

No. 97 INDIAN GREY.	No. 92 SILVER GREY.	No. 93 VERMILION TINT.	No. 46 WHITE.	No. 81 PALE BLUE.	No. 82 TERRA-COTTA.	No. 55 CHOCOLATE.
No. 52 DARK SAGE GREEN.	No. 86 CREAM.	No. 74 BRICK RED.	No. 49 PALE GREY.	No. 68 MAUVE.	No. 90 PALE BUFF.	No. 91 ENGLISH GREY.
No. 75 MAROON.	No. 88 SALMON PINK.	No. 87 OLIVE TINT.	No. 48 STUCCO.	No. 85 PALE GREEN.	No. 47 LIGHT STONE.	No. 80 BRIGHT RED.
No. 53 SALMON TINT.	No. 89 BLUE GREEN.	No. 63 BUFF.	No. 98 PALE ROSE.	No. 94 FRENCH GREY.	No. 70 GOLDEN YELLOW.	No. 71 PEACOCK BLUE.
No. 83 PALE YELLOW	No. 65 CITRON.	No. 99 LILAC.	No. 67 NEUTRAL GREY.	No. 62 LIGHT DRAB.	No. 64 PRIMROSE.	No. 59 STOCK BRICK.
No. 84 DEEP GREEN.	No. 96 PALE SALMON.	No. 72 CEMENT COLOR.	No. 69 AZURE.	No. 73 NEUTRAL BROWN.	No. 95 DUTCH GREY.	No. 66 PALE SAGE GREEN.

DURESCO in all Stock Colours, 30/- per cwt.   PETRIFYING LIQUID, 2/6 per gallon.

MANTEL-PIECES, WITH OVERMANTELS

No. 2959 Mantel-piece, with No. 3469 Overmantel.

Overmantel, with three Bevelled-edge Mirrors, two Pillars, and two Double Shelves.

Width,	... ...	55 ins.
Height,	... ...	37½ ,,
Centre Mirror,	24 × 11	,,
Side Mirrors,	6 × 11	,,
First Shelf,	... 54 × 4	,,
Second Shelf,	30 × 2¾	,,

PRICES.

Overmantel, with Mirrors.

Fine Cast and Painted one coat,

81/ each.

Decorated in Oak, Walnut, &c., or two Colors,

105/ each.

Iron Mantel-piece.

Jambs,	... ...	9 ins.
Projection,	... ...	5½ ,,
Lintel,	... ...	14 ,,
Opening,	...	38 × 38 ,,
Width over Jambs,	...	56 ,,
Height to Shelf,	...	53 ,,
Double Shelf,	... ...	65 × 11 ,,

PRICES.

Mantel-piece.

Fine Cast and Painted one coat,

84/ each.

Decorated in Oak, Walnut, &c, or two Colors,

108/ each.

PRICES, COMPLETE.

No. 2959 Mantel-piece, with No. 3469 Overmantel.

Fine Cast and Painted one coat, ... **165/ per set.**

Decorated in Oak, Walnut, &c., or two Colors, **213/ ,,**

Total height, 90½ inches.

STRATFORD, E., WALTHAMSTOW, N.E., AND LEYTONSTONE, E., LONDON

MANTEL-PIECES, WITH OVERMANTELS

No. 2960 Mantel-piece, with No. 3450 Overmantel.

Overmantel, with one large and two small Bevelled-edge Mirrors and two Balconettes.

Width,	... ...	68 ins.
Height,	... ...	43 ,,
Centre Mirror,	28 × 19	,,
Side Mirrors,	5½ × 8	,,

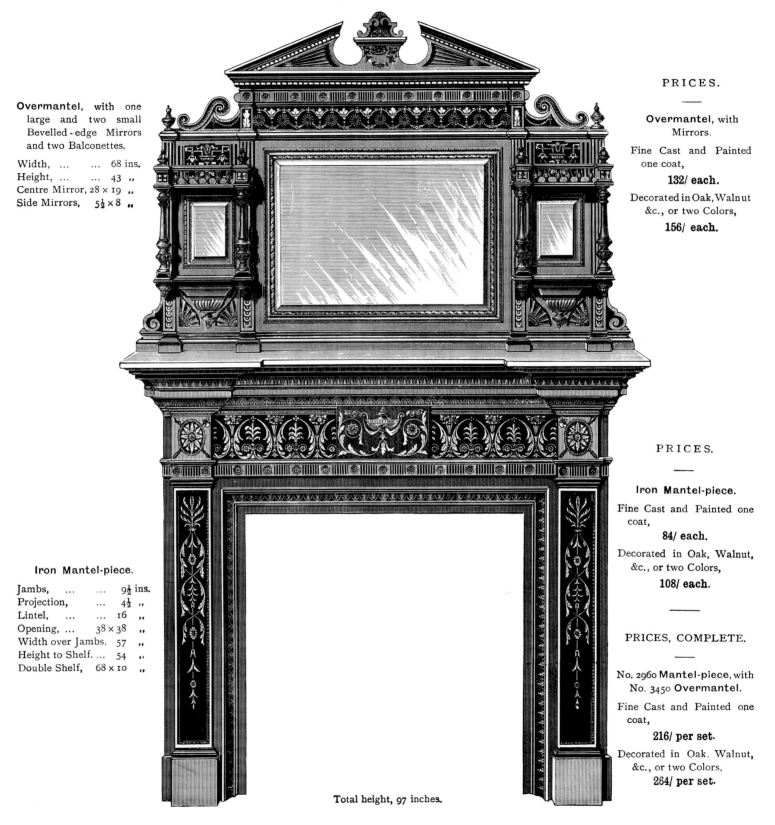

PRICES.

Overmantel, with Mirrors.

Fine Cast and Painted one coat,

132/ each.

Decorated in Oak, Walnut &c., or two Colors,

156/ each.

PRICES.

Iron Mantel-piece.

Fine Cast and Painted one coat,

84/ each.

Decorated in Oak, Walnut, &c., or two Colors,

108/ each.

PRICES, COMPLETE.

No. 2960 **Mantel-piece**, with No. 3450 **Overmantel.**

Fine Cast and Painted one coat,

216/ per set.

Decorated in Oak, Walnut, &c., or two Colors,

264/ per set.

Iron Mantel-piece.

Jambs,	... ...	9½ ins.
Projection,	...	4½ ,,
Lintel,	... ...	16 ,,
Opening,	...	38 × 38 ,,
Width over Jambs,	57	,,
Height to Shelf,	...	54 ,,
Double Shelf,	68 × 10	,,

Total height, 97 inches.

MANTEL-PIECES, WITH OVERMANTELS

No. 2961 Mantel-piece, with No. 3461 Overmantel.

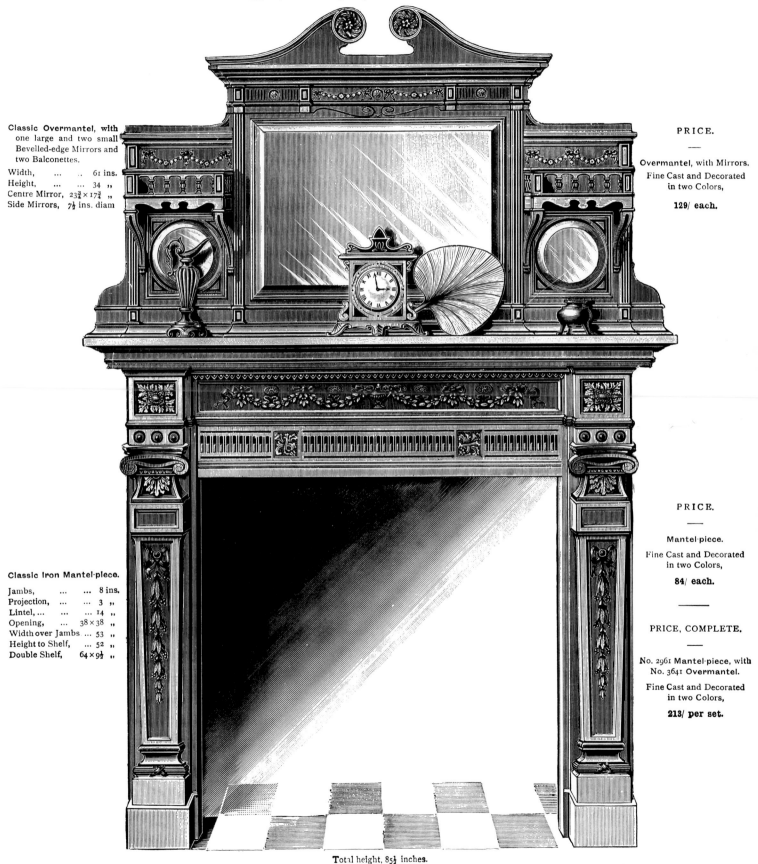

Classic Overmantel, with
one large and two small
Bevelled-edge Mirrors and
two Balconettes.

Width,	... ..	61 ins.
Height,	... ...	34 „
Centre Mirror,	23¾ × 17¾	„
Side Mirrors,	7½ ins. diam	

PRICE.

Overmantel, with Mirrors.
Fine Cast and Decorated
in two Colors,

129/ each.

Classic Iron Mantel-piece.

Jambs,	... ...	8 ins.
Projection,	... ...	3 „
Lintel, ...	... ...	14 „
Opening,	...	38 × 38 „
Width over Jambs	...	53 „
Height to Shelf,	...	52 „
Double Shelf,	64 × 9½	„

PRICE.
—
Mantel-piece.
Fine Cast and Decorated
in two Colors,

84/ each.

———

PRICE, COMPLETE.
—

No. 2961 Mantel-piece, with
No. 3641 Overmantel.

Fine Cast and Decorated
in two Colors,

213/ per set.

Total height, 85½ inches.

MANTEL-PIECES, WITH OVERMANTELS

No. 2962 Mantel-piece, with No. 3442 Overmantel.

Overmantel, in "Louis XIV" Style, with Oval Bevelled-edge Mirror.

Width, ... 54 ins.
Height, ... 35 ,,
Mirror, ... 24 × 18¼ ,,

PRICE.

—

Overmantel, with Mirror.

Fine Cast and Decorated in two Colors,

81/ each.

Iron Mantel-piece, in "Louis XIV" Style.

Jambs, ... 8 ins.
Projection, ... 3½ ,,
Lintel, ... 9 ,,
Opening, ... 38 × 38 ,,
Width over Jambs, 54 ,,
Height to Shelf, 51 ,,
Double Shelf, 66 × 11½ ,,

PRICE.

—

Mantel-piece.

Fine Cast and Decorated in two Colors,

99/ each.

PRICE, COMPLETE.

—

No 2962 Mantel-piece, with No. 3442 Overmantel.

Fine Cast and Decorated in two Colors,

180/ per set.

Total Height, 86 inches.

STRATFORD, E., WALTHAMSTOW, N.E., AND LEYTONSTONE, E., LONDON

MANTEL-PIECES, WITH OVERMANTELS

No. 2963 Mantel-piece, with No. 3443 Overmantel.

Overmantel, with three Bevelled-edge Mirrors.

Width, ... 65 ins.
Height, ... 32 ,,
Three Mirrors, 12 × 21 ,,

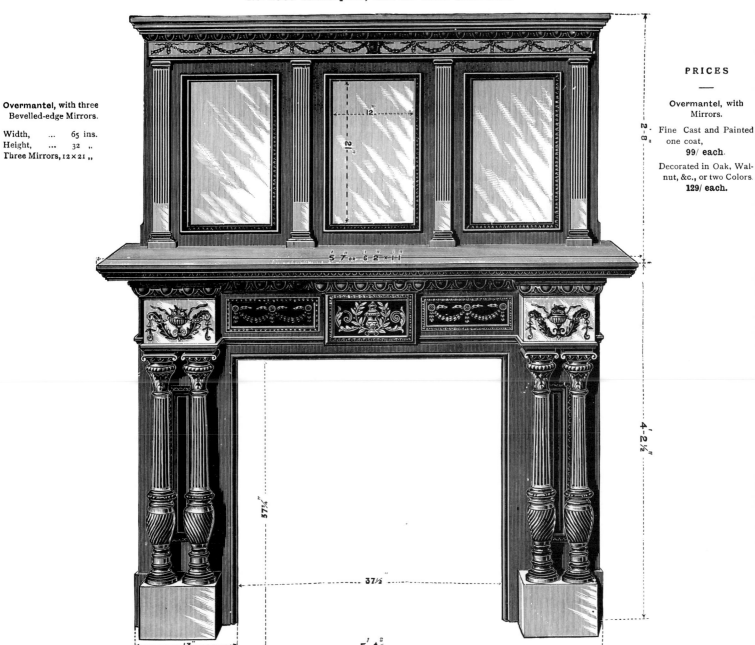

PRICES

Overmantel, with Mirrors.

Fine Cast and Painted one coat,
99/ each.

Decorated in Oak, Walnut, &c., or two Colors.
129/ each.

Massive Iron Mantel-piece, with Sub-bases supporting two Columns to each Pier, Ornamental Capital, and Egg and Tongue Moulding, Double Corniced Shelf.

Piers or Jambs, ...	13 inches.
Projection, ...	8½ ,,
Lintel, ...	11 ,,
Opening, ...	38 × 38 ,,
Width over Jambs, ...	64 ,,
Height to Shelf, ...	50½ ,,
Double Shelf, ...	67 or 74 × 13 ,,

Total height, 82½ inches.

PRICES.

Mantel-piece

Fine Cast and Painted one coat, ...	**210/ each.**
Decorated in Oak, Walnut, &c., or two Colors, ...	**261/ ,,**

PRICES, COMPLETE.

No. 2963 Mantel-piece, with No. 3443 Overmantel.

Fine Cast and Painted one coat, ...	**309/ per set.**
Decorated in Oak, Walnut, &c., or two Colors, ...	**390/ ,,**

MANTEL-PIECES, WITH OVERMANTELS

No. 2964 Mantel-piece, with No. 3444 Overmantel.

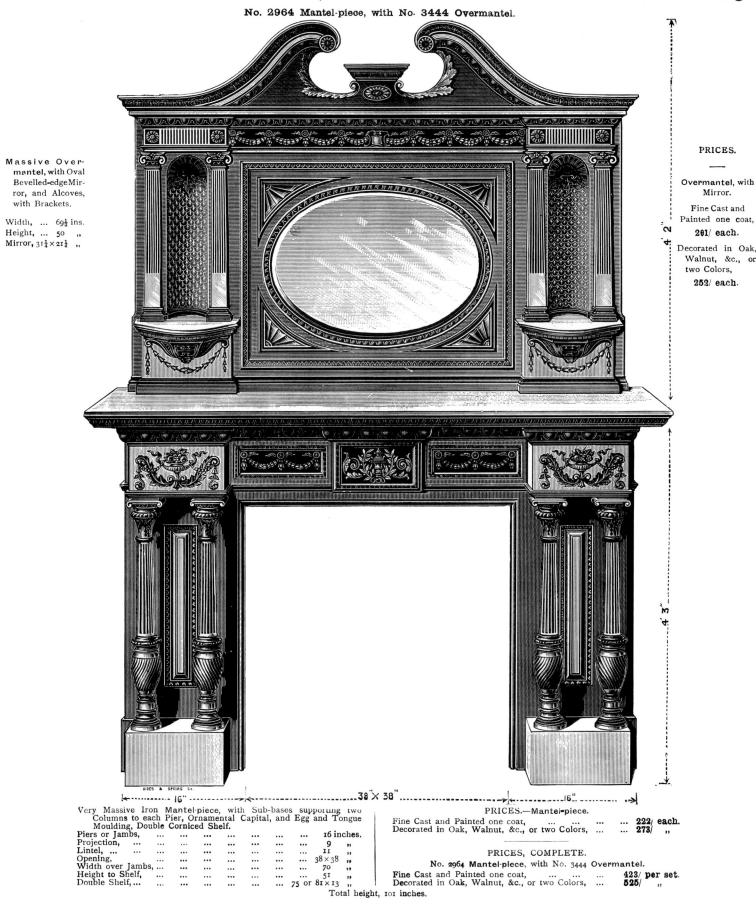

Massive Over-
mantel, with Oval
Bevelled-edge Mir-
ror, and Alcoves,
with Brackets.

Width, ... 69½ ins.
Height, ... 50 ,,
Mirror, 31¼ × 21¼ ,,

PRICES.

Overmantel, with
Mirror.

Fine Cast and
Painted one coat,
201/ each.

Decorated in Oak,
Walnut, &c., or
two Colors,
252/ each.

Very Massive Iron Mantel-piece, with Sub-bases supporting two
Columns to each Pier, Ornamental Capital, and Egg and Tongue
Moulding, Double Corniced Shelf.

Piers or Jambs,	...	...	...	...	...	...	...	16 inches.
Projection,	...	...	...	...	...	...	...	9 ,,
Lintel, ...	...	...	...	...	...	...	...	11 ,,
Opening,	...	...	...	...	...	...	...	38 × 38 ,,
Width over Jambs,	...	...	...	...	...	...	...	70 ,,
Height to Shelf,	...	...	...	...	...	...	...	51 ,,
Double Shelf, ...	...	...	...	...	...	...	...	75 or 81 × 13 ,,

Total height, 101 inches.

PRICES.—Mantel-piece.

Fine Cast and Painted one coat, ... **222/ each.**
Decorated in Oak, Walnut, &c., or two Colors, ... **273/ ,,**

PRICES, COMPLETE.

No. 2964 Mantel-piece, with No. 3444 Overmantel.

Fine Cast and Painted one coat, ... **423/ per set.**
Decorated in Oak, Walnut, &c., or two Colors, ... **525/ ,,**

WOOD CHIMNEY-PIECES

No. 3431 Wood Chimney-piece.

No. 3432 Wood Chimney-piece.

Width of Shelf, 9 inches.

PRICE—Pine,	...	...	...	...	...	...	24/ each.
,, Mahogany,	...	...	...	...	...	...	49/6 ,,
,, Oak,	...	...	...	...	...	...	52/6 ,,
,, Walnut, ...	...	...	...	...	...	...	57/ ,,

Width of Shelf, 10 inches.

PRICE—Pine,	..	...	...	...	...	...	39/ each.
,, Mahogany,	...	...	...	...	...	...	78/ ,,
,, Oak,	...	...	...	...	...	...	84/ ,,
,, Walnut, ...	...	...	...	...	...	...	90/ ,,

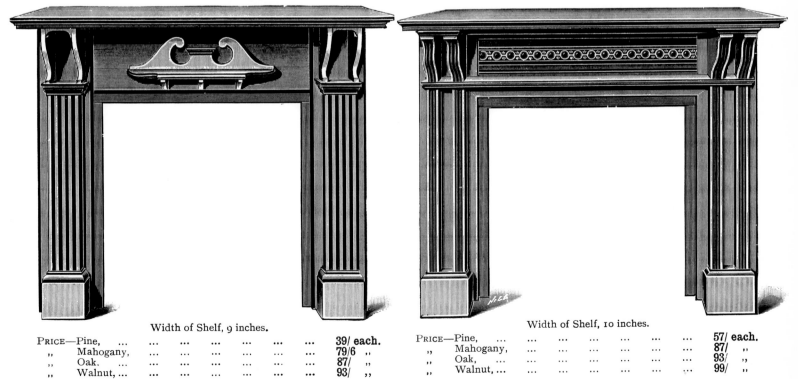

No. 3433 Wood Chimney-piece.

No. 3434 Wood Chimney-piece.

Width of Shelf, 9 inches.

PRICE—Pine,	...	...	...	...	...	...	39/ each.
,, Mahogany,	...	...	...	...	...	...	79/6 ,,
,, Oak. ...	...	...	...	...	...	...	87/ ,,
,, Walnut, ...	...	...	...	...	...	...	93/ ,,

Width of Shelf, 10 inches.

PRICE—Pine,	...	...	...	...	...	...	57/ each.
,, Mahogany,	...	...	...	...	...	...	87/ ,,
,, Oak,	...	...	...	...	...	...	93/ ,,
,, Walnut, ...	...	...	...	...	...	...	99/ ,,

Marble or Enamelled Slate Inner Mouldings, if required, are extra.

WOOD CHIMNEY-PIECES

No. 3435 Wood Chimney-piece.

Width of Shelf, 10 inches.

Openings adjustable.

—

PRICES.

Deal or Pine,	...	...	...	...	**48/ each.**
Mahogany,	...	...	...	...	**84/ ,,**
Oak,	...	...	...	...	**90/ ,,**
Walnut,	...	...	...	...	**93/ ,,**

No. 3436 Wood Chimney-piece.

Width of Shelf, 12 inches.

Openings adjustable.

—

PRICES.

Deal,	...	...	...	...	**102/ each.**
Mahogany,	...	...	...	...	**168/ ,,**
Oak, ...	...	...	...	...	**180/ ,,**
Walnut,	...	...	...	...	**189/ ,,**

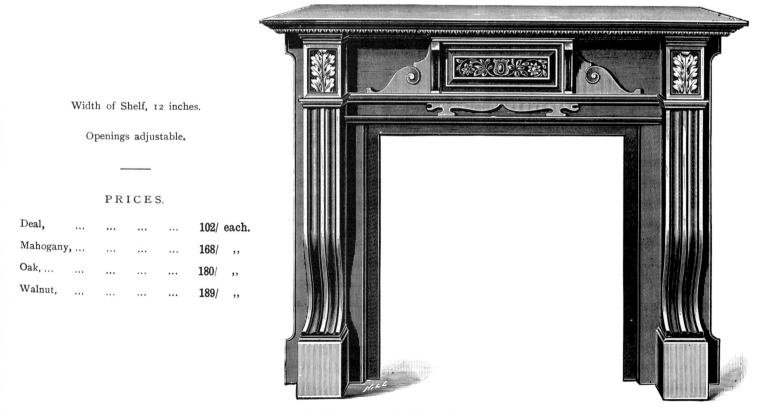

Marble or Enamelled Slate Inner Mouldings, if required, are extra.

STRATFORD, E., WALTHAMSTOW, N.E., AND LEYTONSTONE, E., LONDON

CHIMNEY-PIECES

Manufactured from picked Marble; well made and finished.

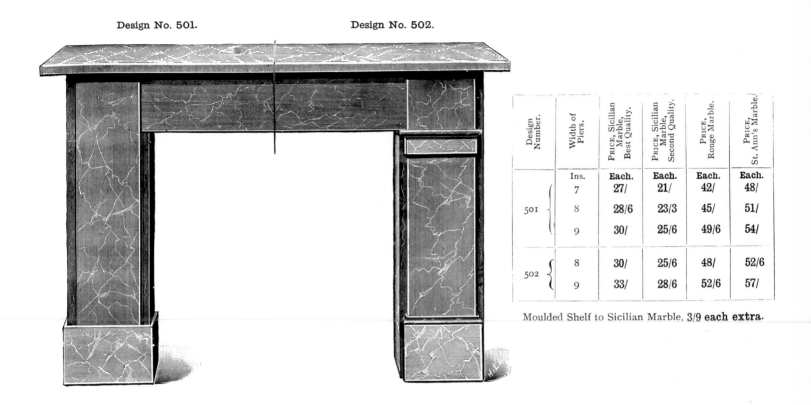

Design No. 501.   Design No. 502.

Design Number.	Width of Piers.	PRICE, Sicilian Marble, Best Quality.	PRICE, Sicilian Marble, Second Quality.	PRICE, Rouge Marble.	PRICE, St. Ann's Marble.
	Ins.	Each.	Each.	Each.	Each.
501	7	27/	21/	42/	48/
	8	28/6	23/3	45/	51/
	9	30/	25/6	49/6	54/
502	8	30/	25/6	48/	52/6
	9	33/	28/6	52/6	57/

Moulded Shelf to Sicilian Marble, 3/9 **each extra.**

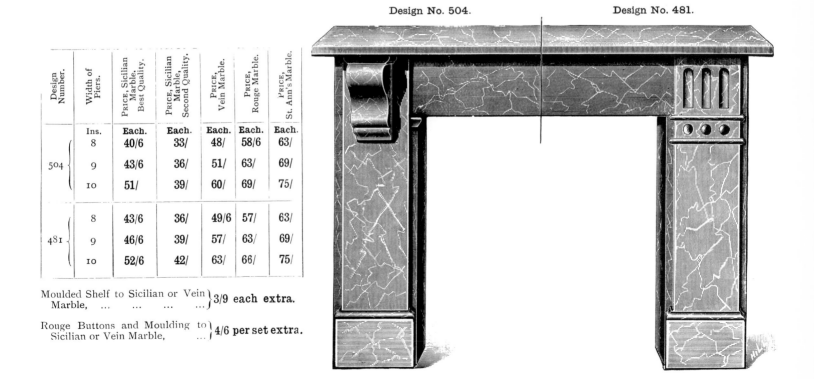

Design No. 504.   Design No. 481.

Design Number.	Width of Piers.	PRICE, Sicilian Marble, Best Quality.	PRICE, Sicilian Marble, Second Quality.	PRICE, Vein Marble.	PRICE, Rouge Marble.	PRICE, St. Ann's Marble.
	Ins.	Each.	Each.	Each.	Each.	Each.
504	8	40/6	33/	48/	58/6	63/
	9	43/6	36/	51/	63/	69/
	10	51/	39/	60/	69/	75/
481	8	43/6	36/	49/6	57/	63/
	9	46/6	39/	57/	63/	69/
	10	52/6	42/	63/	66/	75/

Moulded Shelf to Sicilian or Vein Marble, ... } 3/9 **each extra.**

Rouge Buttons and Moulding to Sicilian or Vein Marble, ... } 4/6 **per set extra.**

CHIMNEY-PIECES

Manufactured from picked Marble; well made and finished.

Design No. 2204.

Design Number.	Width of Piers.	PRICE, Sicilian Marble.	PRICE, Vein Marble.
2204	10 ins.	72/ each.	81/ each.
	11 ,,	78/ ,,	87/ ,,
	12 ,,	84/ ,,	93/ ,,

Rouge Mounts, **7/6 per set extra.**

Sienna ,, 10/6 ,, ,,

Design No. 507.   Design No. 506.

Design Number.	Width of Piers.	PRICE, Sicilian Marble, Best Quality.	PRICE, Sicilian Marble, Second Quality.	PRICE, Vein Marble.	PRICE, Rouge Marble.	PRICE, St. Ann's Marble.
	Ins.	Each.	Each.	Each.	Each.	Each.
	9	—	—	—	—	—
507	10	78/9	63/	† 84/	94/6	99/
	11	84/	69/	† 93/	100/6	105/
	12	90/	78/	† 99/	105/	108/
	9	66/	—	81/	90/	96/
506	10	75/	66/	87/	96/	99/
	11	85/6	72/	99/	102/	105/
	12	97/6	81/	114/	108/	111/

† Rouge Mounts, **7/6 per set extra.**

† Sienna ,, 10/6 ,, ,,

CHIMNEY-PIECES

Manufactured from picked Marble; well made and finished.

Design No. 2205.

Chimney - piece, in Bastard Statuary Marble, with Carved Floral Panels, as drawn, 12-inch Piers; 13-inch Double Shelf.

PRICE, ... **£7 17 6 each.**

Design No. 2206.

Chimney-piece, in Bastard Statuary Marble, with Carved Patras, as drawn, 12-inch Piers; 13-inch Double Shelf.

PRICE, ... **£11 5 0 each.**

CHIMNEY-PIECES,

WHITE MARBLES.

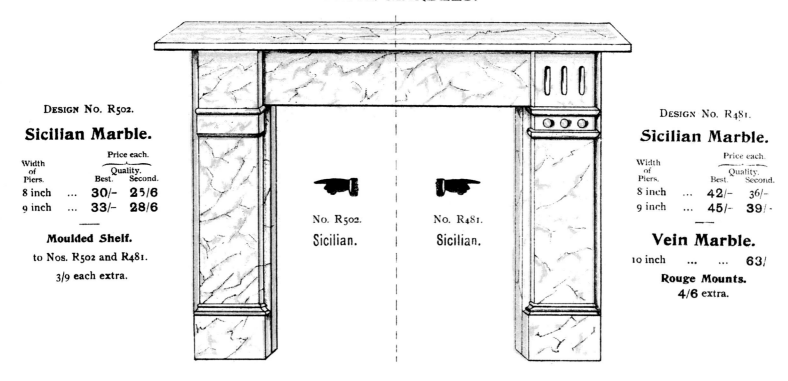

DESIGN No. R502.

Sicilian Marble.

| Width of Piers. | Price each. | |
	Best.	Second.
		Quality.
8 inch ...	30/-	25/6
9 inch ...	33/-	28/6

Moulded Shelf.

to Nos. R502 and R481.

3/9 each extra.

No. R502.
Sicilian.

No. R481.
Sicilian.

DESIGN No. R481.

Sicilian Marble.

| Width of Piers. | Price each. | |
	Best.	Second.
		Quality.
8 inch ...	42/-	36/-
9 inch ...	45/-	39/-

Vein Marble.

| 10 inch ... ... | 63/ |

Rouge Mounts.
4/6 extra.

**We recommend OUR BEST QUALITY, which is manufactured from Pickled Marble, WELL MADE and FINISHED
The Second Quality is only suitable for secondary purposes.**

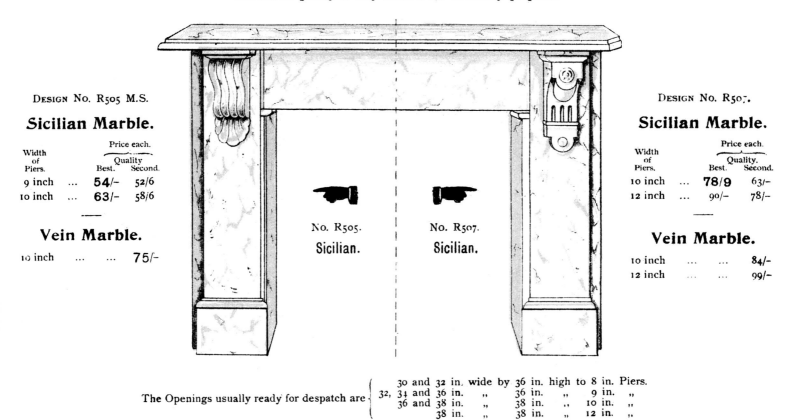

DESIGN No. R505 M.S.

Sicilian Marble.

| Width of Piers. | Price each. | |
	Best.	Second.
		Quality
9 inch ...	54/-	52/6
10 inch ...	63/-	58/6

Vein Marble.

| 10 inch ... ... | 75/- |

No. R505.
Sicilian.

No. R507.
Sicilian.

DESIGN No. R507.

Sicilian Marble.

| Width of Piers. | Price each. | |
	Best.	Second.
		Quality.
10 inch ...	78/9	63/-
12 inch ...	90/-	78/-

Vein Marble.

| 10 inch ... ... | 84/- |
| 12 inch ... ... | 99/- |

The Openings usually ready for despatch are

30 and 32 in. wide by 36 in. high to 8 in. Piers.		
32, 34 and 36 in. ,, 36 in. ,, 9 in. ,,		
36 and 38 in. ,, 38 in. ,, 10 in. ,,		
38 in. ,, 38 in. ,, 12 in. ,,		

STRATFORD, Walthamstow, and Leytonstone.

CHIMNEY-PIECES,

WHITE MARBLES.

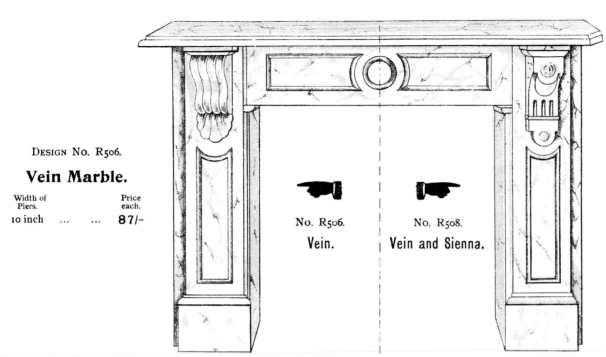

DESIGN No. R506.

Vein Marble.

Width of Piers.		Price each.
10 inch	... ...	87/-

DESIGN No. R508.

Vein Marble. with Sienna Mounts.

Width of Piers.		Price each.
10 inch	... ...	96/-
12 inch	... ..	114/-

No. R506.
Vein.

No. R508.
Vein and Sienna.

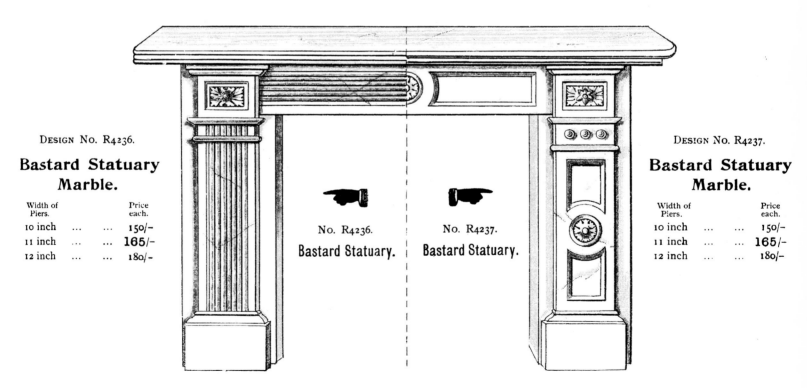

DESIGN No. R4236.

Bastard Statuary Marble.

Width of Piers.		Price each.
10 inch	... ...	150/-
11 inch	... ...	165/-
12 inch	... ...	180/-

DESIGN No. R4237.

Bastard Statuary Marble.

Width of Piers.		Price each.
10 inch	... ...	150/-
11 inch	... ...	165/-
12 inch	... ...	180/-

No. R4236.
Bastard Statuary.

No. R4237.
Bastard Statuary.

MANUFACTURED FROM PICKLED MARBLE. WELL MADE AND FINISHED.

We Stock the above designs with 38 inch by 38 inch Openings in the sizes priced in larger letterpress.

STRATFORD, Walthamstow, and Leytonstone.

CHIMNEY-PIECES,

WHITE MARBLES.

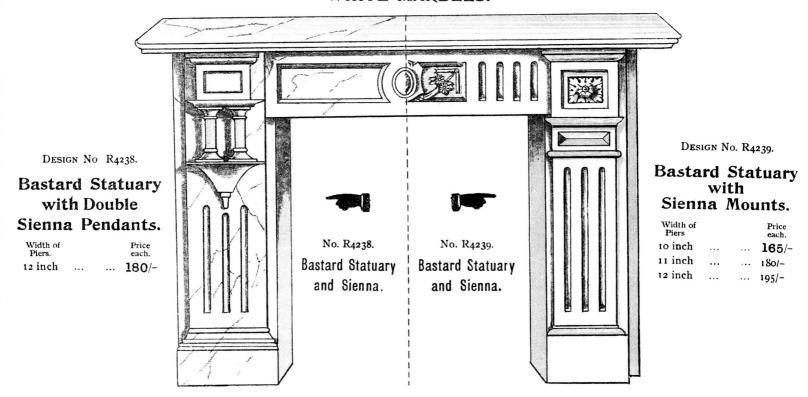

DESIGN No R4238.

Bastard Statuary with Double Sienna Pendants.

Width of Piers.	Price each.
12 inch ...	... 180/-

No. R4238.
Bastard Statuary and Sienna.

No. R4239.
Bastard Statuary and Sienna.

DESIGN No. R4239.

Bastard Statuary with Sienna Mounts.

Width of Piers	Price each.
10 inch ...	... 165/-
11 inch ...	... 180/-
12 inch ...	... 195/-

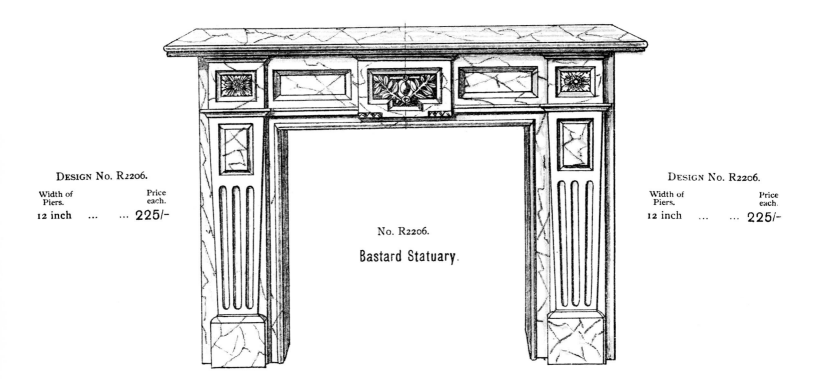

DESIGN No. R2206.

Width of Piers.	Price each.
12 inch ...	... 225/-

No. R2206.

Bastard Statuary.

DESIGN No. R2206.

Width of Piers.	Price each.
12 inch ...	... 225/-

We Stock the above designs with 38 inch by 38 inch Openings in the sizes priced in larger letterpress.

STRATFORD, Walthamstow, and Leytonstone.

TILE GRATES

No. 3250—Russell's Patent "Tit-Bits" Tile Grate.

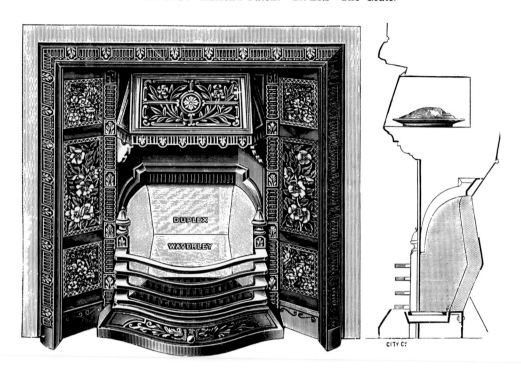

RUSSELL'S Patent " Tit-Bits " Grate, with oven in the canopy, supplies a long-felt want in almost every household, by providing an oven in the canopy of the ordinary dining or breakfast-room grate, in which plates or food can be kept warm. It is almost impossible to point out the numerous instances in which an oven in the breakfast room or dining room would have been an acquisition. Most people are occasionally called away from the table through some cause or other, and the food if not sent into the kitchen to keep warm is, as a matter of course, cold when they return. It is also especially useful where there are children, as some of them are either late at meals or have occasionally to leave the table; the food can then be put into the oven and kept hot, without the trouble and inconvenience of sending it into the kitchen. For the sick room and nursery these Grates will be found very valuable, and all who have used them speak in the highest terms of their usefulness.

The oven is so arranged behind the canopy as not to interfere with the ordinary appearance of a register grate, and it is only by turning down the front plate of canopy, which forms the door, that a good-sized oven is disclosed ; always warm when there is a fire, and ready at any moment for use.

The oven is loose, and draws out to allow of chimney sweeping.

Width,														36	38	40 inches.
Height,														38	38	38 ,,
Fire,														15	15	15 ,,

PRICE (without Tiles), Berlin Black and Ground Front, ...   **69/** each.

,,   ,,   ,,   Superior Finish, ...   **78/** ,,

No. T P 85 Tiles, fitted, **23/3 per set extra.**

The Tiles may be alternated, when so desired, for other patterns shown on lithographed sheets, and the difference in value charged or allowed.

STRATFORD, E., WALTHAMSTOW, N.E., AND LEYTONSTONE, E., LONDON

SPECIAL CHEAP TILE GRATES

No. 529—The "Carlyle" Tile Grate.

No. 1536—The "Campbell" Tile Grate.

With Brick Back, Movable Bars, and Spindled Canopy for Tiles.

Width,								28	30	32	34	36	38	inches.
Height,								36	36	36	36	38	38	,,
Fire,								15	15	15	18	18	18	,,

PRICES, Fine Cast, without Tiles,	...	...	...	**16/6**	**18/** each.
,, Ground and Berlin Black, without Tiles,	...	**25/6**	**27/** ,,		
Ashes Frets, Fine Cast,			**1/1½ each extra.**		
,, Ground and Berlin Black,	...	...	...	**2/3** ,, ,,	

Set B Tiles fitted extra, *see Footnote.*

With Brick Back and Sides to Fire, Movable Bars, and Ashes Fret.

Width,								34	36	38
Height,								36	38	38
Fire,								18	18	18

PRICE, Fine Cast, without Tiles,	...	...	...	**22/6** ea
,, Ground and Berlin Black, without Tiles,	...	...	**31/6**

Set B Tiles fitted extra, *see Footnote.*

No. 3223 Tile Grate

No. 3240 Tile Grate.

Brick forming Back and Half Sides to Fire; Movable Spindle Bars, and Ashes Fret.

Width,	...	...	...	...	30	32	34	36	38	38	40	40	inches.
Height,	...	...	...	...	36	36	36	38	38	38	38	38	,,
Fire,	...	...	...	...	14	14	16	16	16	18	16	18	,,

PRICES, Fine Cast, without Tiles,	...	...	**23/3**	**24/**	**24/9**	**25/6** each.
,, Fine Cast, with Bars and Brick as shown to No. 529, without Tiles,	**17/7½**	**18/4½**	**19/1½**	**19/10½** ,,		

It without Ashes Fret, **1/1½ each less.** If with Lift-off Canopy, **1/1½ each extra.**
Set B Tiles fitted extra, *see Footnote.*

New Design Tile Grate, Semi-slow Fire and Loose Ashes Fret; Reeded Mo Improved "Teale" shape Brick Back and Sides to Fire; Wrought-iron Bars.

Width,	...	...	...	...	...	36	3
Height,	...	...	...	...	...	38	3
Fire,	...	...	...	...	...	18	1

PRICE, Ground and Berlin Black,	...	...	...	...	**45/**

Set C Tiles fitted extra, *see Footnote.*

Tiles fitted to either above Grates.

Set A—Good Colored Tiles, or Tiles and Strips—Seconds, ... **4/6 per set.** | Set C— 6×6 inch Hand-painted Centre, and Colored Tiles and Strips—Firsts, **9/**
,, B— ,, ,, ,, ,, ,, Firsts, ... **6/9** ,, | ,, D—12×6 inch ,, ,, ,, ,, **15/**
Other designs shown on lithographed sheets, at prices quoted on key to same.

SPECIAL CHEAP TILE GRATES

No. 790—The "Caledonia" Tile Grate.

No. 590—The "Goldsmith" Tile Grate.

This is an exceedingly neat and strong design Tile Grate, and a general favourite wherever adopted. Brick forming back and half sides to Fire; good bold Mouldings; Movable Bars of good strength.

Width,								28	30	32	34	36	38	40 inches.
Height,								36	36	36	36	38	38	38 "
Fire,								12	12	14	16	16	16	16 "
PRICES, Fine Cast, without Tiles,								18/	18/9	19/6	20/3	21/	21/9	22/6 each.
" Ground and Berlin Black, without Tiles,								27/	27/9	28/6	29/3	30/	30/9	31/6 "

Ashes Fret to either size, { Fine Cast, ... 1/6 each extra.
{ Ground and Berlin Black, ... 2/3 " "
Set B Tiles fitted extra, *see Footnote.*

New Design Tile Grate, with Brick Back and Sides to Fire, replaceable from front; Removable economical Bars, with Steel Uprights and Ashes Fret.

Width,								30	32	34	36	38	40 inches.
Height,								36	36	36	38	38	38 "
Fire,								12	12	14	16	16	16 "
PRICES, Berlin Black, Third Finish, without Tiles,								28/6	30/	31/6	33/	34/6	36/ each.
" Berlin Black, Second Finish, with Brass }								37/6	39/	40/6	42/	43/6	45/ "
Knobs, without Tiles, }													

Set B Tiles fitted extra, *see Footnote.*

No. 2451—The "Wells" Tile Grate.

No. 2452—The "Gloucester" Tile Grate.

With Spindled Canopy; Ornamental Iron Panel; Brick Back and Sides to Fire; Wrought Vertical Bars; Loose Ashes Fret, with Brass Knob; good bold Mouldings.

Width,											34	36	38	40 inches.
Height,											36	38	38	38 "
Fire,											15	15	17	17 "

PRICE, Special Finish, Bright and Dead Berlin Black, without Tiles, **33/9 each.**
Set C Tiles fitted extra, *see Footnote.*

Entirely New Design Tile Grate, Semi-slow Fire and Loose Ashes Fret; Deep Chair Brick Back and Sides to Fire; Gothic Movable Bars, new shape Canopy; Brass Finials to Bars and Brass Knob to Ashes Fret.

Width,										36	38 inches.
Height,										38	38 "
Fire,										15	15 "

PRICE, Special Berlin Black, relieved with Gilt, ... **37/6 each.**
Set C Tiles fitted extra, *see Footnote.*

Tiles fitted to either above Grates.

Set A—Good Colored Tiles, or Tiles and Strips—Seconds, ... **4/6 per set.** | Set C— 6×6 inch Hand-painted Centre and Colored Tiles and Strips, Firsts, **9/ per set.**
" B— " " " " " Firsts, ... **6/9** | " D—12×6 " " " " " " " " " **15/** "
Other designs shown on lithographed sheets, at prices quoted on key to same.

STRATFORD, E., WALTHAMSTOW, N.E., AND LEYTONSTONE, E., LONDON

FINISHED TILE GRATES

No. 3222.

Tile Grate, Ornamental Canopy; Semi-slow Fire and Ashes Fret; Brick Back; Movable Gothic Bars.

PRICES
(Without Tiles).

No. 3222.

Tile Grate.

Width,	...	32	34	36	38	40	ins
Height,	...	36	36	38	38	38	,,
Fire,	...	17	17	17	17	17	,,

Third Finish,
Berlin Black, } **28/6** **30/ each.**

Second Finish,
Berlin Black, } **34/6** **36/** ,,

No. TP 88 Colored Panel Tiles, fitted,
10/6 per set extra.

No. 3225.

Tile Grate, New Design; Cupola Ornamental Canopy; Semi-slow Fire and Ashes Fret; Chair Brick Back; Movable Gothic Bars.

PRICES
(Without Tiles)

No. 3225.

Tile Grate.

Width,	...	32	34	36	38	inches
Height,	...	36	36	38	38	,,
Fire,	...	16	16	16	16	,.

Third Finish,
Berlin Black,
relieved with } **30/ each.**
Gilt, ...

Special Finish,
Berlin Black,
relieved with } **36/** ,,
Gilt, ...

Set B Colored Tiles and Strips, fitted,
6/9 per set extra.

The Tiles may be alternated, when so desired, for other patterns shown on lithographed sheets, and the difference in value charged or allowed.

STRATFORD, E., WALTHAMSTOW, N.E., AND LEYTONSTONE, E., LONDON

FINISHED TILE GRATES

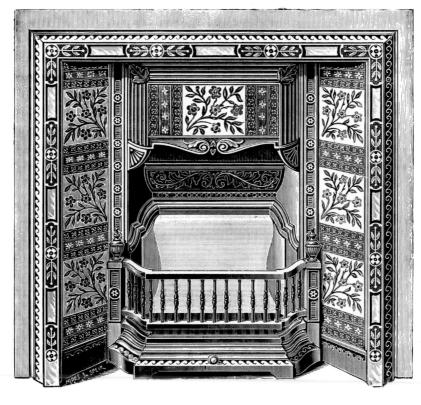

No. 3228.

Tile Grate, with Lift-off Canopy; prepared for Tiles in Canopy and Sides; Turned Spindle Bars, with Brass Knobs; Semi-slow Fire and Ashes Fret; Chair Brick Back.

PRICES
(Without Tiles).

No. 3228.

Tile Grate.

Width,	...	...	30	32	34	36	36	38 ins.
Height,	...	...	36	36	36	38	38	38 ,,
Fire,	...	...	14	14	16	16	18	18 ,,

Third Finish, Berlin Black, }	42/	43/6	45/ each.
Special Finish, Berlin Black, }	45/	46/6	48/ ,,
Second Finish, Berlin Black, }	51/	52/6	54/ ,,
Best Finish, Berlin Black, }	60/	61/6	63/ ,,

Set B Colored Tiles and Strips, fitted in Cheeks and Canopy,
8/3 per set extra.

No. 3229.

Tile Grate, with Improved Brick Back and Sides; Semi-slow Fire and Ashes Fret; Brass Knobs and Movable Bars.

PRICES
(Without Tiles).

No. 3229.

Tile Grate.

Width,	...	...	...	36	38	40 ins.
Height,	...	...	...	38	38	38 ,,
Fire,	...	...	...	17	17	17 ,,

Third Finish, Berlin Black, ...}	45/ each.
Second Finish, Berlin Black, ...}	51/ ,,

No. TP 93 Colored Panel Tiles, fitted.
12/9 per set extra.

The Tiles may be alternated, when so desired, for other patterns shown on lithographed sheets, and the difference in value charged or allowed.

STRATFORD, E., WALTHAMSTOW, N.E., AND LEYTONSTONE, E., LONDON

FINISHED TILE GRATES

No. 3253.

"Sandringham" Tile Grate, for 6-inch Tiles, with Removable Adjustable Canopy (shown partly drawn down), Improved Whole Fire Brick Back and Bars as drawn, or varied in shape, either vertical or horizontal.

PRICES

(Without Tiles).

No. 3253.

"Sandringham" Tile Grate.

Width, ...	30	32	34	34	36	38	36	38	40	40	42	ins
Height, ...	36	36	36	36	38	38	38	38	38	38	38	,,
Fire, ...	14	14	14	16	16	16	18	18	18	21	21	,,

Berlin Black, Third Finish.	69/		72/		81/	ea.
Berlin Black, Second do.,	84/		87/		96/	,,
Berlin Black, First do.,	96/		99/		108/	,,

Electro-bronzed Canopy, **18/ extra.**

No. T 43—Colored Tiles, fitted, **8/3 per set extra.**

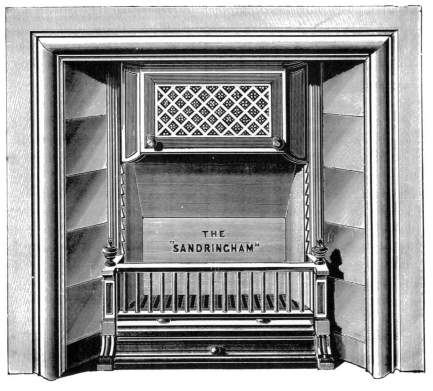

THE "SANDRINGHAM"

No. 3254.

"Sandringham" Tile Grate, for 6-inch Tiles, with Removable Adjustable Canopy, Improved Whole Fire Brick Back and Bars as drawn, or varied in shape, either vertical or horizontal.

PRICES

(Without Tiles).

No. 3254.

"Sandringham" Tile Grate.

Width, ...	36	38	40	40	42	ins.
Height, ...	38	38	38	38	38	,,
Fire, ...	18	18	18	21	21	,,

Berlin Black, Third Finish.	75/		81/	ea.
Berlin Black, Second Finish.	87/		93/	,,
Berlin Black, First Finish.	99/		105/	,,

Self-colored Tiles, fitted, **7/6 per set extra.**

The Tiles may be alternated, when so desired, for other patterns shown on lithographed sheets, and the difference in value charged or allowed.

STRATFORD, E., WALTHAMSTOW, N.E., AND LEYTONSTONE, E., LONDON

FINISHED TILE GRATES

With Hobs.

These Grates are made to combine the quaint appearance of the old fashioned Hob Grates, without their disadvantages of smoky chimneys where bad vents exist.

No. 3298.

Tile Grate, with Hobs; Electro-brass Enrichments on Canopy; Solid Brass Hobs.

PRICES

(Without Tiles).

No. 3298.

Tile Grate.

Width,	...	36 38 or 40 inches.
Height,	...	36 38 or 40 ,,
Fire,	...	18 ,,
Berlin Black, Best Finish,		**120/ each.**

Self-colored Tiles, fitted,
7/6 per set extra.

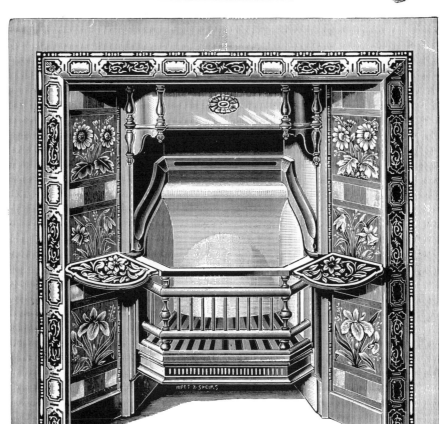

No. 3299.

Tile Grate, with Hobs; Electro-brass Canopy; Solid Brass Hobs, and Ashes Pan.

PRICES

(Without Tiles).

No. 3299.

Tile Grate.

Width,	...	36 38 or 40 inches.
Height,	...	36 38 or 40 ,,
Fire,	...	18 ,,
Berlin Black, Best Finish,		**132/ each.**

No. T P 92 Tiles, fitted,
22/6 per set extra.

The Tiles may be alternated, when so desired, for other patterns shown on lithographed sheets, and the difference in value charged or allowed.

TILE GRATES

The "Sandringham" Grate.

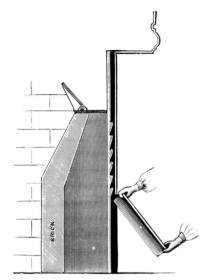

Section showing method of Removing
Canopies.

No. 3252.—18-in. Fire.

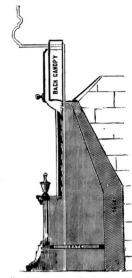

Section showing both Canopies
in position.

THIS Grate is provided with two canopies, one in front of the other. The front canopy works upon a rack (cast on to the front), and stops at any point, enabling a bright cheerful fire to be immediately produced, or the draught regulated at will. The advantage of this arrangement is obvious, as a sluggish draught can be at once quickened, or a nearly-extinguished fire revived, by merely lowering the front canopy to the desired point. Both canopies are easily removable, leaving an open space over the brick, through which the back of the fire can be built up *with the Grate in position*, and the chimney more easily and effectually swept, than in grates of other construction.

The back and sides of the fire are entirely of fire brick of an improved form, by which the maximum of heat is deflected into the room, and also the greater portion of the smoke, as well as the noxious gases generated by combustion, arrested and consumed; thus, not only increasing the heating power of the Grate, but preventing the vitiation of the atmosphere.

The bars are fitted with vertical steel spindles placed close together, which tend to make the fire burn more slowly; but should a quicker combustion be desired, the ordinary horizontal bars may be substituted. After first lifting out the bars, both canopies are easily removable by passing same down a groove in front of the rack at each side of the Grate.

The Advantages of the "Sandringham" Grate may be summed up as follows :—

EASY REGULATION OF THE DRAUGHT.

A BRIGHT FIRE IMMEDIATELY OBTAINABLE.

GREATLY INCREASED HEATING POWER.

FREE ACCESS TO THE CHIMNEY FOR FIXING AND SWEEPING.

ECONOMY OF FUEL.

CONSUMPTION OF SMOKE AND DELETERIOUS GASES.

CONTROLLED OR PERFECT COMBUSTION.

PERFECT CURE FOR SMOKY CHIMNEY.

It is very necessary that the back plate or canopy remain stationary on the top rack when the Grate is in use, as if allowed to drop out of position it will render the front canopy unworkable.

Various designs of Tile Grates with the "Sandringham" arrangement are shown on the preceding and following pages

STRATFORD, E., WALTHAMSTOW, N.E., AND LEYTONSTONE, E., LONDON

TILE GRATES

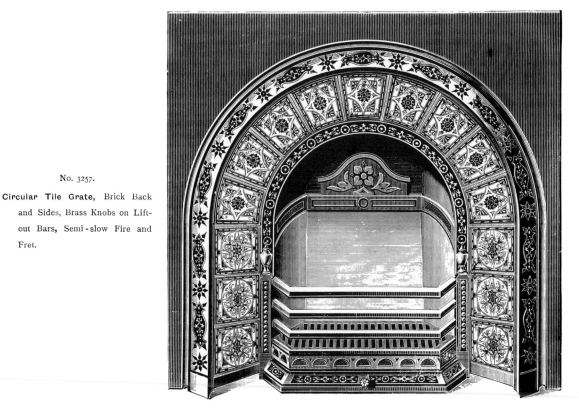

No. 3257.

Circular Tile Grate, Brick Back and Sides, Brass Knobs on Lift-out Bars, Semi-slow Fire and Fret.

PRICE
(With Tiles inclusive).

No. 3257.
Circular Tile Grate.

Width,	...	...	38	40 inches.
Height	...	...	38	38 ,,
Fire,	...	...	18	18 ,,

Berlin Black. Best Finish, with Tiles as drawn, fitted, } **99/ each.**

THE "SANDRINGHAM"

No. 3258.

"Sandringham" Circular Tile Grate, with Removable Adjustable "Sandringham" Canopy, Improved Whole Fire Brick Back; Spindle Bars, with Brass Knobs; Semi-slow Combustion Fire and Fret.

PRICES
(Without Tiles).

No. 3258.
"Sandringham"
Circular Tile Grate.

Width,	...	...	36	38	40 inches.
Height,	...	...	38	38	38 ,,
Fire,	...	...	18	18	18 ,,

Berlin Black, Third Finish, ... } **99/ each.**

Berlin Black, Second Finish, ... } **111/ ,,**

Berlin Black, Best Finish, ... } **123/ ,,**

Electro-bronzed Canopy, ... } **18/ ,, extra.**

Electro-bronzed Canopy, Moulding, and Fret, ... } **51/ ,, ,,**

No. T P 87 Tiles, fitted,
18/ per set extra.

The Tiles may be alternated, when so desired, for other patterns shown on lithographed sheets, and the difference in value charged or allowed.

TILE GRATES

Architects' Special Designs, suitable for Wood Chimney-pieces.

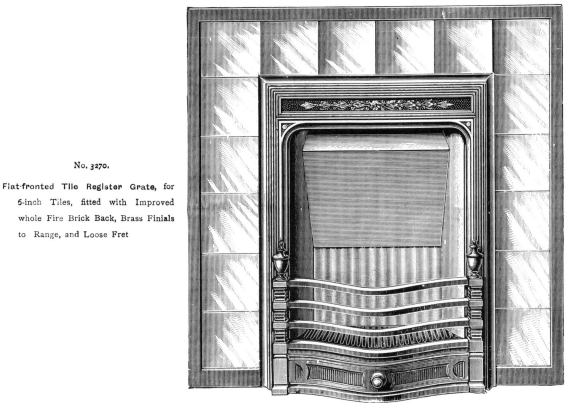

No. 3270.

Flat-fronted Tile Register Grate, for 6-inch Tiles, fitted with Improved whole Fire Brick Back, Brass Finials to Range, and Loose Fret

PRICES

(Without Tiles.)

No. 3270.

Flat-fronted Tile Register Grate.

Width,	...	...	...	40 inches.
Height,	...	...	...	39 „
Fire,	...	...	...	18 „

Berlin Black, Third Finish, ... **60/ each.**

„ Special „ ... **66/** „

„ Best „ ... **72/** „

Self-colored Tiles, fitted, **12/ per set extra.**

No. 3295.

"Queen Anne" Tile Register Grate, for 6-inch Tiles, fitted with whole Brick Back, Polished Brass Dogs, and Inner and Outer Mouldings, Vertical or Horizontal Bars, with Brass Finials and Fret.

PRICES

(Without Tiles).

No. 3295.

"Queen Anne" Tile Register Grate.

Width, ...	...	32	36	38	40 inches.
Height, ...	...	36	38	38	38 „
Fire, ...	...	14	18	18	18 „

	With Dogs.	Without Dogs.
Berlin Black, Second Finish,	165/	129/ ea.
„ First „	171/	135/ „

Self-colored Tiles, fitted, **9/9 per set extra.**

The Tiles may be alternated, when so desired, for other patterns shown on lithographed sheets, and the difference in value charged or allowed

TILE GRATES

Architects' Special Designs, suitable for Wood Chimney-pieces.

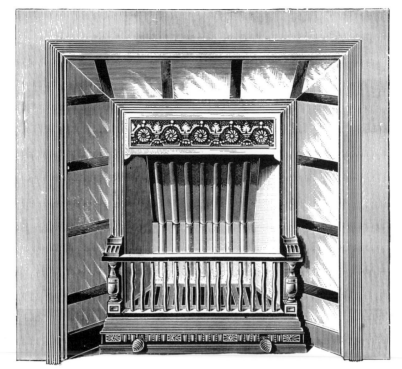

No. 3296.

Tile Grate, with Brass Inner and Outer Mouldings; with 6-inch Tiles (Self-color Tiles and Strips) all round on the splay; New Milner Back Grate Bottom, and two Brass Knobs to Ashes Fret; complete, as drawn.

PRICES.

—

No. 3296.

Tile Grate.

Width,	...	...	...	38	40 inches.
Height,	...	...	...	38	38 ,,
Fire,	...	...	...	18	18 ,,

Berlin Black, Best Finish, complete, with Tiles, ... } **150/ each.**

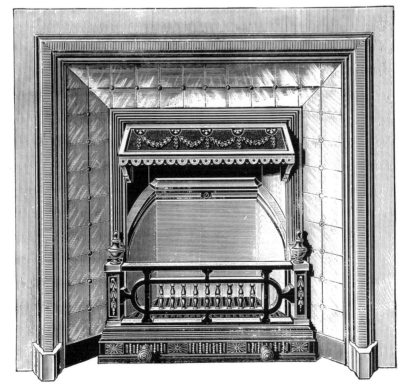

No. 3297.

Tile Grate, with Brass Inner and Outer Mouldings, Brass Finials on Bars, Two Brass Knobs to Ashes Fret; fitted with 3-inch Self-color Tiles, set with Brass Studs to fit 6-inch Panels all round on the splay; Projecting Canopy; Metal Back, lined with brick in three parts; complete, as drawn.

PRICES.

—

No. 3297.

Tile Grate.

Width,	...	...	...	38	40 inches.
Height,	...	...	...	38	38 ,,
Fire,	...	...	...	18	18 ,,

Berlin Black, Best Finish, complete, with Tiles, ... } **201/ each.**

The Tiles may be alternated, when so desired, for other patterns shown on lithographed sheets, and the difference in value charged or allowed.

STRATFORD, E., WALTHAMSTOW, N.E., AND LEYTONSTONE, E., LONDON

HIGH-CLASS INTERIORS

No. 2447 Interior.

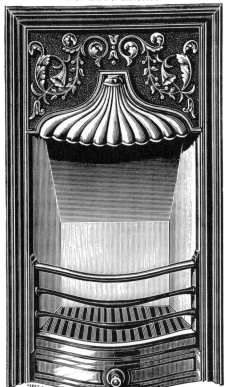

No. 2448 Interior.

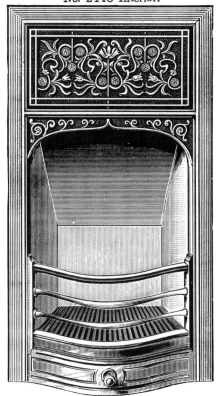

With Canopy, Plain Solid Brick Back, Grate Bottom, and Ashes Fret.

Width,					20	22	24	inches.
Height,	...	...	...	...	38	38	38	,,
Fire,	...	...	...	...	16	16	16	,,

PRICE, Fine Cast and Blacked, ... **43/6 each.**
,, Berlin Black, Third Finish, ... **48/**
,, ,, Second ,, ... **54/** ,,
,, ,, Best ,, ... **60/** ,,
Electro-bronzed Canopy, **15/** each extra.

With Plain Milner Back, Grate Bottom, and Ashes Fret.

Width,					18	20	22	24	inches.
Height,	...	...	...	...		36 or 38			,,
Fire,	...	...	...	...	14	14	16	18	,,

PRICE, Cast and Blacked, ... **45/ each.**
,, Berlin Black, Third Finish, ... **49/6** ,,
,, ,, Second ,, ... **54/** ,,
,, ,, Best ,, ... **60/** ,,

No. 2449 Interior.

No. 2450 Interior.

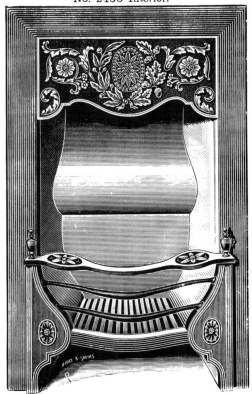

With Brass Repoussé Panel, Vertical Bars, Brick-lined Metal Back, Grate Bottom, and Ashes Fret.
Sizes made, from 24 inches wide × 38 inches high. Fire, 18 inches.
PRICE, Berlin Black, Best Finish, ... **120/ each.**
,, If with Cast-iron Panel, all Berlin Black, ... **99/** ,,

With Brass Repoussé Panel and new Brick Back, as shown; Top Bar with Trivets and Brass Knobs; Grate Bottom.
Sizes made, from 24 inches wide × 38 inches high. Fire, 18 inches.
PRICE, Best Finish, ... **132/ each.**

HIGH-CLASS INTERIORS

No. 2495 Interior.

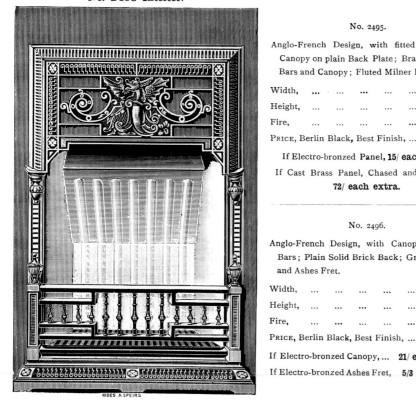

No. 2496 Interior.

No. 2495.

Anglo-French Design, with fitted Perforated Canopy on plain Back Plate; Brass Knobs on Bars and Canopy; Fluted Milner Back.

Width,	... ...	24 inches.
Height,	... ...	38 ,,
Fire,	... ...	18 ,,

PRICE, Berlin Black, Best Finish, ... **90/ each.**

If Electro-bronzed **Panel, 15/ each extra.**

If Cast Brass Panel, Chased and Polished, **72/ each extra.**

No. 2496.

Anglo-French Design, with Canopy; Vertical Bars; Plain Solid Brick Back; Grate Bottom, and Ashes Fret.

Width,	... ...	24 inches.
Height,	... ...	38 ,,
Fire,	... ...	18 ,,

PRICE, Berlin Black, Best Finish, ... **90/ each.**

If Electro-bronzed Canopy, ... **21/ each extra.**

If Electro-bronzed Ashes Fret, **5/3** ,,

No. 2497 Interior.

No. 2498 Interior.

No. 2497.

Anglo-French Design, with Canopy fitted with Brass Pillars and Finials; Brick-lined Metal Back; Vertical Bars, with Brass Knobs.

Width,	... ...	24 inches.
Height,	... ...	38 ,,
Fire,	... ...	18 ,,

PRICE, Berlin Black, Best Finish, ... **120/ each.**

If with Electro-bronzed Canopy and Dome, **27/ each extra.**

If with Bronzed Fret, **5/3 each extra.**

No. 2498.

With Electro-bronzed Canopy, Dome and Pilasters; Cast Brass Pillars and Knobs on Canopy; Dog Bar Range, with Cast Brass Pillars, Feet, Fret, and Finials; Brick-lined Metal Back.

Width,	... ...	24 inches.
Height,	... ...	38 ,,
Fire,	... ...	18 ,,

PRICE, Berlin Black, Best Finish, ... **219/ each.**

A lithograph, in colors, of this Interior supplied on application.

OXFORD COLLEGE AND PARSON GRATES

No. 2491 College Sham.

No. 2492 Oxford College Grate.

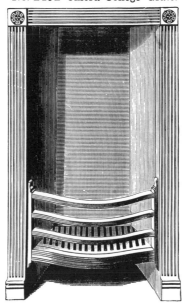

No. 2493 Parson Grate.

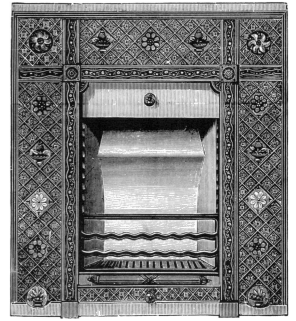

Width,	...	15	18	21	24	inches.
Height,	...		29 to 38			,,
Fire,	...	11	14	17	20	,,
Fine Cast,	...	10/6	12/	13/6	15/	each.
Berlin Black, Third Finish,		15/	16/6	18/	21/	,,
Berlin Black, Second Finish,		19/6	21/	22/6	24/	,,

Bricks, Damper, and Bottom Grate to suit,
15/ per set extra.

With Flat or Curved Bars, complete with
Bricks, Register Door and Frame.

Width,	...	15	17	19	21 inches.
Height,	...	30	30	30	30 ,,
Fire,	...	12	14	16	18 ,,
Fine Cast,		22/6	24/	25/6	27/ each.

If Rubbed and Black, **3/ each extra.**

With Blower and whole Fire-brick Back, Loose Horizontal
Bars, with Loose Fret.

Width,	...	22	24	26	28	30	32	34	36	38	inches.
Height,	...	36	36	36	36	36	36	36	38	38	,,
Fire,	...	12		14			16	18	20		,,
Fine Cast and Blacked,		45/		46/6			49/6	51/	54/		each.
Berlin Black, Second Finish,		52/6		54/			57/	58/6	61/6		,,
Berlin Black, Best Finish,		63/		64/6			67/6	69/	72/		,,

If without Blower, **6/ less.**
If Slow Combustion, **3/ extra.**

No. 2494 Parson Grate.

No. 2494.

Parson Grate, with whole Fire-brick Back and Lift-out Range, with
Loose Ashes Fret.

Width,	...	...	...	...	30	32	34	36	36	38	40 inches.
Height,	...	...	...	...	36	36	36	36	38	38	38 ,,
Fire,	...	...	...	...			12			15	,,
Fine Cast and Blacked,	...		...				40/6			42/	each.
Berlin Black, Special Finish,	...						46/6			48/	,,
,, Best Finish,	...						57/			60/	,,

Steel Blower, **6/ extra.**

STRATFORD, E., WALTHAMSTOW, N.E., AND LEYTONSTONE, E., LONDON

PARSON GRATES

No. 2293 Parson Grate.

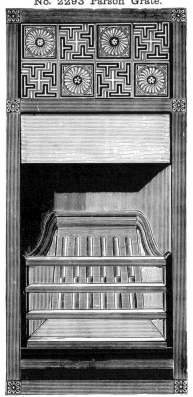

No. 2294 Parson Grate.

With Blower.

Width,				18	20	22	24 inches.
Height,	...	...	...	36	36	36	36 ,,
Fire,	...	...	...	14	16	18	20 ,,
PRICES, Fine Cast,		...		16/6	18/	19/6	21/ each.
,, Berlin Black,		...		25/6	27/	28/6	30/ ,,

If with Solid Milner Brick Back, **10/6 each extra.**

For Tiles at sides, Blower, Slow Combustion.

Width,	...	...	...	...	33	36	38	40 inches.
Height,	...	...	...	...	36	36	36	36 ,,
Fire,	...	...	...	...	15	16	18	20 ,,
PRICES, Fine Cast,	...	...	...	21/	22/6	24/	25/6 each.
,, Berlin Black,		...	...	30/	31/6	33/	34/6 ,,

Self-colored Tiles fitted, **7/6 per set extra,** or No. T 5 Embossed Tiles, **17/6 per set extra.**

If with Solid Milner Brick Back, **10/6 each extra.**

No. 2289 Parson Grate Sham.

Width,	...	...	...	...	...	...	...	36	36	38 inches.
Height,	...	...	...	...	...	...	...	38	38	38 ,,
Fire,	...	...	...	...	...	...	...	14 or 16	16	18 ,,
PRICE, Fine Cast,	...	...	...	...	...	...			27/ each.	
,, Berlin Black, Third Finish,		...	...	...				36/ ,,		
,, ,, Second Finish,		...	...	...				45/ ,,		

Bricks for forming Bottom, Back, and Sides, **9/ per set extra.**

If fitted with Sliding Blower in Front, **6/ each extra.**

If fitted with Iron Back Metal and Brick Back, **16/6 per set extra.**

If fitted with Brick, Damper, and Stool, **16/6 per set extra.**

The Pattern can be had with Tiles at Sides, similar to No. 2294.
Prices on application.

CURB FENDERS

IRON

No. 2175 Curb Fender.

Inside sizes—

30, 36, 39, 42, 45. and 48 × 12 inches.

No. 2175.

Section, 2 × 2⅞ inches.

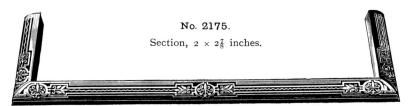

PRICES—No. 2175.

Fine Cast and Blacked,
5/3 each.

Ground and Berlin Blacked,
9/9 each.

No. 2177 Curb Fender.

Inside sizes--

30, 36, 39, 42, 45, and 48 × 12 inches.

No. 2177.

Section, 2½ × 4 inches.

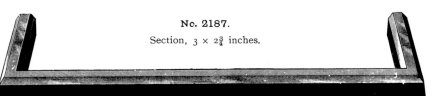

PRICES—No. 2177.

Fine Cast and Blacked,
6/9 each.

Ground and Berlin Blacked,
11/3 each.

No. 2187 Curb Fender.

Inside sizes—

30, 36, 39, 42, 45, and 48 × 12 inches.

No. 2187.

Section, 3 × 2¾ inches.

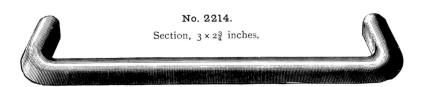

PRICES—No. 2187.

Fine Cast and Blacked,
9/ each.

Ground and Berlin Blacked,
13/6 each.

No. 2214 Curb Fender.

Inside sizes--

36, 39, 42, 45, and 48 × 12 inches.

No. 2214.

Section, 3 × 2¾ inches.

PRICES—No. 2214.

Fine Cast and Blacked,
9/9 each.

Berlin Black, Best Finish,
15/ each.

No. 2215 Curb Fender.

Inside sizes—

36, 39, 42, 45, 48, and 54 × 12 inches.

No. 2215.

Section, 4¼ × 3¼ inches.

PRICES—No. 2215.

Best Finish, **22/6 each.**

Best Finish, with Brass Beading,
33/ each.

No. 2216 Curb Fender.

Inside sizes—

42, 45, and 48 × 12 inches.

No. 2216.

Section, 3½ × 4 inches.

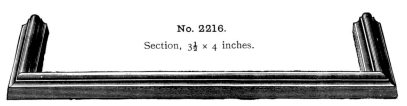

PRICES--No. 2216.

Rubbed and Blacked, **22/6 each.**

Ground and Berlin Blacked,
28/6 each.

Ditto, Ditto, Best Finish,
34/6 each.

MARBLE CURB FENDERS

BLOCK SECTIONS.

No. 561, New.

No. 562, New.

No. 563, New.

	No. 561, New.	No. 562, New.	No. 563, New.	
PRICES, Sicilian Marble,	30/	30/	39/	each.
,, Vein Marble,	37/6	39/9	47/3	,,
,, Rouge Royal Marble,	27/	27/	31/6	,,
,, St. Ann's Marble,	27/	27/	31/6	,
,, Black Marble,	28/6	28/6	31/6	,,
,, Bastard Statuary Marble,	51/	51/	60/	,,

Stock size, 48 × 12 inches inside.

STRATFORD, E., WALTHAMSTOW, N.E., AND LEYTONSTONE, E., LONDON

CURB FENDERS AND DOGS
⸺ BERLIN BLACK AND BRASS ⸺

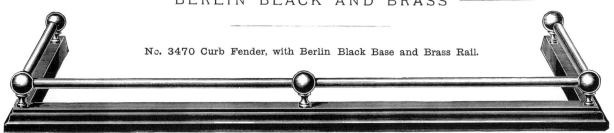

No. 3470 Curb Fender, with Berlin Black Base and Brass Rail.

Inside sizes—42, 45, 48 × 12 inches deep.　　No. 3470 Curb Fender, as drawn, PRICE, **15/9 each.**　　Dogs to match, **7/6 per pair.**

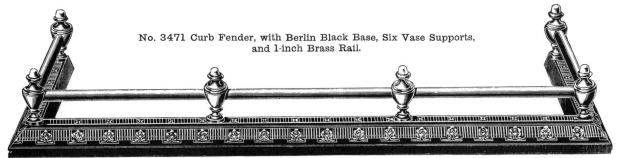

No. 3471 Curb Fender, with Berlin Black Base, Six Vase Supports, and 1-inch Brass Rail.

Inside sizes— 36, 42, 48 × 12 inches deep.　　No. 3471 Curb Fender, as drawn, PRICE, **24/ each.**　　Dogs to match, **15/ per pair.**

No. 3472 Curb Fender, with Berlin Black Chamfered Base, Seven Ball Supports, and ⅞-inch Brass Rail.

Inside sizes—42, 48, 54 × 12 inches deep.　　No. 3472 Curb Fender, as drawn, PRICE, **25/6 each.**　　Dogs to match, **15/ per pair.**

No. 3473, Complete Set, Berlin Black and Brass.

No. 3474.

PRICE, **6/ per pair.**

No. 3475.

PRICE, **7/6 per pair.**

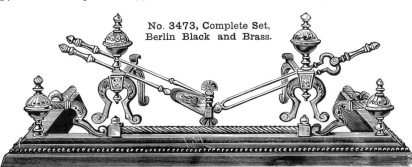

Inside sizes of Curb — 48 × 12 inches.

Curb,	...	...	...	...	...	...	...	99/ each.
Irons,	...	...	...	...	...	...	...	30/ per set.
Stops,	...	...	...	...	...	...	...	4/6 each.
Dogs,	...	...	...	...	...	...	...	37/ per pair.
PRICE, complete,	...	...	...	...	...	...	170/6 per set.

No. 3476.

PRICE, **7/6 per pair.**

No. 3477.

PRICE, **9/ per pair.**

No. 3478.

PRICE, **10/6 per pair.**

No. 3479.

PRICE, **15/ per pair.**

CURB FENDERS AND DOGS
POLISHED BRASS

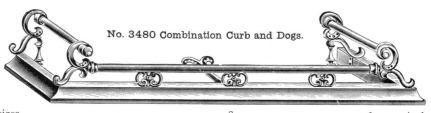

No. 3480 Latest Design

Combined Curb and Dogs.

No. 3480 Combination Curb and Dogs.

In Brass—well finished.

| Inside sizes, | ... | ... | ... | ... | ... | ... | 48 | 51 | 54 | 57 | 60 × 12 inches deep. |
| Prices, | .. | ... | ... | ... | ... | ... | 43/6 | 45/ | 48/ | 49/6 | 52/6 each. |

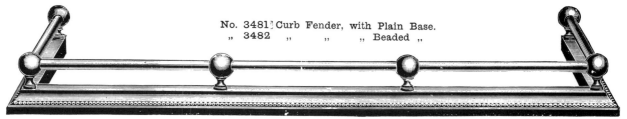

No. 3481 Curb Fender, with Plain Base.
„ 3482 „ „ „ Beaded „

Inside sizes—42, 45, 48 × 12 inches deep and 5 inches high.

No. 3481 Plain Curb Fender, Price, 27/9 each. Dogs to match, 9/ per pair.
„ 3482 Reeded „ „ „ 39/9 „ „ „ 24/ „

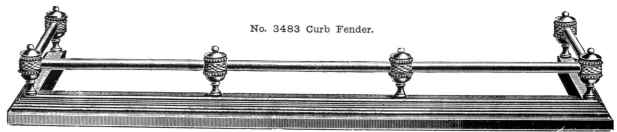

No. 3483 Curb Fender.

Inside sizes—42, 45, 48 × 12 inches deep and 6½ inches high. No. 3483 Curb Fender, Price, 54/ each. Dogs to match, 7 inches high, 21/ per pair.

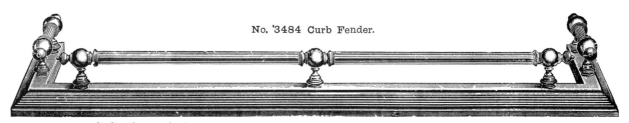

No. 3484 Curb Fender.

Inside sizes—42, 45, 48 × 12 inches deep and 6 inches high. No. 3484 Curb Fender, Price, 69/ each. Dogs to match, 7 inches high, 21/ per pair.

BRASS DOGS

No. 3521.

Price, 6/9 per pair.

No. 3522.

Price, 14/3 per pair.

No. 3523.

Price, 21/ per pair.

No. 3524.

Price, 22/6 per pair.

STRATFORD, E., WALTHAMSTOW, N.E., AND LEYTONSTONE, E., LONDON

CURB FENDERS AND DOGS

POLISHED BRASS

No. 3485 Curb Fender and Set.

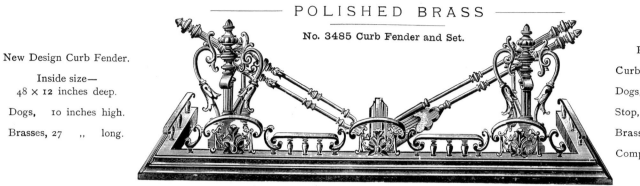

New Design Curb Fender.

Inside size—
48 × 12 inches deep.

Dogs, 10 inches high.

Brasses, 27 „ long.

PRICES.—No. 3485.

Curb Fender, 60/ each.

Dogs, ... 22/6 per pair.

Stop, ... 7/6 each.

Brasses, ... 18/9 per set.

Complete,... 108/9 „

No. 3486 Curb Fender.

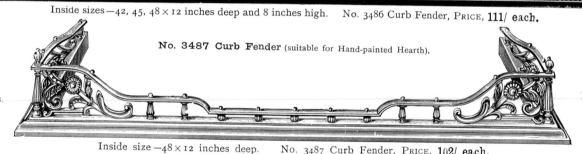

Scrolls
in
Brass
or
Copper.

Dogs
to match,
PRICE,
33/
per pair.

Inside sizes—42, 45, 48 × 12 inches deep and 8 inches high.   No. 3486 Curb Fender, PRICE, 111/ each.

No. 3487 Curb Fender (suitable for Hand-painted Hearth).

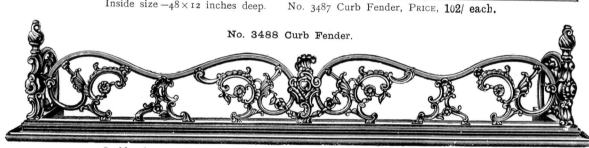

Brass Base
and
Copper Spindles.

Dogs to match,
13½ inches high,
43/6 per pair.

Brasses to match,
26 inches long,
28/6 per set.

Inside size—48 × 12 inches deep.   No. 3487 Curb Fender, PRICE, 102/ each.

No. 3488 Curb Fender.

In Cast Brass,
Louis XV.
Style.

Suite
complete,
PRICE,
459/ each.

Inside size—54 × 12 inches deep.   No. 3488 Curb Fender, PRICE, 279/ each.
Dogs to match, 90/ per pair ; Brasses to match, 72/ per set ; Stops, 18/ each.—Shown on page 155.

BRASS DOGS

No. 3525.

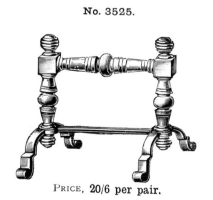

PRICE, 20/6 per pair.

No. 3526.

PRICE, 22/6 per pair.

No. 3527.

PRICE, 30/ per pair.

No. 3528.

PRICE, 42/ per pair.

STRATFORD, E., WALTHAMSTOW, N.E., AND LEYTONSTONE, E., LONDON

FIRE IRONS, BERLIN BLACK

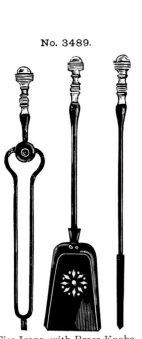

No. 3489.

Fire Irons, with Brass Knobs.
PRICE, 9/ per set.

No. 3490.

Fire Irons, with Copper and Brass Handles.
PRICE, 12/9 per set.

No. 3491.

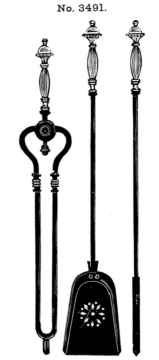

Fire Irons, with Copper and Brass Handles.
PRICE, 15/ per set.

No. 3492.

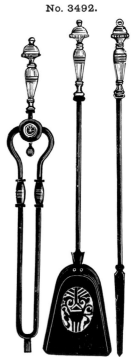

Fire Irons, with Brass Handles.
PRICE, 16/6 per set.

STOPS, BERLIN BLACK AND BRASS

No. 3510.

PRICE, 2/3 each.

No. 3511.

PRICE, 5/3 each.

No. 3512.

PRICE, 4/6 each.

No. 3513.

PRICE, 7/6 each.

FIRE BRASSES, POLISHED BRASS

BRASS POKERETTES

No. 3493.

24 inches long.
PRICE, 8/3 per set.

No. 2197. No. 2198.

24 inches long.
PRICE, 13/6 per set.

26 inches long.
PRICE, 15/9 per set.

No. 3494.

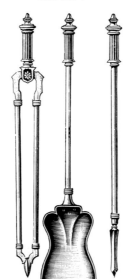

24 inches long.
PRICE, 15/9 per set.

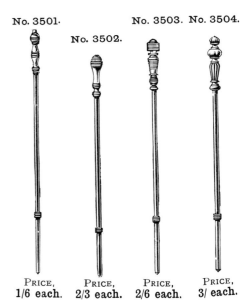

No. 3501.

No. 3502.

No. 3503. No. 3504.

PRICE, 1/6 each.

PRICE, 2/3 each.

PRICE, 2/6 each.

PRICE, 3/ each.

STOPS, POLISHED BRASS

No. 3514.

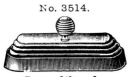

PRICE, 3/9 each.

No. 3515.

PRICE, 6/ each.

No. 3516.

PRICE, 8/3 each.

No. 3517.

PRICE, 9/ each.

FIRE BRASSES, DOGS, AND TRIVETS

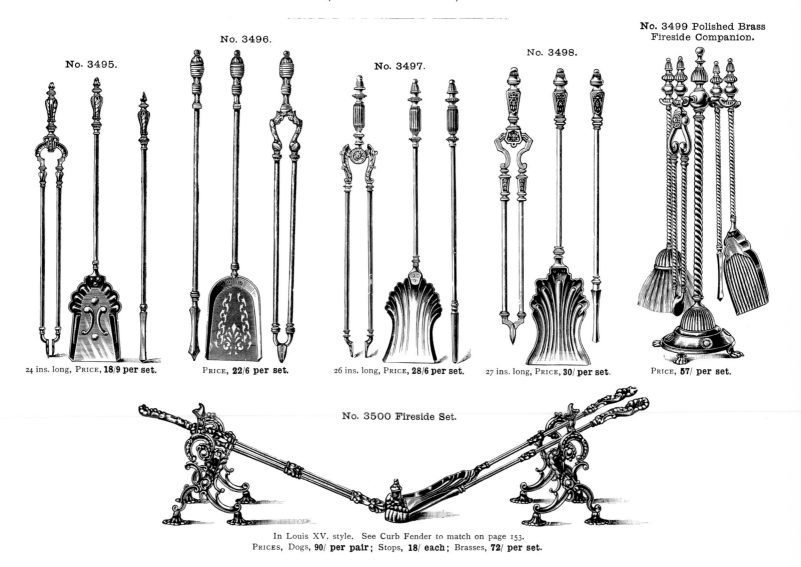

No. 3495.

No. 3496.

No. 3497.

No. 3498.

No. 3499 Polished Brass Fireside Companion.

24 ins. long, PRICE, **18/9 per set.**

PRICE, **22/6 per set.**

26 ins. long, PRICE, **28/6 per set.**

27 ins. long, PRICE, **30/ per set.**

PRICE, **57/ per set.**

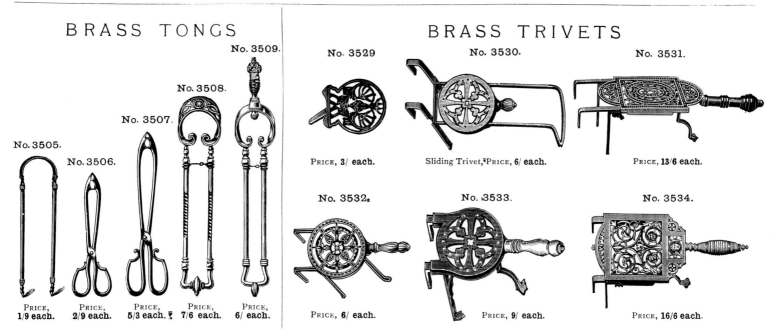

No. 3500 Fireside Set.

In Louis XV. style. See Curb Fender to match on page 153.
PRICES, Dogs, **90/ per pair**; Stops, **18/ each**; Brasses, **72/ per set.**

BRASS TONGS

No. 3509.

No. 3508.

No. 3507.

No. 3505.

No. 3506.

PRICE, **1/9 each.**

PRICE, **2/9 each.**

PRICE, **5/3 each.**

PRICE, **7/6 each.**

PRICE, **6/ each.**

BRASS TRIVETS

No. 3529.

No. 3530.

No. 3531.

PRICE, **3/ each.**

Sliding Trivet, PRICE, **6/ each.**

PRICE, **13/6 each.**

No. 3532.

No. 3533.

No. 3534.

PRICE, **6/ each.**

PRICE, **9/ each.**

PRICE, **16/6 each.**

FENDERS, SCRAPERS, AND TABLES

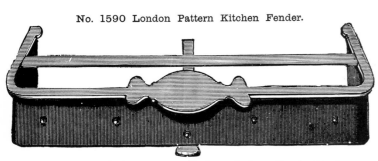

No. 1590 London Pattern Kitchen Fender.

No. 3535 Manchester Pattern Kitchen Fender.

Top Bar, $1\frac{1}{2} \times \frac{3}{16}$ inches ; Return Ends, 12 inches ; Depth, 6 inches.

Sizes Made,	...	...	36	42	48	54	60 inches.
PRICES,	...	...	8/3	9/6	10/6	11/3	12/ each.

Top Bar, $1\frac{1}{2} \times \frac{3}{16}$ inches ; Return Ends, 12 inches ; Depth, 6 inches.

Sizes made,	...	...	42	48	54	60	66 inches.
PRICES,	...	...	12/9	14/3	15/	16/6	18/ each.

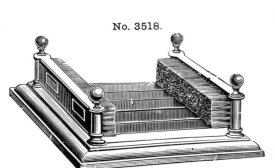

No. 3518.

No. 3519.

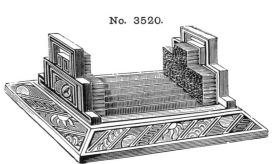

No. 3520.

Berlin-black Scraper, with Brushes and Pan.

Sizes, ...	...	15	18	21	24 inches wide.
PRICES,	...	14/3	16/6	18/	21/ each.

Gothic Berlin-black Scraper.

Size,...	..	...	14 inches wide.
PRICE,	...	...	9/ each.

Berlin-black Scraper, with Brushes and Pan.

Sizes, ...	...	...	15	18	24 inches wide.
PRICES,	...	...	19/6	21/	24/ each.

If without Brushes, 7/6 less.

No. 2421 Table, Round Top.

No. 2423 Table, Oblong Top.

No. 2422 Table, Round Top.

Height, 28 inches.

PRICE, with Cast-iron Ornamental Top as drawn, Fine Cast and Painted one Coat, any Color, ... } 9/9 ea.

Ironwork only, with Bearing Frame, but without Top, Fine Cast and Painted one Coat, any Color, ... } 7/6 ,,

Marble Tops for above, extra.

Size,	...	...	...	...	21 ins.
Round Edge Sicilian Rouge or St. Ann's,					12/ ea.

Height, 28 inches with Bearing Frame to receive Top.

Sizes,	...	...	...	36×20	42×20	48×20 ins.
PRICE, Ironwork only (without Top), Fine Cast and Painted one Coat, any Color, ... }				15/9	16/6	18/ ea.
Ditto, Bronzed,	...	...	...	20/3	21/	22/6 ,,

Marble Tops for above, extra.

Round Edge Rouge or St. Ann's,	12/	15/	18/ ,,
Sicilian, ...	...	14/3	16/6	19/6 ,,

This is a very handsome and useful Table, and is exceedingly good value. Height, 30 inches.

PRICE, Ironwork only (without Top), Fine Cast and Painted one Coat, any Color, ... } 15/9 ea.

Ditto, Bronzed,... ... ... 21/ ,,

Marble Tops for above, extra.

Sizes, ...	...	...	24	27	30 ins. diam.
Round Edge Sicilian Rouge or St. Ann's, }			13/6	16/6	19/6 each.

STRATFORD, E., WALTHAMSTOW, N.E., AND LEYTONSTONE, E., LONDON

COAL BOXES AND CABINETS—WOOD

No. 3550 Coal Box.

With Galvanized Lining and Brass Hand Scoop.

PRICE—In Oak, Walnut, or Mahogany,
15/9 each.

No. 3556 Coal Cabinet.

38 inches high.

With Carved Front, Galvanized Lining, and Brass Hand Scoop.

PRICE—In Oak, Walnut, or Mahogany, on Castors, **66/ each.**

No. 3551 Coal Box.

With Galvanized Lining, Brass Hand Scoop, and Carved Front.

PRICE—In Oak, Walnut, or Mahogany,
24/ each.

No. 3552 Coal Box.

With Galvanized Lining and Brass Hand Scoop.

PRICE—In Oak, Walnut, or Mahogany,
27/9 each.

No. 3553 Coal Box.

With Galvanized Lining and Brass Hand Scoop.

PRICE—Inlaid Rosewood, Brass Handle,
42/ each.

No. 3554 Coal Cabinet.

23 inches high.

With Brass Handles, Galvanized Lining, and Brass Hand Scoop.

PRICE—In Oak, Walnut, or Mahogany,
49/6 each.

No. 3557 Coal Cabinet.

38 inches high.

With Galvanized Lining and Brass Hand Scoop.

PRICE—Inlaid Rosewood, with Bevelled-edge Mirror at back, on Castors,
90/ each.

No. 3555 Coal Cabinet.

23 inches high.

With Galvanized Lining, Brass Hand Scoop, and Carved Front.

PRICE—In Oak, Walnut, or Mahogany, on Castors, **57/ each.**

STRATFORD, E., WALTHAMSTOW, N.E., AND LEYTONSTONE, E., LONDON

ASHES PANS AND UMBRELLA STANDS

───── ASHES PANS ─────

No. 3567.—Pierced Bright Front and Beads, Black Venetians, ... } 3/9 each.

No. 3568.—Pierced Bright Front and Beads, all Bright Venetians, ... } 6/9 ,,

No. 3569.—Pierced Bright Front, Black Venetians, with Brass Beads, ... } 6/9 ,,

No. 3570.—Pierced Brass Front, all Brass Venetians, ... } 9/ ,,

No. 3571.—Gothic Ashes Pan, Plain Brass Front, Black Venetians, Brass Beads and Moulding, ... } 9/ each.

No. 3572.—All Brass, Plain Front, Brass Venetians, Brass Beads and Moulding, ... } 10/6 ,,

No. 3573.—All Brass Ashes Pan, with Brass Gadroons, 11 7-inch Flutes, } 13/6 each.

N.B.—The above prices are for the ordinary stock sizes; special sizes made to order, charged extra. A paper template is requisite with special sizes.

UMBRELLA STANDS—CAST IRON

No. 3581 Umbrella Stand.

With loose Tray.
PRICE, Fine Cast, ... **7/6 each.**
,, Bronzed and Painted, **15/** ,,

No. 2428 Umbrella Stand.

With two loose Trays.
PRICE, Fine Cast, ... **10/6 each.**
,, Painted, ... **11/3** ,,
,, Bronzed, ... **15/** ,,

No. 3582 Corner Umbrella Stand.

PRICE, Bronzed, **13/6 each.**

No. 3583 Umbrella Stand.

PRICE, Bronzed, **21/ each.**

UMBRELLA STANDS—BRASS

No. 3577 Corner Umbrella Stand.

In Polished Brass, with Iron Base.
PRICE, **15/ each.**

No. 3578 Umbrella Stand.

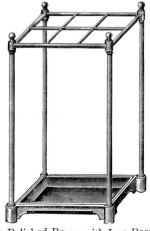

In Polished Brass, with Iron Base.
Size, 13 × 8⅜ inches.
PRICE, 4 Holes, ... **15/ each.**
,, 6 ,, ... **16/6** ,,
,, 8 ,, ... **19/6** ,,
,, 12 ,, ... **22/6** ,,

No. 3579 Umbrella Stand.

In Copper and Brass, with Iron Base.
PRICE, **48/ each.**

No. 3580 Umbrella Stand.

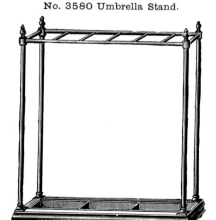

In Polished Brass.
PRICE, with Iron Base, 15 ins., **33/ each.**
,, ,, ,, 21 ,, **42/** ,,
,, with Brass Base, 15 ,, **42/** ,,
,, ,, ,, 21 ,, **57/** ,,

COAL VASES AND SCOOPS

No. 3565 "The Eastbourne" Coal Scoop.

18 ins. long.
Japanned, with Brass Handle and Hand Scoop.

PRICE—Plain Art Colors, ... **18/ each.**
,, As drawn, ... **24/** ,,

No. 3560 "The Leamington" Coal Vase.

With Lining and Hand Scoop.

PRICE—All Brass, ... **48/ each.**
,, ,, Copper, ... **48/** ,,

No. 3562 "The Saxon" Coal Vase.

With Lining and Hand Scoop.

PRICE—Brass, with "Louis" Panel, }
Hammered Top and Sides, } **81/ each.**
,, Ditto, with Plain Top and }
Sides, ...} **66/** ,,

No. 3559 "The Norman" Coal Vase.

Japanned, with Lining and Hand Scoop.

PRICE, as Drawn, ... **28/6 each.**

No. 3564 "The Gloucester" Coal Vase.

With strong Seamless Body, 13 ins. diameter inside,
Wrought-iron Frame.

		PRICE, Without Lining.	PRICE, With Lining.	
Copper Body, Hammered all over,		87/	96/	**each.**
Brass	,, ,,	87/	96/	,,
Copper	,, Fluted	69/	78/	,,
Brass	,, ,,	69/	78/	,,
Copper	,, Plain	60/	69/	,,
Brass	,,	60/	69/	,,

No. 3563 "The Hastings" Coal Vase.

With Lining and Hand Scoop.

PRICE—All Brass, with Ebony Mounts, **90/ each.**
,, Copper, with Brass Handle and }
Ebony Mounts, ...} **93/** ,,

No. 3558 "The Surrey" Coal Vase.

11½ ins. wide.
Japanned on Tinned Iron, with Brass Handle and
Knob.

PRICE—Black, with Fillet, ... **15/9 each**
,, ,, Gold Line, **18/** ,,
,, Ornamented, as drawn, }
Black Ground, ...} **21/** ,,

No. 3566 "The V.R." Coal Scoop.

With Wrought-iron Mounts and Hand Scoop.

		Small.	Large.	
Size, ...		11	12 ins. wide.	
PRICE—Copper Body, Plain,		45/	54/	**each.**
,, Brass ,, ,,		45/	52/6	,,
,, Copper ,, Hammered } all over, }		63/	72/	,,
,, Brass ,, ,,		60/	69/	,,

No. 3561 "The Bedford" Coal Scoop.

With strong Seamless Body, 18 ins. long; Wrought-
iron Mounts and Hand Scoop.

PRICE—Copper, with Hammered Back, **75/ each.**
,, Brass ,, ,, ,, **75/** ,,

FIRE SCREENS.

No. 3541.—FIRE SCREEN.

Brass Frame and Leaded Light Centre.

No. 3541—Width, 18 in.; Height, 30 in.,
Price 24/ each.

No. 3542, or with Wings—Width, 28 in.;
Height, 25 in., **Price 39/ each.**

No. 3543.—FIRE SCREEN.

Wrought Iron Frame.

Width, 25 in.; Height, 31½ in. extreme.

With Floral Centre	**36/**	**each.**
With Tinted Glass (plain)	**30/**	„
With Leaded Centre, as No. 3544	**36/**	„

No. 3544.—FIRE SCREEN

Brass and Copper Frame, with Leaded Centre.
Width, 19¼ in.; Height, 34 in.
Price 75/ each.

No. 3545.— FIRE SCREEN.

Brass Frame and Bevelled Plates, and Leaded.
Width, 21 in.; Height, 31 in.,
Price 96/ each.

With Leaded Centre, as No. 3541 ... **81/ each.**
      „   „   as No. 3546 ... **96/** „

MANY OTHER DESIGNS, BOTH CHEAPER AND MORE EXPENSIVE, ARE DISPLAYED IN OUR SHOW ROOMS.

No. 3546.— FIRE SCREEN.

Wrought Iron, Brass & Copper Frame, Leaded Painted Centre.
Width, 26 in.; Height, 34 in.
Price 99/ each.

With Leaded Centre, as No. 3544 ... **96/ each.**

STRATFORD, E., WALTHAMSTOW, N.E., AND LEYTONSTONE, E., LONDON.

BUILDERS' IRONMONGERY.
LOCKS.

No. 2002. Rim Lock.   No. 2169. Padlock.   No. 2025. Rim Lock.

No.		6 inch.
2001	Serviceable Rim Lock, Unbushed	18/- per doz.
2002	Strong ditto, Brass Bushed	23/3 ,,
2007	Strong Lock, Wrought Iron Bolts, with Scotch Spring Open Cap, drilled-through Furniture	26/7½ ,,
2014	Do., do., do., Brass Bushed, do., do.	28/10½ ,,

No.		Per doz.
2166	Japanned Tumbler, Brass Bushed	10/6
2167	Galvanized, Brass Shackle & Rivets	18/-
2168	Two-Lever Brass Padlock	27/9
2169	Four-Lever do., do.	45/-

No.		6	7	8 inch.
2025	Brass Bolt, Scotch Spring, Open Cap Rim Lock, with drilled-through Furniture	32/3	—	— doz
2005	Heavy Iron Bolt Rim Lock, Odd Ward, fully Bushed, Open Plate	39/-	48/9	69/- ,,
2006	Superior finish, Palace motion, fully Bushed, Brass Bolt	51/9	62/3	83/3 ,,

No. 2015. Rim Lock.   No. 2034 Rim Draw-Back Lock.   No. 2113. Rim Lock.

No.		6 inch.
2015	Stamped Steel Case, Round End, Iron Bolt, with drilled-through Furniture	24/9 doz.
2020	Do., do., Brass Bolt, do., do.	27/- ,,

No.		5½ × 3½ inch
2034	Rim Draw-Back Lock and Night Latch combined, Kahala Bronze, one Lever, without Stop, two keys	54/- doz.
2035	Do., do., with Stop, do., do.	58/6 ,,

No.		6 inch.
2113	Heavy Cast Case, Iron Bolt, Elizabethan design, Rim Lock	38/3 doz.
2114	Do., do., Brass Bolt, do., do.	45/9 ,,

No. 2009. Rim Dead Lock.   No. 2011. 2-Lever Rim Dead Lock.

No. 2008.
Fine Ward, Unbushed.

4	5	6 inch.
13/6	14/7½	17/3 doz.

No. 2009.
Do., do., Brass Bushed.

4	5	6 inch.
15/9	17/3	20/7½ doz.

No. 2010.
Strong Brass Bushed Dead Lock.

4	5	6 inch.
24/-	25/10½	30/- doz.

No. 2011.
Two-Lever Dead Lock Brass Bolt.

6	7	8 inch.
57/-	72/9	93/- doz.

No. 2036. Rim Draw-Back Lock.   No. 2012. Plate Lock.

 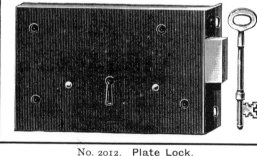

No. 2036.
Fine Ward, Cover Plate, Single Staple.

7	8	9 inch.
36/4½	37/10½	57/- doz.

No. 2037.
Fine Ward, Cover Plate, Double Staple, with Back Slide.

7	8	9	10 inch.
47/3	48/9	67/6	90/-doz.

No. 2012.
Fine Plate Lock.

7	8	10 inch.
15/9	18/9	26/3 doz.

No. 2013.
Do., do., Bushed.

7	8	10 inch.
28/6	32/3	39/- doz.

IRON GATE LOCKS.

No.		
2042	Plain Self-Color Iron Draw-Back Lock	26/7½ per doz.

No.		
2041	Flanged Iron Draw-Back Lock	33/9 per doz.

No.		
2094	One Iron Bolt Flanged Rim Gate Lock	41/3 per doz.
	Brass Bolt do.	48/- ,,

STRATFORD, Walthamstow and Leytonstone.

BUILDERS' IRONMONGERY.

LOCKS.

No. 2016. Mortice Lock.

No.		5 in.
2016	Japanned Case, Round End, Sash Ward	20/7½ doz.
2017	Japanned Case, Round End, Iron Bolt	25/10½ ,,
2017B	Japanned Case, Round End, Brass Bolt	28/6 ,,

No. 2023. Mortice Lock.

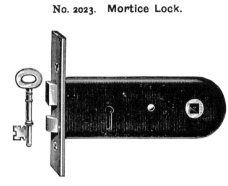

No.		5 in.
2023	Centre Bit, Brass Bolt ..	27/- doz.
2018	Half Rabbeted, Japanned Case Round End, Sash Ward ..	39/- ,,

No. 2021. Mortice Lock.

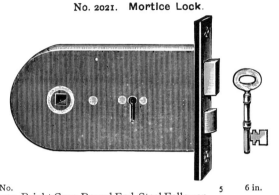

No.		5	6 in.
2021	Bright Case, Round End, Steel Follower Bushed 48/4½		51/9 doz.
2022	Half Rabbeted do. do. do. ..57/-		62/3 ,,
2024	Brass Roller Bolt, with Nickel Plated Steel Keys .. .. —		49/6 ,,

---

No. 2043. Mortice Sash Lock.

2	2½	3 inch.
39/-	42/-	45/- per doz.

No. 2175. Full Rabbeted Mortice Lock.

No. 2174. Half Rabbeted.

2	2½	3 inch.
48/9	54/-	58/6 per doz.

No. 2175. Full Rabbeted.

2	2½	3 inch.
81/-	84/-	87/9 per doz.

No. 2172. Mortice Sash Dead Lock.

2	3	4 inch.
31/6	36/-	42/- per doz.

No. 2173. Mortice Sash Latch.

2	2½	3 inch.
24/-	27/-	30/- per doz.

No. 2048. Cupboard Lock.

No.	3	3½	4 in.
2046	Japanned.. 2/7½	3/-	3/4½ doz.
2047	Do. Strong 4/10½	5/3	5/7½ ,,
2048	Bright .. 8/7½	9/-	9/4½ ,,
2049	Do. Strong Brass Bolt } 11/3	12/-	12/9 ,,

	2	2½	3 in.
2130	All Brass.. 8/3	9/-	9/4½ doz.
2132	Do. Lever 12/9	14/3	15/9 ,,
2133	Do. 2 ,, 20/7½	21/9	23/3 ,,

No. 2134. Cut Cupboard Lock.

No.		2	2½	3 in.
2134	Brass	12/-	13/6	15/- doz.
2135	,,		20/3	21/-	22/6 ,,
2136	,,		24/-	25/6	26/3 ,,

No. 2160. Brass Till Lock.

No.		2¼	2½	2¾ in.
2160	Brass ..	8/3	9/-	9/6 doz.
2161	,,	..11/7½	12/9	13/10½ ,,
2162	2 Lever do.	18/-	18/9	19/6 ,,
2163	6 ,, ,,	36/9	37/6	39/- ,,

No. 2200. Scandinavian Padlock.

No.		doz.
2200	Scandinavian Padlock, with two keys and fast Shackles	15/9
2201	Do. do. Six Tumbler	18/-

YOUNG & MARTEN, Merchants and Manufacturers,
BUILDERS' IRONMONGERY.

BRASS DOOR FURNITURE.

No. 2052.

No.		Per doz. sets. 4	4½	5	6	7	8 in.
2051	Brass Latch Furniture	4/10½	6/-	—	—	—	—
2052	„ Rim do. ..	—	—	7/6	8/7½	9/9	—
2150	„ Drilled-thro' do.	—	—	8/3	9/4½	10/6	

No. 2060.

No.		6 in.
2060	Mineral Rim Furniture ..	6/9 doz. sets
2151	Do. Mortice „	7/10½ „

No. 2145.

No.		6 in.
2145	1¾ in. Stamped Reeded Brass Rim Furniture, Wilkes' Spindling ..	13/10½ doz. sets

No. 2059.

No.		6	7	8 in.
2059	Vaughan's Brass Rim Furniture, with Cast Roses	8/7½	9/9	11/7½ doz. sets

No. 2056.

No.		6	7	8 in.
2152	Mace's Brass Rim Furniture, with Cast Roses	12/9	—	— doz. sets
2056	Do.,do.,Strong do.	14/7½	17/3	21/- „

No. 2054.

No.		6 in.
2153	Brass Mortice Furniture, Stamped Roses, Wilkes' Spindling	19/1½ doz. sets
2054	Do., do., Cast Roses ..	33/9 „

No. 2057.

No.		6 in.
2154	Mace's Mortice Furniture Stamped Roses	18/9 doz. sets
2057	Strong do., with Cast Roses	27/- „

No. 2155.

No.		6 in.
2155	Mace's Reeded Mortice Furniture	52/6 doz. sets
2156	Do., do., Pitts' Spindling ..	57/9 „

No. 2148.

No.		6 in.
2148	Mace's Brass Polished Fluted Mortice Furniture ..	47/3 doz. sets
2149	Do., Rim do.	36/9 „

BRASS REEDED AND REPOUSSÉ FINGER PLATES.

No. 2240. **No. 2241.** **No. 2242.** **No. 2243.** **No. 2244.** **No. 2245.**

		Long	Short.				Long	Short.
No. 2240.	Reeded Brass Finger Plates..	10/6 ..	9/- doz.	No. 2243.	Polished Brass Perforated Repoussé Finger Plates,		24/-	20/3 doz
No. 2241.	„ „ „	15/- ..	12/- „	No. 2244.	„ „ Reeded „ „ „		14/3	11/3 „
No. 2242.	Polished Brass Repoussé Finger Plates ..	15/9 ..	11/3 „	No. 2245.	„ „ Embossed „ „ „		16/1½	13/1½ „

STRATFORD, Walthamstow and Leytonstone.

CHINA DOOR FURNITURE.

No. 2053.

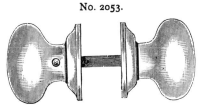

No.		White.	Black.	White and Gold.	Black and Gold.	
2053	Wilkes' Patent	12/-	14/3	20/3	22/6	per doz. sets

No. 2058.

No.		White.	Black.	White and Gold.	Black and Gold.	
2058	Brass Roses and Self-adjusting Spindles	18/-	20/3	25/6	28/6	per doz. sets

No. 2210.

Section of Brass Rose.

No		White.	Black.	White and Gold.	Black and Gold.	
2210	China Mortice Furniture, with Fancy Brass Rose, Pitts' Spindling ..	18/-	20/3	26/3	27/9	per doz. sets
2211	Do., do., Mace's Patent..	24/-	26/3	32/3	33/9	,,

No. 2075.

No.		Cream.	Black.	Pink & Gold on Cream.	
2075	Queen Anne Mortice Furniture	19/6	20/3	30/-	per doz. sets

No. 2212.

No.		Cream.	Black.	Cream and Gold.	Black and Gold.	
2212	Reeded Mortice Furniture	14/3	15/-	22/6	23/3	per doz. sets

No. 2213.

No.		Cream.	Black.	Cream and Gold.	Black and Gold.	
2213	Reeded Mortice Furniture,	15/9	16/6	24/-	24/9	per doz. sets

CHINA FINGER PLATES.

No. 2071.   No. 2072.   No. 2220.   No 2074.

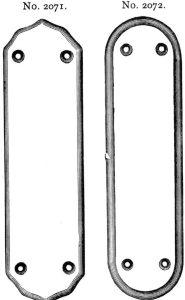

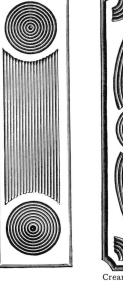

No. 2081.
WHITE CHINA CENTRE DOOR KNOBS.

2½ in., 9/- ; 2¾ in., 11/3 per dozen.

No. 2082.
BLACK CHINA CENTRE DOOR KNOBS.

2½ in., 11/3 ; 2¾ in., 12/9 per dozen.

No.		White.	Cream.	Black.	White & Gold.	Cream, Pink, and Gold.	Black & Gold.	
2071	China Finger Plates, long or short..	4/6	—	6/-	12/-	—	12/9	doz.
2072	Round End Finger Plates	4/10½	—	6/4½	12/9	—	13/6	,,
2220	Square End Reeded ..	6/-	6/9	7/6	—	—	—	,,
2074	Queen Anne Finger Plates	—	6/9	7/6	—	15/-	—	,,

CHINA DOOR NUMBERS.

39

No.		1 or 2 Figures.	3 Figures	
2086	Black Figures on White, 3½ × 2¼ inches..	7/1½	9/-	per doz
2087	Gold Figures on Black ,, ,, ..	12/9	18/-	

YOUNG & MARTEN, Merchants and Manufacturers,

BUILDERS' IRONMONGERY.

IRON DOOR KNOCKERS.

No. 2271.

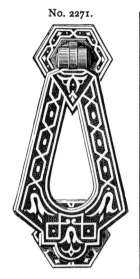

No. 2271.

Adamantine, Bronzed.

15/- per doz.

No.		Doz.
2101	Japanned Iron, 9¾ × 3¼ in. ...	11/3
,,	Bronzed Iron, 9¾ × 3¼ in. ...	13/6
2102	Japanned Iron, 8¾ × 2¾ in. ...	9/-
,,	Bronzed Iron, 8¾ × 2¾ in. ...	11/3

No. 2103.

No. 2103.

Enamelled, Bronzed Iron.

12/- per doz.

No. 2106.

No. 2106.

Kahala, Bronzed.

18/- per doz.

No. 2104.

No. 2104.

Kahala, Bronzed or Berlin Blacked
Letter Plate & Knocker

18/- per doz.

No. 2272.

No. 2272.

Japanned Iron, 12/- per doz

No. 2073.

Adamantine, Bronzed.

12/9 per doz.

IRON DOOR KNOBS.

No. 2274.

No. 2274.

Adamantine, Bronzed.

12/- per doz.

No. 2076.

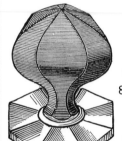

Gothic Pattern.

Japanned.

2¼	2½	2¾ inch
8/7½	9/9	10/6 doz.

Bronzed.

2¼	2½	3 inch
9/4½	10/6	12/-

No. 2078.

Ornamental
Kahala, Bronzed
2½ inch.

13/6 per doz.

No. 3093.

SPRING CUPBOARD CATCH

Kahala, Bronzed .. 11/3 per doz.

IRON POSTAL HANDLES AND LETTER PLATES.

No. 3045. Postal Handle.

No.		Doz.
3045.	Kahala, Bronzed, Postal Handle	27/-
2126	Brown, Bronzed or Berlin Black do., with Reeded Brass Grip	40/6

No. 3039. Letter Plate.

No. 3039.	Kahala, Bronzed ..	9/9 doz.
No 3040.	"Vertical" do., do...	9/9 ,,

No. 3044. Letter Plate.

No. 3044. Kahala, Bronzed .. 15/9 per doz.

No. 2271.

No. 2271.
Bronzed Iron Frame
with Solid Brass
Flap and Letters.

14/3 per doz.

No. 2276. Combination Postal Handle.

No. 2276 { Adamantine, Bronzed, Combination Postal Handle and Knocker .. } 27/- per doz.

No. 3043.

Brass
Letter Plate.

No. 3043.	All Brass, Bronzed and Relieved ..	27/- per doz.
,, 2277.	Polished Brass ditto, 8½ inch	54/- ,,
No. 2277	Bronzed and Relieved same price as Polished.	

STRATFORD, Walthamstow and Leytonstone.

BRASS DOOR KNOCKERS.

No. 2121.   No. 2108.   No. 2109.   No. 2127.   No. 2116.   No. 2128.

Polished Brass, 4/1½ each.   Polished Brass, 4/1½ each.   Polished Brass, 5/3 each.   Polished Brass, 5/7½ each.   Polished Brass, 4/6 each.   Polished Brass, 14/3 each.

No. 2123.

COMBINATION KNOCKER.

BRASS DOOR KNOBS.

No. 2100.   No. 2079.   No. 2129

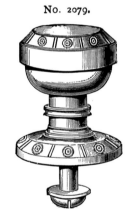

Polished Brass, 9/9 each.

Polished Brass, 4/1½ each.   Bronzed & Relieved, 7/1½ ea.   Polished Brass, 2⅝in., 10/10½ ea.
Polished Brass, 6/9 each.   ,,   ,, 3¼,,   16/10½ ,,

COMBINATION KNOCKERS.

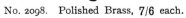

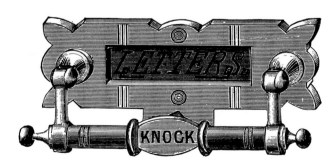

No. 2098.   Polished Brass, 7/6 each.   No. 2099.   Polished Brass, 8/7½ each.

STRATFORD, Walthamstow and Leytonstone.

BRASS POSTAL HANDLES.

No. 2122.　Polished Brass, 6/4½ each.

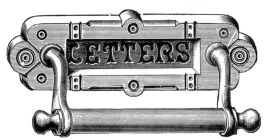

No. 3047.　Polished Brass, 6/- each.

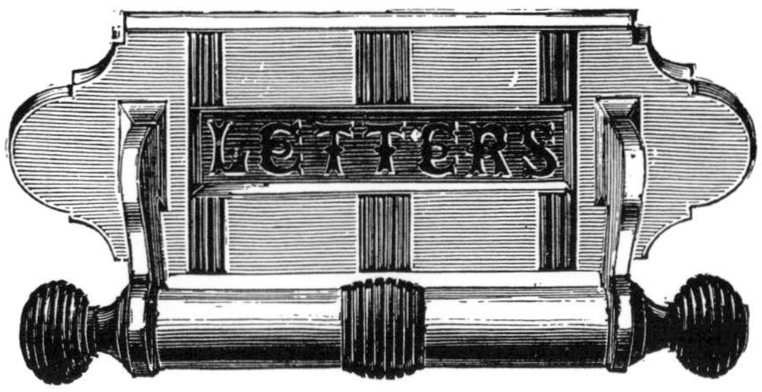

No. 3049.　Polished Brass, 7/10½ each.

No. 2137.　Polished Brass, 10/1½ each.

No. 2138.　Polished Brass, 7/1½ each.

No. 2139.　Polished Brass, 7/6 each.

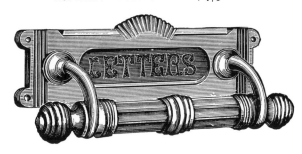

No. 2062.

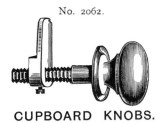

CUPBOARD KNOBS.

No.		1	1⅛	1¼	1⅜	1½ inch	
2066	Japanned Iron	8/7½	9 9	11/7½	—	14/7½	per gross
2067	Brass	15/9	19/10½	24/9	28/6	32/3	,,
2068	White China ..	12/9	—	13/6	—	15/9	,,
2069	Black ,, ...	14/3	—	15/-	—	17/3	,,
2065	White and Gold ..	—	—	4/6	—	4/10½	per doz.
2070	Black and Gold ..	—	—	4/10½	—	5/3	,,

CUPBOARD TURNS.

No.					1¼ in.	1½ in.	
2062	Brass	..	..	..	3/9	4/10½	per doz.
2063	White China ..	..	..	..	4/10½	5/3	,,
2064	Black	..	..	..	5/3	6/-	,,
2088	White and Gold China	..	..	..	8/3	9/-	,,
2089	Black and Gold ,,	..	..	..	9/-	9/9	,,

BUTTONS.

No. 3011.　No. 3012. 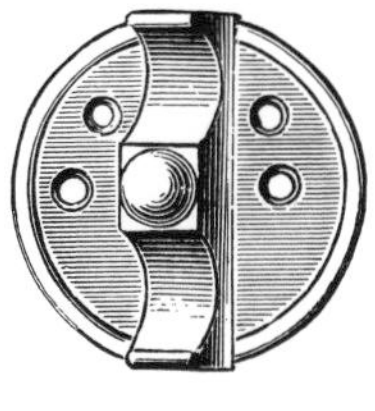　No. 3013.

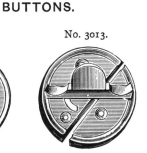

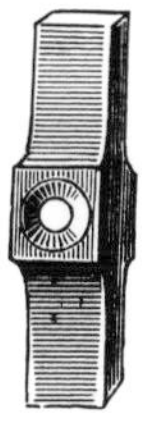

No. 3010.

No.			1½	1¾	2	2¼	2½ inch	
3010	Japanned Iron ..	..	—	—	3/9	4/10½	6/-	per gross
3011	Brass	..	10/6	12/4½	13/10½	22/1½	24/9	,,
3012	Brass Button on Plate	..	—	4/10½	6/-	—	—	per doz.
3012	Japanned Iron on Plate	..	—	1/6	1/10½	—	—	,,
3013	Brass Button on Plate	..	—	6/-	6/9	—	—	,,

JAPANNED SHELF BRACKETS.

No.	3 × 4	4 × 5	5 × 6	6 × 8	8 × 10	9 × 15	10 × 12	12 × 18 inches.
3060	1/6	1/10½	2/7½	3/9	6/4½	9/-	8/3	15/9 per doz.

Shop Door Latches, Cupboard Door Fastenings, Letter Plates, and Centre Door Knobs.

No. YS5133.
Bronzed Iron Cupboard Catch.

Size, 2½ ins. by 2 ins.
Price, 4/4 per doz.

No. YS5149. Shop Door Latch.

Bronzed Iron Case, Ebonized Lever Handles.
A Thoroughly Reliable Latch for Hard Wear.
No. YS5149. Price, 4/4 each.
No. Y2190. Nickel-plated Blackwood Lever Handles. Price, 10/8 each.

No. Y2192. Shop Door Lock.

Kahala Bronzed Shop Door Lock and Latch with 2 Keys and Bronzed Iron Handles.
Price, 7/4 each.

No. Y2442.

No. Y2068.

Cupboard Turns.

No.							1¼ in.	1½ in.	
Y2442	Brass	..	..	..	..	..	3/4	4/4	per doz.
Y2063	White China					..	4/4	4/8	,,
Y2064	Black ,,	..	..			..	4/8	5/4	,,
Y2088	White and Gold China			..	..		7/4	8/-	,,
Y2089	Black and Gold ,,	..	..	..			8/-	8/8	,,

Cupboard Knobs.

No.				1	1⅛	1¼	1½ inch.
Y2066	Japanned Iron	..	..	7/9	8/8	11/8	— per gross.
Y2067	Brass	..	..	14/-	17/9	21/-	,,
Y2068	White China	..	..	14/-	—	16/8	19/- ,,
Y2069	Black ,,	..	..	16/8	—	18/8	21/- ,,
Y2065	White and Gold	..	..	—	—	21/-	36/- ,,
Y2070	Black and Gold	..	..	—	—	40/-	48/- ,,

No. Y3012.

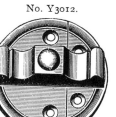

Brass and Iron Cupboard Buttons.

No. Y3013.

No. Y3011.

Sizes	..	..	..	1½	1¾	2	2¼	2½ in.
No. Y3010.	Japanned Iron Button	2/-	2/8	3/4	4/4	5/4 per gross.
,, Y3011.	Brass	..	..	9/4	11/-	12/4	20/-	22/- ,,
,, Y3012.	Brass Button on Plate	—	4/-	5/-	6/-	6/8 per dozen.
,, Y30121.	Iron	..	..	—	1/4	1/8	2/8	,,
,, Y2013.	Brass Button on Plate, with Thumb Bit	—	5/-	5/4	6/8	— ,,

No. Y3039. Letter Plate.

Bronzed Iron.
Price, 9/- per doz.

No. Y3048. Letter Plate.

Size, 7 ins.
Polished Brass.
Price, 2/- each.

No. Y3043. Letter Plate. Polished Brass.

Sizes	..	6 × 2¼	7 × 3¼	8 × 4	10 × 4 ins.
Aperture	..	4¼ × 1	4¾ × 1⅜	6 × 1⅝	8 × 2 ,,
Price	..	2/-	3/-	5/-	8/- each.

No. Y2274.
Bronzed Iron Centre Knob.

Price, 11/- doz.

No Y2076. Gothic Centre Knob.

Size, 2½ ins
Japanned, 8/8 doz. Bronzed, 10/- doz.

No. Y2078.
Bronzed Iron Centre Knob.

Size, 2¼ ins. Price, 12/- doz.

No. Y2129. Brass Centre Knob.

Handsome Polished Brass Hall Door Knob. Price, 7/4 each.

YOUNG & MARTEN, Ltd., Merchants and Manufacturers,

STEEL LOCKS, BRACKETS, DOOR FURNITURE, AND MISCELLANEOUS WIRE CORDS, &c.

No. Y1999. MACHINE-MADE STEEL RIM LOCK.

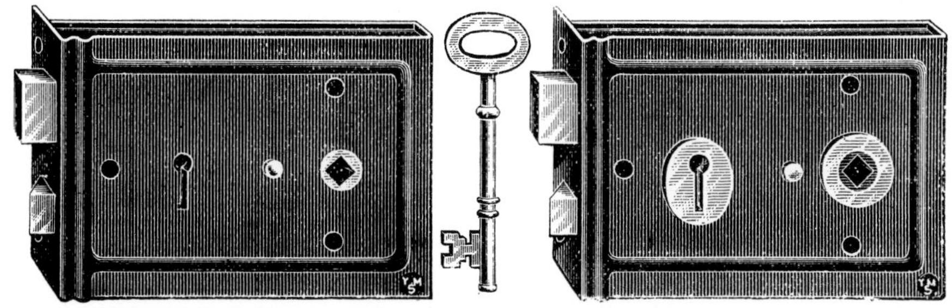

We are frequently asked for a Rim Lock lower in price than our No. Y2001 (shown on page 242). We have therefore introduced the Lock illustrated above. It is made of light stamped steel, with malleable bolts and fittings. When fixed it has a very neat appearance, and in strength is equal to a much more expensive Lock. We recommend it specially for cottage property and any light doors. Suitable furniture is illustrated on page 247.

No. Y1999.—6-inch Ornamental Dead Black Case, without Furniture, Price, 12/- per dozen.
,, Y2000.—The same Lock, Brass Bushed .. .. ,, 16/- ,,

No. Y1988. BUILDERS' BRANDING IRONS.

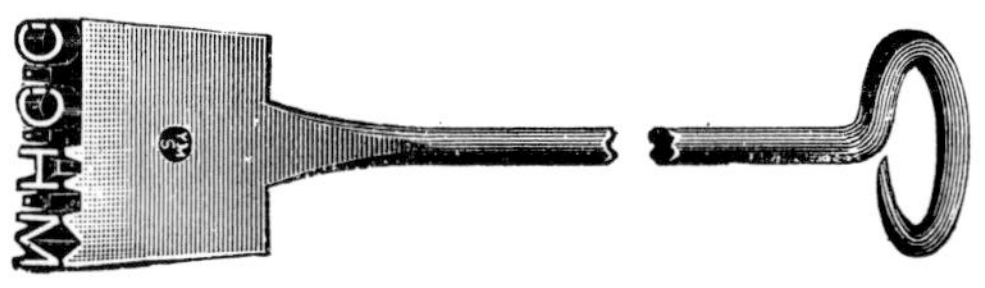

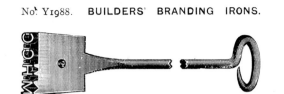

Made to Order.

Initials or Name cut in solid steel, in any size.

Size of Letters	2	3	4	5	6	8	10	letters,
$\frac{1}{4}$ and $\frac{5}{16}$ inch ..	3/-	3/4	4/6	5/4	6/8	8/8	10/-	each.
$\frac{3}{8}$,, $\frac{1}{2}$,, ..	3/9	4/6	5/4	7/8	9/-	10/6	12/-	,,
$\frac{5}{8}$,, $\frac{3}{4}$,, ..	6/-	7/8	9/-	10/6	12/-	15/-	18/-	,,
$\frac{7}{8}$,, 1 ,, ..	8/-	9/-	10/6	12/-	15/-	18/-	21/-	,,

REEDED FINGER PLATES.

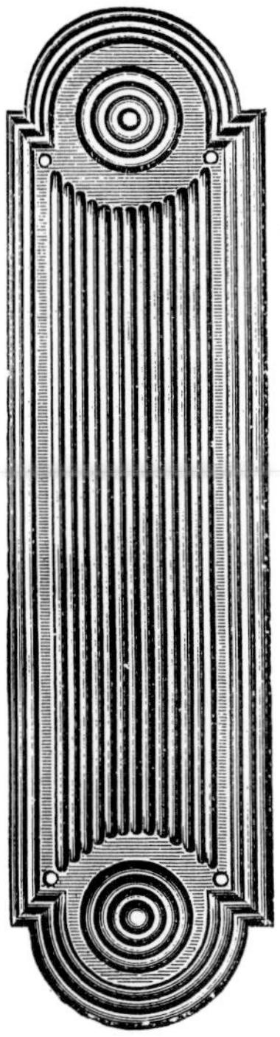

No. Y1320.

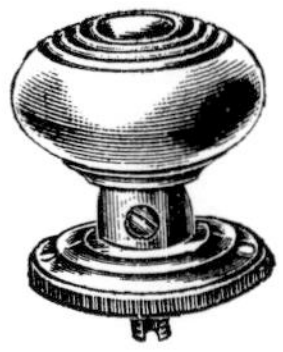

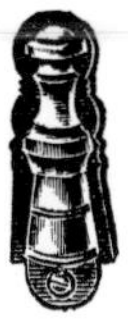

PRICE.

Per doz.

Mortice Furniture, Maces', Y1320 .. 24/-
Rim Furniture, Y1321 20/-
Finger Plates, Long, Y1322 .. .. 8/-
Finger Plates, Short, Y1322 .. .. 7/-

No. Y1992.

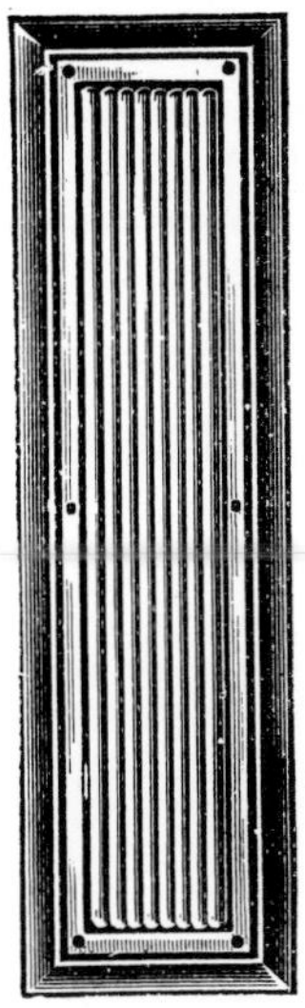

An entirely new design in reeded plates, with bold bevelled edges, giving a far superior appearance to the ordinary flat-reeded plate.
Long .. 11/4 per doz.
Short .. 9/- ,,

No. Y1994. OVAL BRASS FURNITURE.

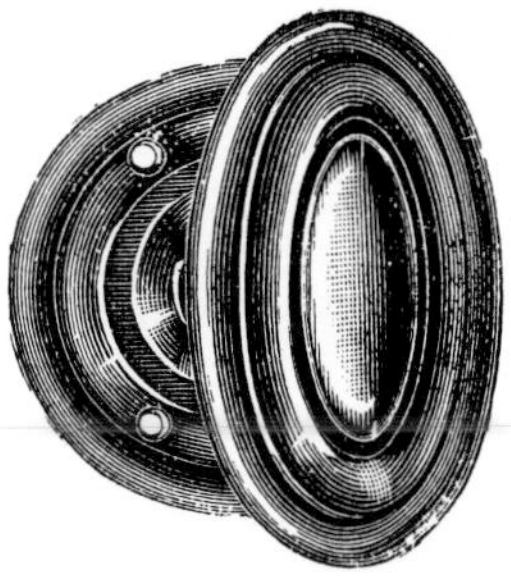

The special feature of this Furniture is its strength. It is made in stamped brass, highly polished, and is **lined with steel plate.** It has a more artistic appearance than the ordinary round knobs, and cannot, under any circumstances, be bruised or indented.

PRICE.

Pitt's Rose .. 4/- per set.

No. Y1995. FLUTED-BRASS MORTICE FURNITURE.

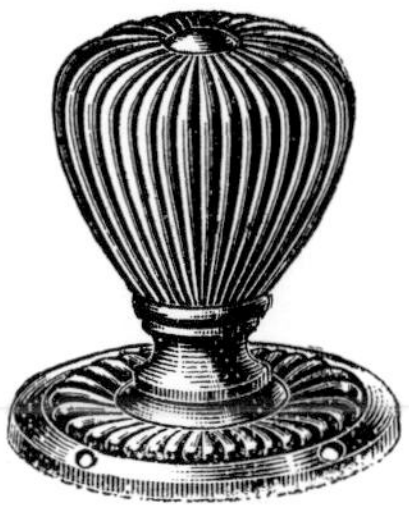

An entirely new shape in "Queen Anne" Furniture.

Gives a firm and pleasant grip, and has a most effective appearance when fixed.

PRICE.

Pitt's Rose ... 4/6 per set.

No. Y2451. "QUEEN ANNE" FURNITURE.

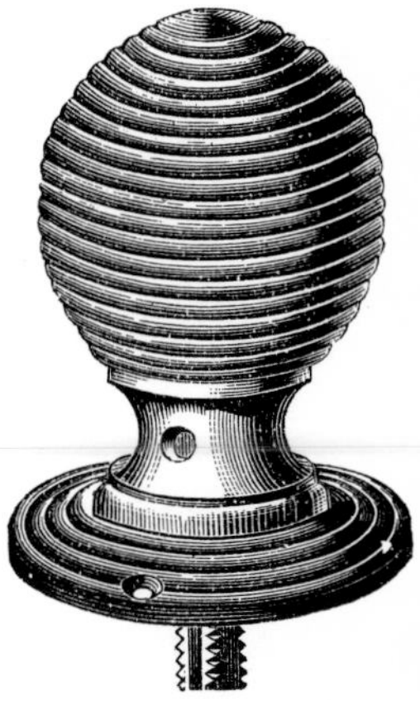

This Furniture is in solid brass, and is the strongest, heaviest, and best made in this pattern. Suitable for best work.

PRICES, per dozen.

No. Y2127.—Maces' Rose Rim Furniture 26/8
No. Y2451.—Maces' Rose Mortice Furniture 40/-

No. Y1985. WROUGHT-STEEL SHELF BRACKET.

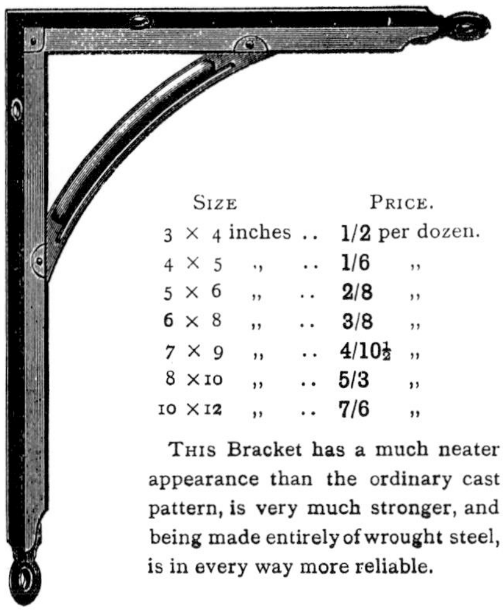

Size	Price.
3 × 4 inches ..	1/2 per dozen.
4 × 5 ,, ..	1/6 ,,
5 × 6 ,, ..	2/8 ,,
6 × 8 ,, ..	3/8 ,,
7 × 9 ,, ..	4/10½ ,,
8 × 10 ,, ..	5/3 ,,
10 × 12 ,, ..	7/6 ,,

This Bracket has a much neater appearance than the ordinary cast pattern, is very much stronger, and being made entirely of wrought steel, is in every way more reliable.

No. Y1997 BRASS CUPBOARD TURN.

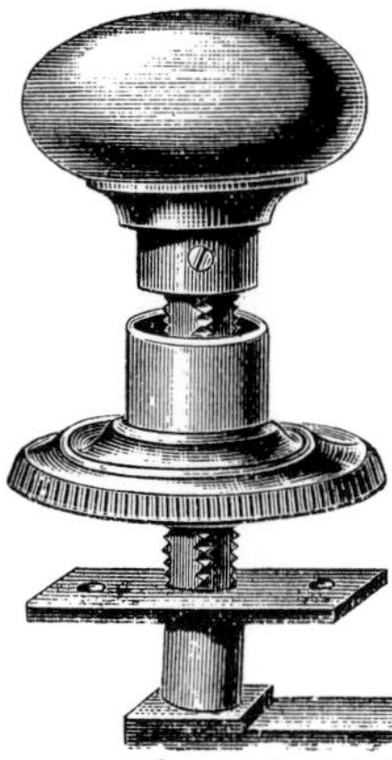

This is a very much superior article to the brass cupboard turns generally used. It is made with Maces' Patent Rose, ensuring a smooth and easy action. Recommended for best work.

PRICE ... 10/- per dozen.

FLEXIBLE COPPER WIRE CORD.

Gilt for Picture Wire. Self-colour for Sashes.

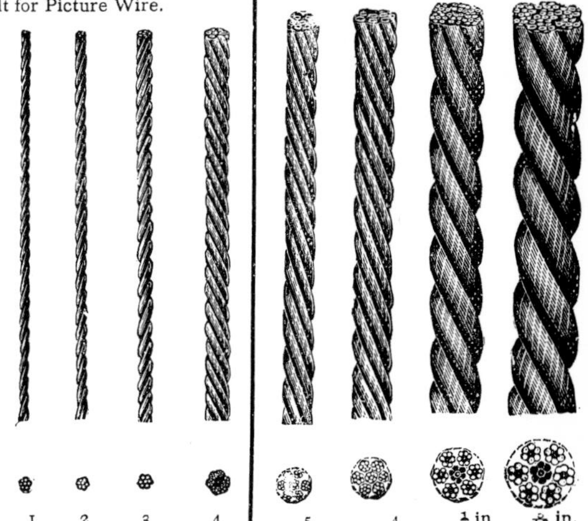

Nos. ..	1	2	3	4	5	4	¼ in	$\frac{5}{16}$ in.
Working Load	4	7	14	28	75	112	168	224 lbs
Price, per 100 feet.	1/2	2/-	3/8	9/-	13/6	22/6	24/-	31/6

GALVANIZED WIRE CLOTHES LINES } Size No. 5 (as above). In 50 or 100 feet lengths. 1/- 1/8 each.

STRATFORD, Walthamstow, Leytonstone, Millwall, & Brentford.

SASH FASTENERS.

No. 3052.	No. 2250.	No. 3054.	No. 3055.
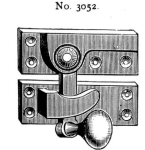	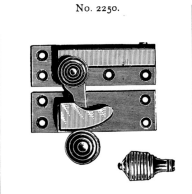		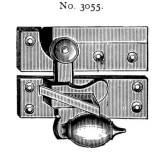

No.		Doz.
3052	Bronzed Iron, with Brass or China Knob	3/4½
3053	Do. do.	4/6
3051	All Brass, with Brass or China Knob	4/6
3052	Do. do.	6/-
3053	Do. do.	9/9

No.		Doz.
2250	All Brass, Reeded Knob	8/3
2251	Do. do.	9/9

No.		Doz.
3054	Cast Brass, with Brass or China Knob	11/3
3151	Walker's Patent, with Plain Brass Knob	18/-
3152	Do. do. China Knob	19/6
3153	Do. Reeded Brass Knob	21/9

No.		Doz
3055	With Drop Catch, Brass or China Knob	13/1½
3156	Willett's Patent, Brass Dead and Relieved	13/10½
3157	Do. Strong Polished Brass do.	17/7½
3158	Do. Extra Strong do.	24/9

PATENT FLUSH SASH FASTENER,

Patent 11/2/92, No. 2713.

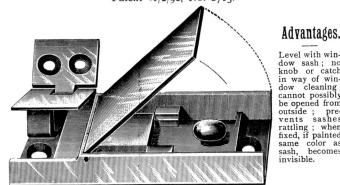

Advantages.

Level with window sash; no knob or catch in way of window cleaning; cannot possibly be opened from outside; prevents sashes rattling; when fixed, if painted same color as sash, becomes invisible.

Price, Solid Cast Brass Polished .. 18/- | 2¾ | 3½ inch. 22/6 per doz.

SASH LIFTS.

No. 3301.	No. 3300.	No. 3067.
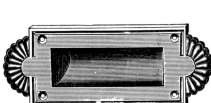		

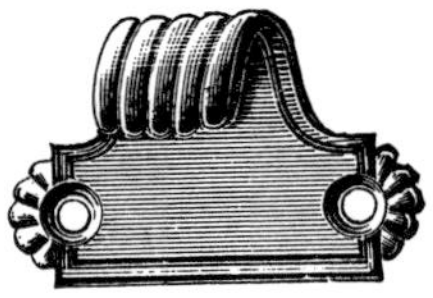

No. 3074.
Japanned Iron. 1/1½ doz.

No. 3066.
Stamped Brass ditto, 2/3 doz.

No.		
3301	(Registered) Brass ..	5/7½ per doz.
		2½ 3 inch
3072	Japanned Iron ..	1/6 2/- per doz.
3073	Brass do. ..	7/10½ ,,

No. 3300 (Registered).
1¾	2	2¼ inch.
1/10½	2/7½	3/- doz.

Cast Brass Jointed,
8/3 per dozen.

No. 3302. **SASH HANDLE.**	No. 3303. **DRAWER PULL.**	No. 3042. **LIFTING HANDLE.**
	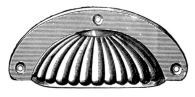	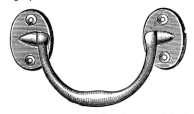

No.		3	3¼	3½	4 inch.
3064	Japanned Iron..	1/6	1/10½	2/7½	3/4½ per doz.
3065	Brass	4/6	4/10½	6/-	7/10½ ,,
			2½	3	3½ inch.
3302	Stamped Brass do. ..		3/9	4/1½	4/6 per doz.

No.		Nos. 1	2	3	
3304	Japanned Iron	10 6	12/-	18/- per gross
3079	Cast Brass	..	49/6	,,
3303	Stamped Brass (Registered),	40/6		,,

No.		2¼	2½	3	3½ inch.
3042	Japanned Iron,	2/3	3/-	4/1½	5/3 doz. pairs
3075	Brass ditto	6/4½	7/10½	9/4½	11/3 ,,

No. 3121. **BRASS DRESSER HOOKS.** No. 3124. **BRASS CUP HOOKS.**

	¾	1	1⅛	1¼	1⅜	1½ inch.
	5/3	7/1½	8/3	9/4½	11/3	12/9 gross

	¾	1	1⅛	1¼	1⅜	1½ inch.
	6/9	9/9	11/7½	15/9	19/1½	22/6 gross

CASEMENT STAYS AND FASTENERS.

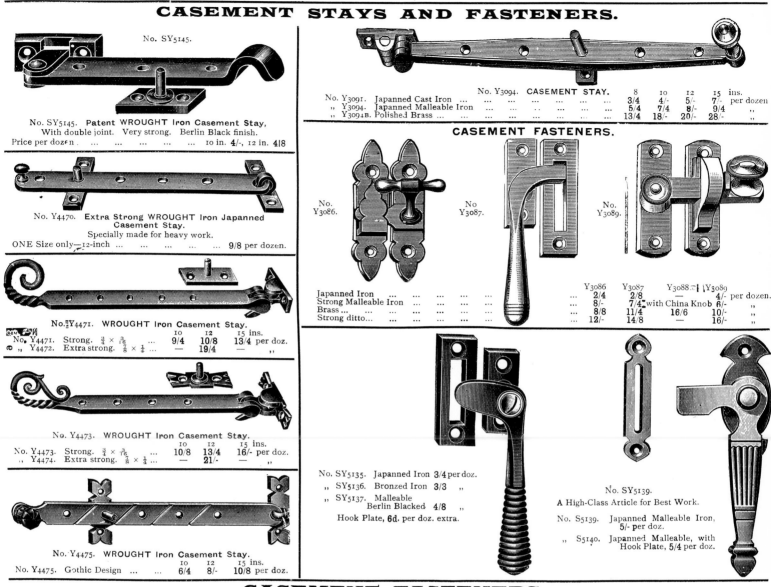

No. SY5145.

No. SY5145. Patent WROUGHT Iron Casement Stay,
With double joint. Very strong. Berlin Black finish.
Price per dozen ... ... 10 in. **4/-**, 12 in. **4|8**

No. Y4470. Extra Strong WROUGHT Iron Japanned Casement Stay.
Specially made for heavy work.
ONE Size only—12-inch ... ... **9/8** per dozen.

No. Y4471. WROUGHT Iron Casement Stay.

	10	12	15 ins.
No. Y4471. Strong. $\frac{3}{4} \times \frac{3}{16}$ ...	9/4	10/8	13/4 per doz.
„ Y4472. Extra strong. $\frac{5}{8} \times \frac{1}{4}$ ...		19/4	„

No. Y4473. WROUGHT Iron Casement Stay.

	10	12	15 ins.
No. Y4473. Strong. $\frac{3}{4} \times \frac{3}{16}$ ...	10/8	13/4	16/- per doz.
„ Y4474. Extra strong. $\frac{5}{8} \times \frac{1}{4}$ ...	—	21/-	„

No. Y4475. WROUGHT Iron Casement Stay.

	10	12	15 ins.
No. Y4475. Gothic Design	6/4	8/-	10/8 per doz.

No. Y3094. CASEMENT STAY.

	8	10	12	15 ins.
No. Y3091. Japanned Cast Iron ...	3/4	4/-	5/-	7/- per dozen
„ Y3094. Japanned Malleable Iron ...	5/4	7/4	8/-	9/4 „
„ Y3094B. Polished Brass ...	13/4	18/-	20/-	28/- „

CASEMENT FASTENERS.

No. Y3086. **No Y3087.** **No. Y3089.**

	Y3086	Y3087	Y3088	Y3089
Japanned Iron	2/4	2/8	—	4/- per dozen.
Strong Malleable Iron ...	8/-	7/4 with China Knob		6/- „
Brass	8/8	11/4	16/6	10/- „
Strong ditto... ...	12/-	14/8		16/- „

No. SY5135. Japanned Iron **3/4** per doz.
„ SY5136. Bronzed Iron **3/3** „
„ SY5137. Malleable Berlin Blacked **4/8** „
Hook Plate, **6d.** per doz. extra.

No. SY5139.
A High-Class Article for Best Work.

No. S5139. Japanned Malleable Iron, **5/-** per doz.
„ S5140. Japanned Malleable, with Hook Plate, **5/4** per doz.

CASEMENT FASTENERS.

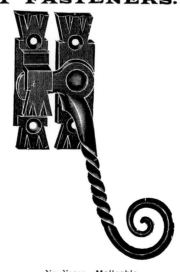

No. Y3240. Malleable.
Square Handle, Very Strong.
No. Y3240. Hook Plate ... **5/4** per doz.
„ Y3241. Slotted Plate **4/8** „

No. Y3243. WROUGHT Iron.
Extra Strong.
Made with Hook Plate only.
5/4 per dozen.

No. Y3244. Malleable.
No. Y3244. Hook Plate ... ... **8/-** per doz.
„ Y3245. Slotted Plate ... **7/4** „
„ Y3246. Extra large and very strong Hook Plate ... **18/-** „
„ Y3247. Ditto. Slotted Plate **16/-** „

No. Y3224. Malleable.
No. Y3224. Hook Plate ... ... **10/-** per doz.
„ Y3225. Slotted Plate ... **9/4** „
„ Y3226. Extra Strong Hook Plate ... ... **21/-** „
„ Y3227. Ditto. Slotted Plate **19/4** „

All above Casement Fasteners are illustrated with Hook Plate.

STRATFORD, Walthamstow, Leytonstone, Millwall, & Brentford.

CORNICE POLES

STRAIGHT CORNICE POLE

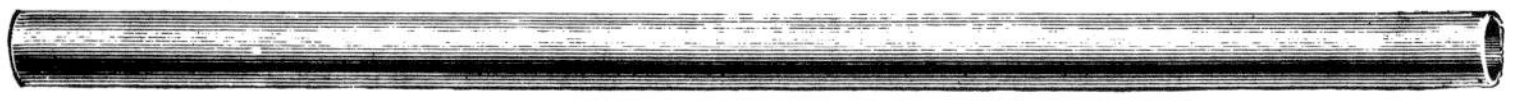

Sizes, ...	I	1¼	1½	1¾	2	2¼	2½	3	inches.
No. 8840.—Polished and Lacquered Brass, ...	/9	/10½	1/	1/1½	1/3	1/10½	2/	3/	per foot.
No. 8841.—Stained Wood — Mahogany, Walnut, or Pine, ...			/2	/3½	/6	/9			,,
No. 8842.—Solid Mahogany or Birch, ...			/6¾	/8¼	/11	1/4½			,,
,, 8843.—Solid Walnut, Oak, Ash, or Ebonized, ...			/10½	1/	1/3	1/7½			,,

2-BEND BAY CORNICE POLE

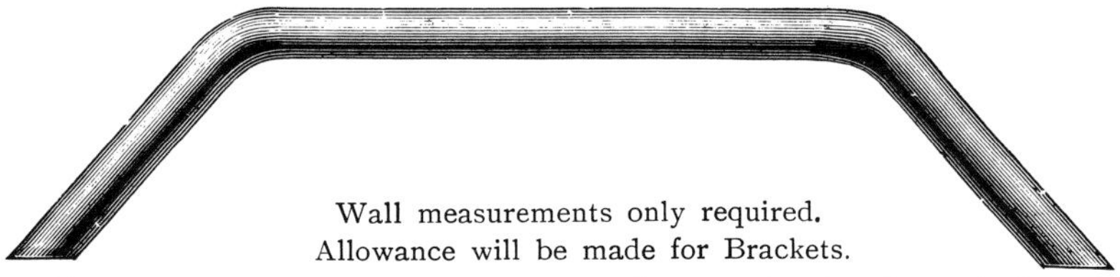

Wall measurements only required.
Allowance will be made for Brackets.

Sizes, ...	I	1¼	1½	1¾	2	2¼	2½	2¾	3	inches.
No. 8844.—Polished and Lacquered Brass, ...	1/4½	1/7½	1/9	2/3	2/6	3/	3/3	3/9	4/6	per foot.
No. 8845.—Stained Wood — Mahogany, Pine, or Walnut, ...	/10½	1/3	1/9	—	2/3					,,
No. 8846.—Solid Mahogany or Birch, ...	1/3	1/9	2/3	—	3/					,,
,, 8847.—Solid Walnut, Oak, Ash, or Ebonized, ...	1/9	2/3	2/9	—	3/6					,,

4-BEND BAY CORNICE POLE

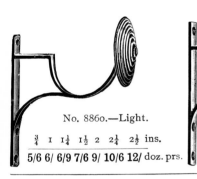

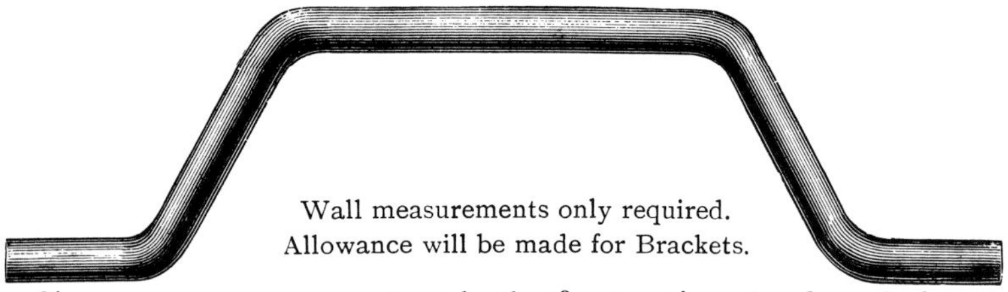

Wall measurements only required.
Allowance will be made for Brackets.

Sizes, ...	I	1¼	1½	1¾	2	2¼	2½	2¾	3	inches.
No. 8850.—Polished and Lacquered Brass, ...	1/7½	1/10½	2/	2/9	2/9	3/3	3/9	4/6	5/	per foot.
No. 8851.—Stained Wood — Mahogany, Pine, or Walnut, ...			1/6	1/9	2/3	—	2/9			,,
No. 8852.—Solid Mahogany or Birch, ...			1/10½	2/3	2/9	—	3/			,,
,, 8853.—Solid Walnut, Oak, Ash, or Ebonized, ...			2/3	2/7½	3/3	—	3/6			,,

6-BEND BAY CORNICE POLE

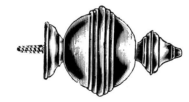

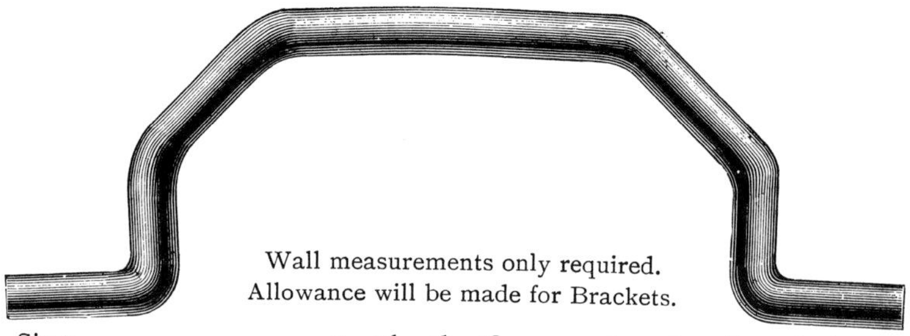

Wall measurements only required.
Allowance will be made for Brackets.

Sizes, ...	I	1¼	1½	1¾	2	2¼	2½	2¾	3	inches.
No. 8856.—Polished and Lacquered Brass, ...	1/9	2/	2/3	2/9	3/	3/9	4/3	5/	6/	per foot.
No. 8857.—Stained Wood — Mahogany, Pine, or Walnut, ...			1/10½	2/4½	2/9	—	3/			,,
No. 8858.—Solid Mahogany or Birch, ...			2/7½	3/	3/4½	—	3/6			,,
,, 8859.—Solid Walnut, Oak, Ash, or Ebonized, ...			3/	3/6	3/9	—	4/			,,

CORNICE POLE BRACKETS

No. 8860.—Light.

¾	1	1¼	1½	2¼	2½	ins.
5/6	6/	6/9	7/6	9/	10/6 12/	doz. prs.

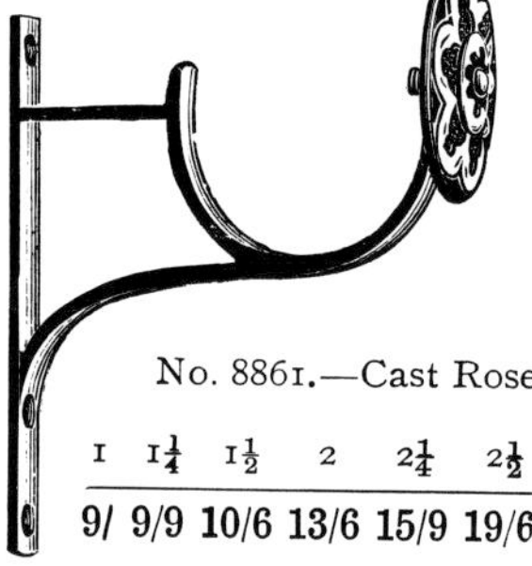

No. 8861.—Cast Rose, Medium.

1	1¼	1½	2	2¼	2½	3	ins.
9/	9/9	10/6	13/6	15/9	19/6	22/6	doz. prs.

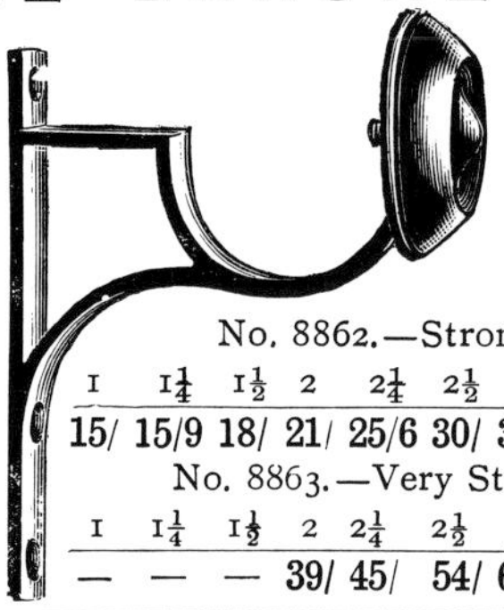

No. 8862.—Strong.

1	1¼	1½	2	2¼	2½	3	ins.
15/	15/9	18/	21/	25/6	30/	39/	doz. prs.

No. 8863.—Very Strong.

1	1¼	1½	2	2¼	2½	3	ins.
—	—	—	39/	45/	54/	66/	doz. prs.

No. 8866.—Medium.

1	1¼	1½	2	2¼	2½	3	ins.
7/6	8/3	9/	12/	13/6	16/6	19/6	doz.

No. 8867.—Strong.

1	1¼	1½	2	2¼	2½	3	ins.
9/	10/6	12/9	15/	16/6	18/	21/	doz.

CORNICE POLE ENDS

No. 8870.—Polished Brass.

1	1¼	1½	2	2½	ins.
/10½	1/	1/1½	1/9	2/6	per pair.
9/	10/6	12/	18/	27/	doz. pairs.

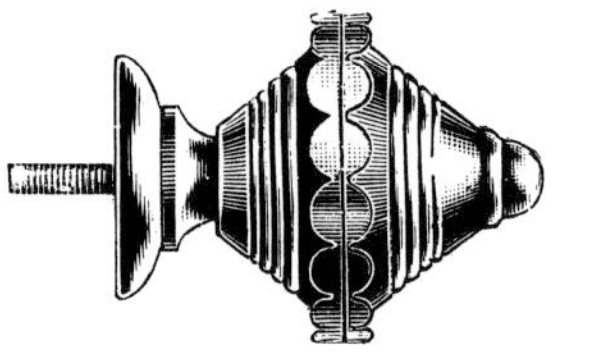

No. 8874.—Polished Brass.

¾	1	1¼	1½	2	2½	ins.
1/	1/6	1/9	2/	2/9	4/	per pair.

No. 8875.—Polished Brass.

1½	2	2½	3	ins.
2/6	3/6	5/	5/9	per pair.

Sizes, ...	3	3½	4	4½	5	ins.
No. 8877. — Stained Wood—Mahogany, Walnut, or Pine, ...	9/	10/6	15/	21/	30/	doz. prs.
No. 8878.—Solid Mahogany or Birch, ...	16/6	21/	25/6	31/6	45/	,,
No. 8879.—Solid Walnut, Oak, Ash, or Ebonized, ...	27/	33/	39/	45/	60/	,,

HARCOURT'S PATENT CORNICE POLE JOINT

As tubing is always kept in stock by ironmongers, by the use of the joint a Cornice Pole may be fitted to any window in a few minutes, at a minimum cost. It can be carried outside or inside any angle. It suits either brass-cased, all brass tube, or wood poles. It renders brazing of angles or bends unnecessary. Any ironmonger may make his own Cornice Poles. It allows of old poles and rods being used when change of house is made.

Outside Diam., ...	¾	1	1¼	1½	1¾	2	ins.
No. 8880, ...	20/	24/	32/	40/	54/	60/	per doz.

Prices include Hard Wood Plugs.

CORNICE POLE RINGS—BEST FINISH

	I	1¼	1½	1¾	2	2¼	2½	2¾	3	3½	ins.
No. 8881.—Brass, Light,	8/3	9/	10/6	12/	13 6	15/9	—	—	—	—	p. grs.
No. 8882.—Brass, Medium, ...		13/6	18/		19/6	22/6	25/6	—	—		,,
No. 8883.—Brass, Strong, ...		27/	30/		33/	36/	48/				,,
No. 8886.—Stained Wood—Mahogany, Walnut, or Pine,		10/6	13/6		19/6	24/	33/				,,
No. 8887.—Solid Mahogany or Birch, ...		19/6	24/		27/	30/	54/				,,
No. 8888.—Solid Walnut, Oak, Ash, or Ebonized, ...		33/	40/		45/	54/	80/				,,

PORTIERE RODS, CURTAIN BANDS, AND PICTURE ROD FURNITURE

BRASS PORTIERE RODS, COMPLETE WITH RINGS

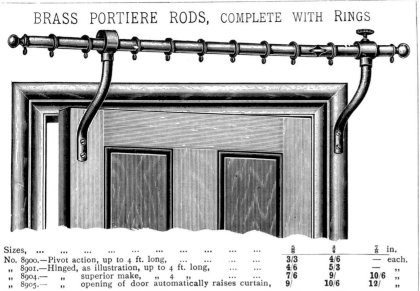

Sizes, ...	$\frac{5}{8}$	$\frac{3}{4}$	$\frac{7}{8}$ in.
No. 8900.—Pivot action, up to 4 ft. long, ...	**3/3**	**4/6**	— each.
„ 8901.—Hinged, as illustration, up to 4 ft. long, ...	**4/6**	**5/3**	— „
„ 8904.— „ superior make, „ 4 „ ...	**7/6**	**9/**	**10/6** „
„ 8905.— „ opening of door automatically raises curtain,	**9/**	**10/6**	**12/** „

BRASS CURTAIN BAND

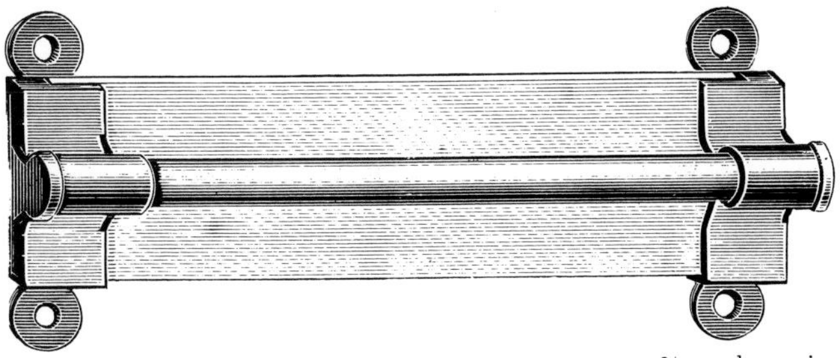

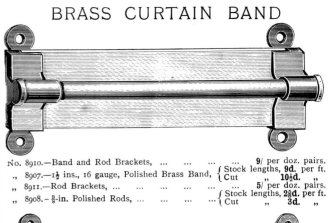

No. 8910.—Band and Rod Brackets, ... **9/** per doz. pairs.
„ 8907.—1½ ins., 16 gauge, Polished Brass Band, { Stock lengths, **9d.** per ft. / Cut „ **10½d.** „
„ 8911.—Rod Brackets, ... **5/** per doz. pairs.
„ 8908.—$\frac{3}{8}$-in. Polished Rods, ... { Stock lengths, **2$\frac{5}{8}$d.** per ft. / Cut „ **3d.** „

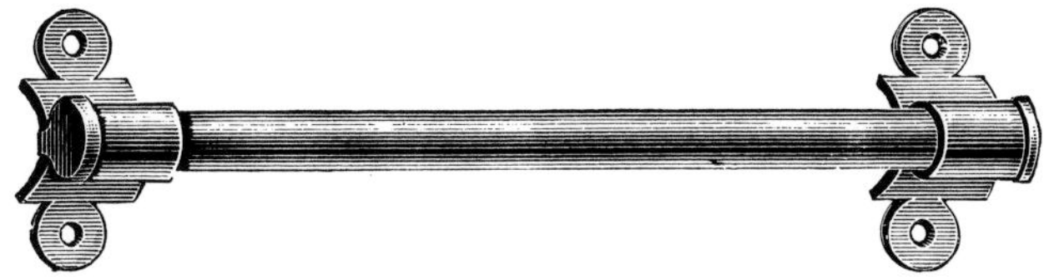

POLISHED AND LACQUERED BRASS-CASED TUBING

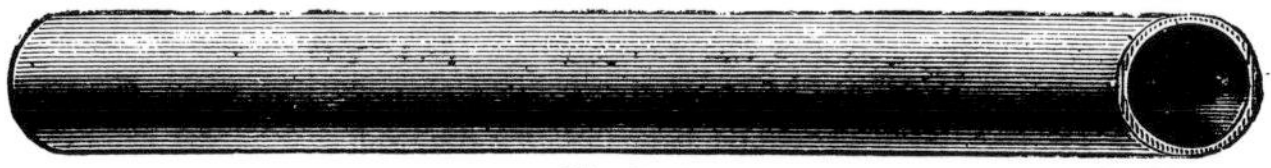

No. 8908.

Sizes, ...	$\frac{5}{16}$	$\frac{3}{8}$	$\frac{1}{2}$	$\frac{5}{8}$	$\frac{3}{4}$	$\frac{7}{8}$	1	1¼	1½ ins.
Stock lengths, about 13 ft., ...	**/2$\frac{5}{8}$**	**/2$\frac{5}{8}$**	**/3$\frac{3}{8}$**	**/4**	**/4¾**	**/5½**	**/6¾**	**/9¾**	**1/0¾** per ft.
Cut lengths, ...	**/3**	**/3**	**/3¾**	**/4½**	**/5½**	**/6½**	**/7¾**	**1/**	**1/3** „

No. 8909.—Solid Brass Tube, Polished and Lacquered.

Sizes, ...	$\frac{3}{8}$	$\frac{1}{2}$	$\frac{5}{8}$	$\frac{3}{4}$	$\frac{7}{8}$	1	1¼	1½ ins.
PRICE, ...	**/4½**	**/6**	**/7½**	**/9**	**/10½**	**1/**	**1/3**	**1/6** per ft.

PICTURE ROD BRACKETS

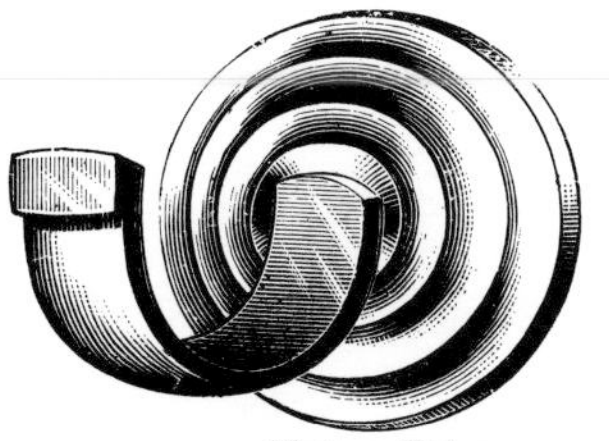

Plate or Drive.

	$\frac{5}{8}$	$\frac{3}{4}$	$\frac{7}{8}$	1	1¼ ins.
No. 8925. Light.	—	—	**3/9**	—	— p. doz.
No. 8926. Medium,	**4/**	**4/9**	**5/3**	**6/6**	**8/3** p. doz.
No. 8927. Strong Cast Rose,		**6/9**	**7/6**	**8/3**	**9/** p. doz.

No. 8928.—Cast Polished.

Size,	$\frac{3}{4}$	$\frac{7}{8}$	1	1¼ ins.
PRICE,	**9/9**	**10/6**	**11/3**	**15/** per doz.

PICTURE CHAIN

(Full Size.)

No. 8915.
7/6 per doz. yards

No. 8916.
Smaller.
6/9 per doz. yards.

No. 8917.
Larger.
9/ per doz. yards.

CHAIN HOOKS

(Half Size.)

No. 8918.
PRICE, **5/3** per gross.

No. 8919.—Smaller.
PRICE, **4/6** per gross.

No. 8920.
PRICE, **5/3** per gross.

PATENT WALL BOSS OR PICTURE SUSPENDER

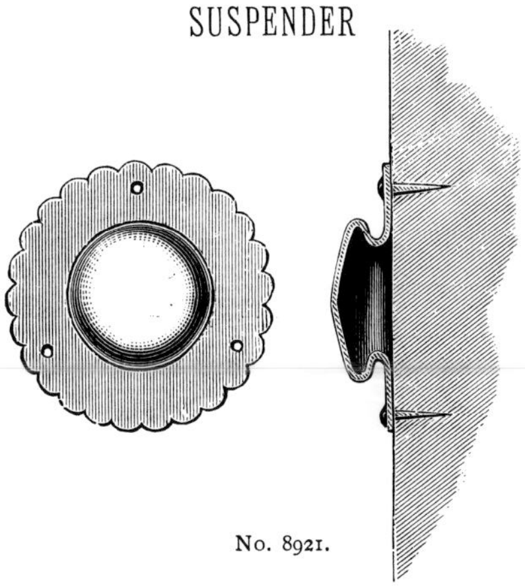

No. 8921.

Will carry a picture upwards of 56 lbs. weight.
Will not cut the cord.

Sizes, ...	1½	2 ins.
PRICES, ...	**1/6**	**1/10½** per doz.
„ ...	**16/6**	**21/** „ gross.

PICTURE ROD ENDS

No. 8930.—Bright.

Sizes,	$\frac{5}{8}$	$\frac{3}{4}$	1 in.
PRICES,	**2/9**	**3/**	**4/6** per doz.
„	**30/**	**31/6**	**51/** „ gross.

No. 8931.—Polished.

Sizes,	$\frac{5}{8}$	$\frac{3}{4}$	$\frac{7}{8}$	1	1¼	1½ ins.
PRICES,	**3/**	**3/6**	**4/6**	**5/3**	**6/9**	**9/9** per doz.
„	**33/**	**37/6**	**48/**	**60/**	**72/**	**112/** „ gross.

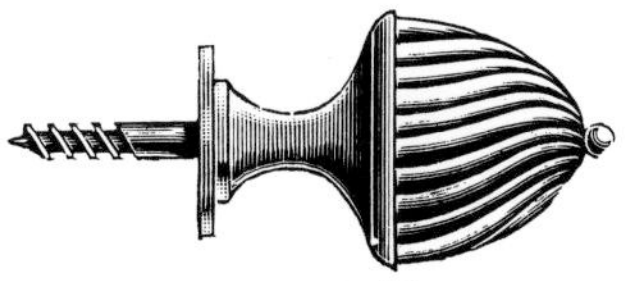

No. 8932.—Bright.

Sizes, ...	$\frac{3}{4}$	$\frac{7}{8}$	1	1¼ ins.
PRICES, ...	**3/9**	**5/**	**6/**	**7/6** per doz.
„ ...	**42/**	**52/6**	**63/**	**78/** „ gross.

No. 8936.—Cast Polished.

Sizes,	$\frac{3}{4}$	$\frac{7}{8}$	1	1$\frac{1}{8}$	1¼ ins.
PRICES,	**12/**	**13/6**	**16/6**	**24/**	**33/** per doz.

No. 8938.—Wood Plugs for Ends, Nos. 8930, 8931, and 8932, ½ in., **2/3**; $\frac{5}{8}$ in., **3/**; ¾ in., **3/9**; $\frac{7}{8}$ in., **4/**; 1 in., **4/6**; 1¼ ins., **6/9** per gross.

PICTURE RODS AND MOULDING HOOKS

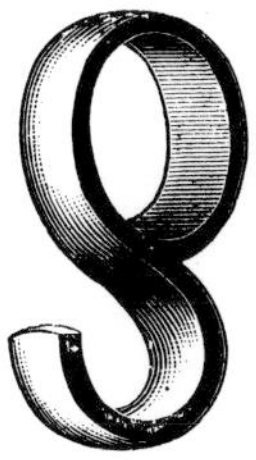

No. 8940.

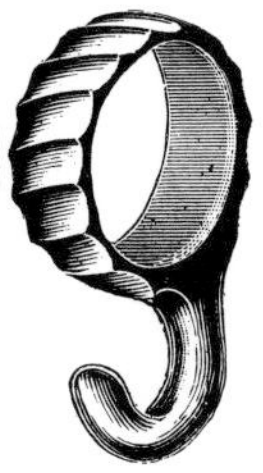

No. 8942.

Sizes,	$\frac{5}{8}$	$\frac{3}{4}$	$\frac{7}{8}$	1	1$\frac{1}{8}$	1¼ ins.
No. 8940,	**2/**	**2/3**	**2/9**	**3/6**	**4/6**	**5/6** p doz.
„ 8942, Polished,		**4/6**	**5/3**	**6/**	**6/9**	**7/6** „

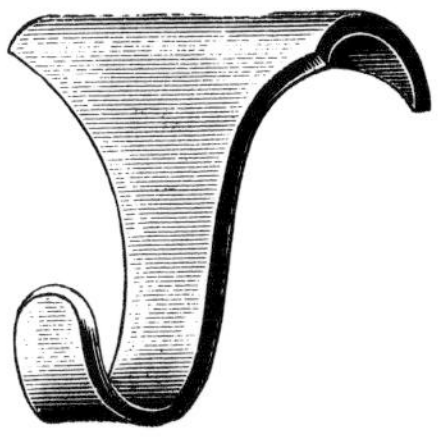

Polished.
No. 8945.—Small.
1/3 p. doz.; **13/6** p. gross.
No. 8946.—Larger.
1/6 p. doz.; **15/** p. gross.
No. 8947.—Best.
2/ p. doz.; **21/** p. gross.

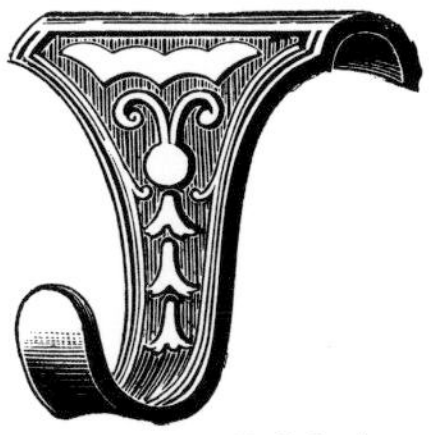

No. 8950.—Polished.
2/ p. doz.; **19/6** p. gross.

No. 8951.—Smaller.
1/3 p. doz.; **13/6** p. gross.

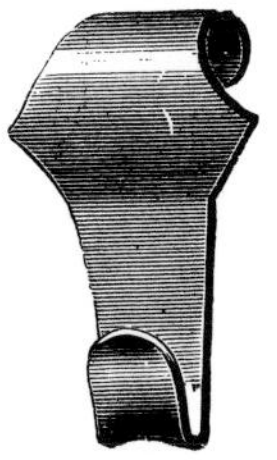

No. 8952.
Polished.
2¼ ins. long.
1/9 per doz.
19/6 per gross.

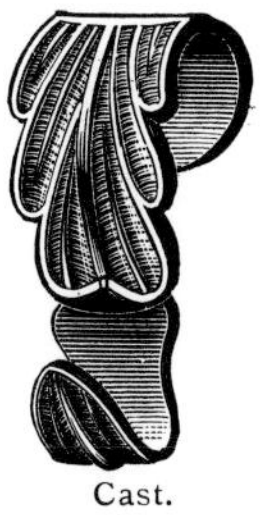

Cast.
No. 8954.
3/ per doz.
No. 8955.
2/ per doz

WINFIELD'S NEW PICTURE MOULDING HOOK
WITH ANTI-FRICTION ROLLER.

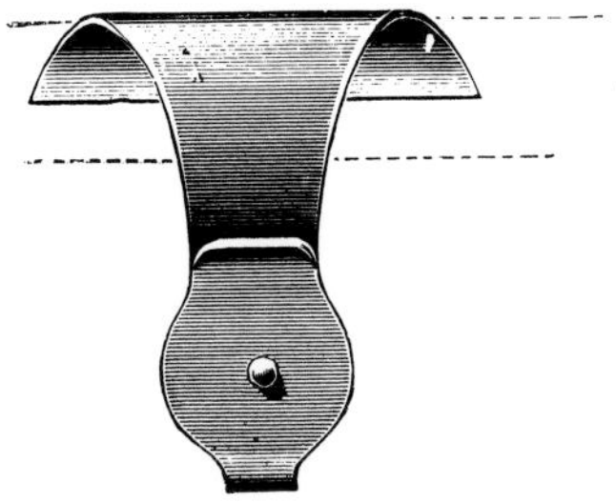

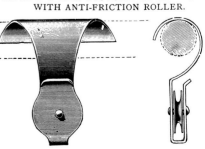

FRONT ELEVATION

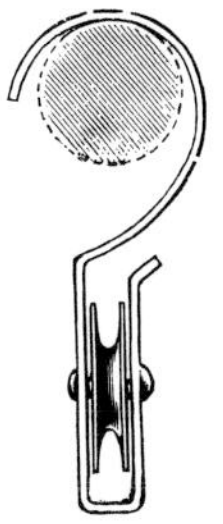

SIDE ELEVATION

No. 8957.—Small size, **6/**; No. 8958.—Large size, **6/9** per doz.

CRANK BELL FITTINGS

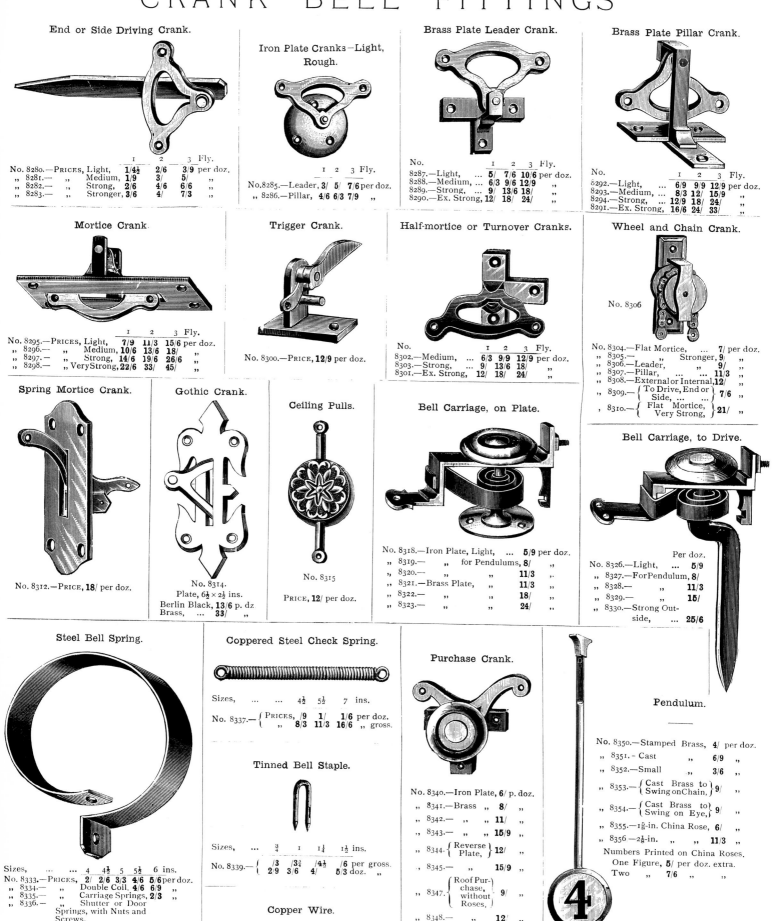

End or Side Driving Crank.

	1	2	3 Fly.
No. 8280.—Prices, Light,	1/4½	2/6	3/9 per doz.
„ 8281.— „ Medium,	1/9	3/	5/ „
„ 8282.— „ Strong,	2/6	4/6	6/6 „
„ 8283.— „ Stronger,	3/6	4/	7/3 „

Iron Plate Cranks—Light, Rough.

	1	2	3 Fly.
No. 8285.—Leader,	3/	5/	7/6 per doz.
„ 8286.—Pillar,	4/6	6/3	7/9 „

Brass Plate Leader Crank.

No.	1	2	3 Fly.
8287.—Light, ...	5/	7/6	10/6 per doz.
8288.—Medium, ...	6/3	9/6	12/9 „
8289.—Strong, ...	9/	13/6	18/ „
8290.—Ex. Strong,	12/	18/	24/ „

Brass Plate Pillar Crank.

No.	1	2	3 Fly.
8292.—Light, ...	6/9	9/9	12/9 per doz.
8293.—Medium, ...	8/3	12/	15/9 „
8294.—Strong, ...	12/9	18/	24/ „
8291.—Ex. Strong,	16/6	24/	33/ „

Mortice Crank.

	1	2	3 Fly.
No. 8295.—Prices, Light,	7/9	11/3	15/6 per doz.
„ 8296.— „ Medium,	10/6	13/6	18/ „
„ 8297.— „ Strong,	14/6	19/6	26/6 „
„ 8298.— „ Very Strong,	22/6	33/	45/ „

Trigger Crank.

No. 8300.—Price, **12/9** per doz.

Half-mortice or Turnover Cranks.

No.	1	2	3 Fly.
8302.—Medium, ...	6/3	9/9	12/9 per doz.
8303.—Strong, ...	9/	13/6	18/ „
8301.—Ex. Strong,	12/	18/	24/ „

Wheel and Chain Crank.

No. 8306

No. 8304.—Flat Mortice, ...	7/ per doz.
„ 8305.— „ Stronger,	9/ „
„ 8306.—Leader,	9/ „
„ 8307.—Pillar, ...	11/3 „
„ 8308.—External or Internal,	12/ „
„ 8309.— { To Drive, End or Side, ...	7/6 „
„ 8310.— { Flat Mortice, Very Strong,	21/ „

Spring Mortice Crank.

No. 8312.—Price, **18/** per doz.

Gothic Crank.

No. 8314.
Plate, 6½ × 2½ ins.
Berlin Black, **13/6** p. dz
Brass, ... **33/** „

Ceiling Pulls.

No. 8315
Price, **12/** per doz.

Bell Carriage, on Plate.

No. 8318.—Iron Plate, Light, ...	5/9 per doz.
„ 8319.— „ for Pendulums,	8/ „
„ 8320.— „ „	11/3 „
„ 8321.—Brass Plate, „	11/3 „
„ 8322.— „ „	18/ „
„ 8323.— „ „	24/ „

Bell Carriage, to Drive.

	Per doz.
No. 8326.—Light, ...	5/9
„ 8327.—For Pendulum,	8/
„ 8328.— „	11/3
„ 8329.— „	15/
„ 8330.—Strong Outside, ...	25/6

Steel Bell Spring.

Sizes, ...	4	4½	5	5½	6 ins.
No. 8333.—Prices,	2/	2/6	3/3	4/6	5/6 per doz.
„ 8334.— Double Coil.		4/6	6/9		„
„ 8335.— Carriage Springs,		2/3			„
„ 8336.— Shutter or Door Springs, with Nuts and Screws. Small, 3/ ; Large, 4/6					„

Coppered Steel Check Spring.

Sizes, ...	4½	5½	7 ins.
No. 8337.— { Prices,	/9	1/	1/6 per doz.
{ „	8/3	11/3	16/6 „ gross.

Tinned Bell Staple.

Sizes, ...	¾	1	1¼	1½ ins.
No. 8339.— {	/3	3/¾	4/¼	/6 per gross.
{	2/9	3/6	4/	5/3 doz. „

Copper Wire.

Price, ... **1/1½** per lb.

Purchase Crank.

No. 8340.—Iron Plate, 6/ p. doz.
„ 8341.—Brass „ 8/ „
„ 8342.— „ „ 11/ „
„ 8343.— „ „ 15/9 „
„ 8344. { Reverse Plate, } 12/ „
„ 8345.— 15/9 „
„ 8347. { Roof Pur- chase, without Roses, } 9/ „
„ 8348.— „ 12/ „

Pendulum.

No. 8350.—Stamped Brass,	4/ per doz.
„ 8351.- Cast „	6/9 „
„ 8352.—Small „	3/6 „
„ 8353.— { Cast Brass to Swing on Chain, }	9/ „
„ 8354.— { Cast Brass to Swing on Eye, }	9/ „
„ 8355.—1⅝-in. China Rose,	6/ „
„ 8356 —2½-in. „ „	11/3 „

Numbers Printed on China Roses.
One Figure, **5/** per doz. extra.
Two „ **7/6** „ „

CRANK BELLS AND BELL PULLS

HOUSE BELLS

Diam. at Mouth.		Weight.
2⅜ ins.	...	5 oz.
2⅝ „	...	6 „
2¾ „	...	7 „
3 „	...	8 „
3⅛ „	...	9 „
3¼ „	...	10 „
3½ „	...	12 „
3¾ „	...	14 „
4 „	...	16 „
4⅛ „	...	18 „
4¼ „	...	20 „
4½ „	...	24 „
5 „	...	32 „
5½ „	...	40 „

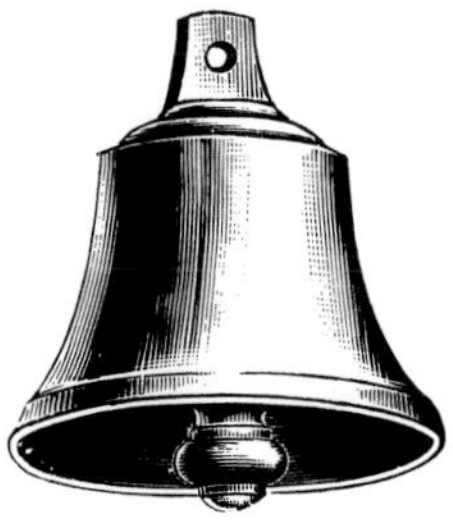

No. 8360.—Turned Edge and Dipped.
PRICE, ... **1/3** per lb.
No. 8361.—Polished and Lacquered.
PRICE, ... **2/3** per lb.
No. 8362.—Polished and Lacquered, Best Quality.
PRICE, ... **2/6** per lb.

YARD AND TURRET BELLS

Diam. at Mouth.		Approx. Weight.
6 ins.	...	3 lbs.
6½ „	...	4 „
7 „	...	5 „
7¼ „	...	7 „
7¾ „	...	8 „
8 „	...	10 „
8½ „	...	11½ „
9 „	...	14 „
9½ „	...	17 „
10 „	...	21 „
11 „	...	30 „
12 „	...	40 „
13 „	...	52 „
14 „	...	70 „
15 „	...	84 „

No. 8363.

No. 1 Quality,	... ...	**1/9** per lb.
„ 2 „	... ...	**1/7½** „
„ 3 „	... ...	**1/6** „

SCHOOL OR FACTORY BELLS

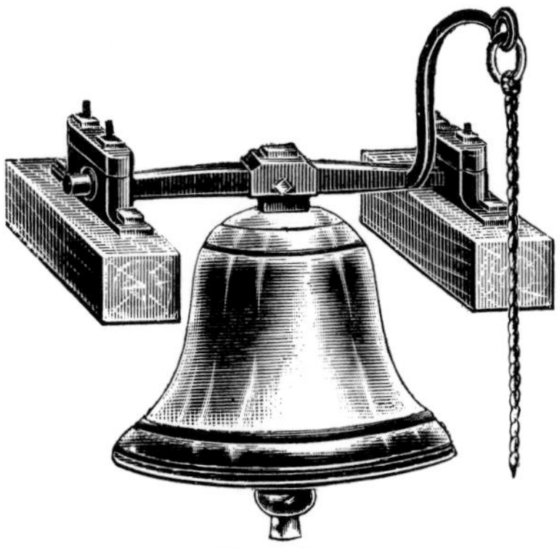

No. 8365.

Represents a School, Factory, Alarm, or Plantation Bell, with wrought-iron stock and cranked lever, cast-iron journeys, gun-metal bearings, with long pins and nuts for fixing.

PRICES.

Diam. at Mouth.	Quality No. 3.	Quality No. 1.
8 inches,	**30/**	**33/**
9 „	**36/**	**42/**
10 „	**48/**	**54/**
11 „	**63/**	**72/**
12 „	**75/**	**87/**
13 „	**99/**	**114/**

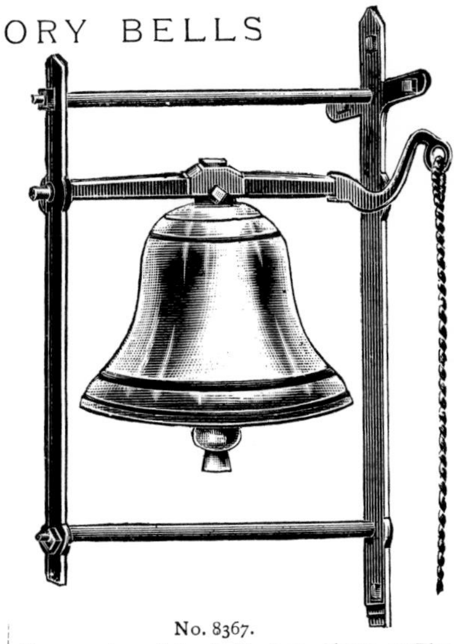

No. 8367.

Represents a School, Factory, Alarm, or Plantation Bell, with wrought-iron frame for fixing against a building, to be rung from the outside.

Diam. at Mouth.	PRICES, Complete.
9 inches,	**57/**
10 „	**75/**
13 „	**144/**

No. 8368.
The same, but to ring from the inside.

9 inches,	**60/**
10 „	**78/**
13 „	**147/**

N.B.—In ordering, the thickness of the wall should be given.

ALARM BELLS

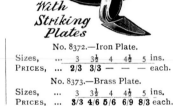

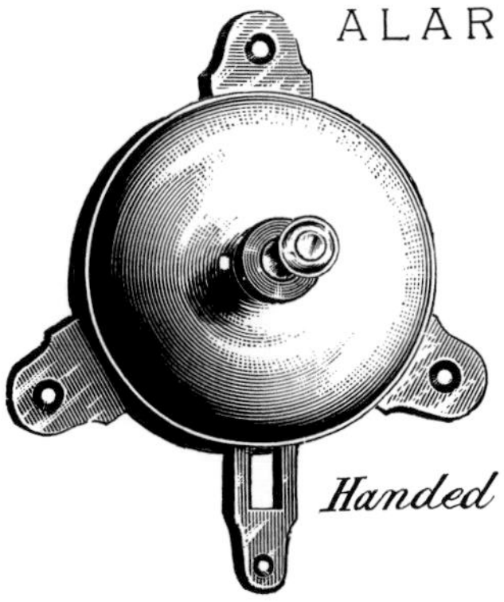
Handed

No. 8370.—Iron Plate.

Sizes,	3	3½	4	4½	5 ins.
PRICES,	**2/3**	**3/3**	—	—	— each.

No. 8371.—Brass Plate.

Sizes,	3	3½	4	4½	5 ins.
PRICES,	**3/3**	**4/6**	**5/6**	**6/9**	**8/3** each.

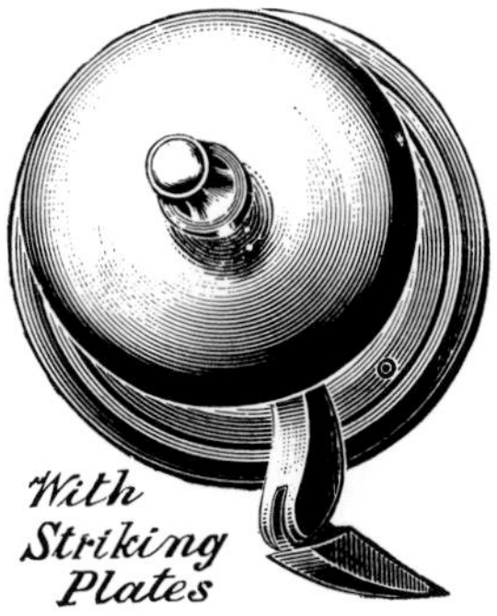
With Striking Plates

No. 8372.—Iron Plate.

Sizes,	3	3½	4	4½	5 ins.
PRICES,	**2/3**	**3/3**	—	—	— each.

No. 8373.—Brass Plate.

Sizes,	3	3½	4	4½	5 ins.
PRICES,	**3/3**	**4/6**	**5/6**	**6/9**	**8/3** each.

SHOP DOOR BELLS

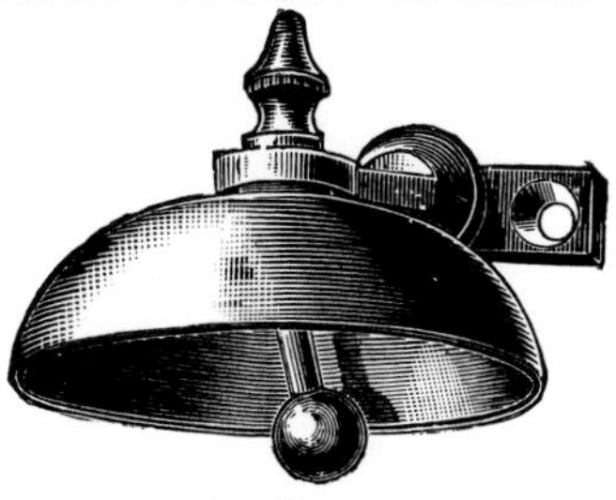

Cast Gongs.
No. 8375.—Bronzed Iron Fixed Arm.

Sizes,	3	3½	4 inches.
PRICES,	**19/6**	**27/**	— per dozen.

No. 8376.—Brass Swivel Arm to throw out of action.

Sizes,	3	3½	4 inches.
PRICES,	**27/**	**33/**	**42/** per dozen.

BRASS SLIDE BELL PULLS

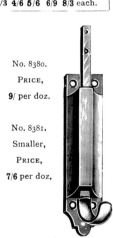

No. 8380.
PRICE,
9/ per doz.

No. 8381.
Smaller,
PRICE,
7/6 per doz.

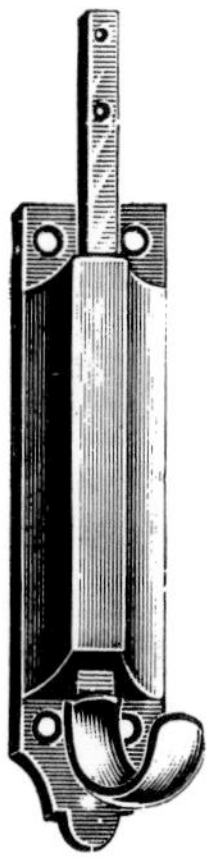

No. 8382.
PRICE,
9/9 per doz.

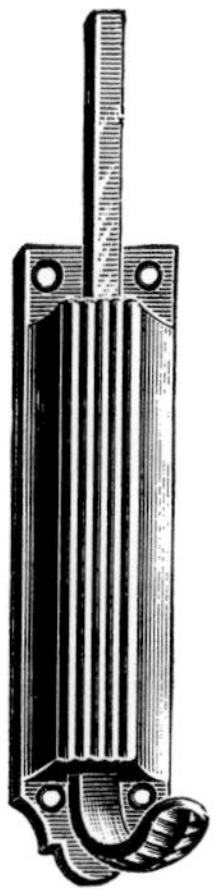

No. 8383.
PRICE,
15/9 per doz.

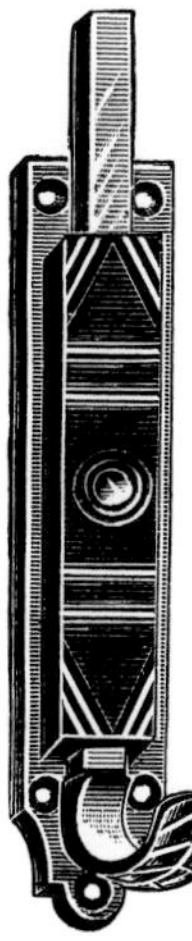

No. 8384.
PRICE,
22/6 per doz.

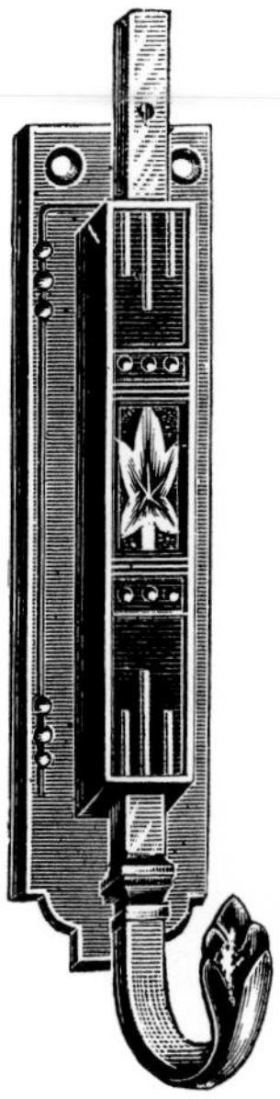

BRASS PLATE BELL PULLS, HALF SIZE

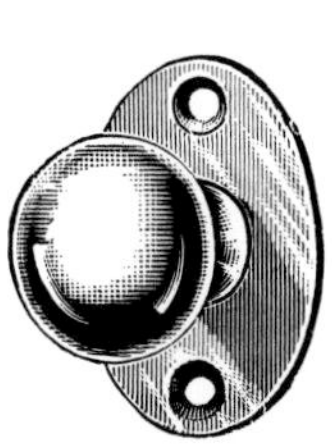

No. 8387.—Polished.
Sizes, 1¾ 2 2½ 3 ins.
PRICES, **5/6** **6/** **7/6** **9/9** p. doz.

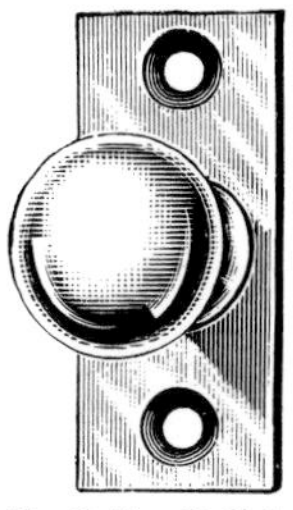

No. 8388.—Polished.
Size, 2½×1¼ ins.
PRICE, **10/6** p. doz.

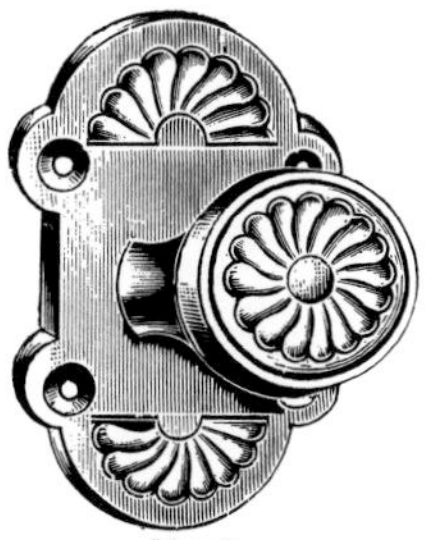

No. 8390.
Polished or Steel Bronzed.
Size, ... 3×1¾ ins.
PRICE, ... **15/** p. doz.

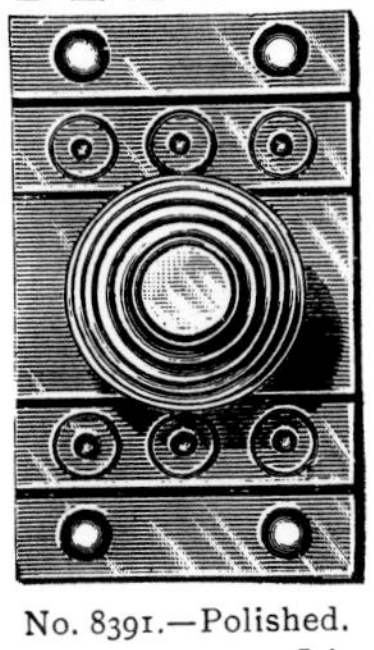

No. 8391.—Polished.
Size, ... 3×1⅞ ins.
PRICE, ... **19/6** p. doz.

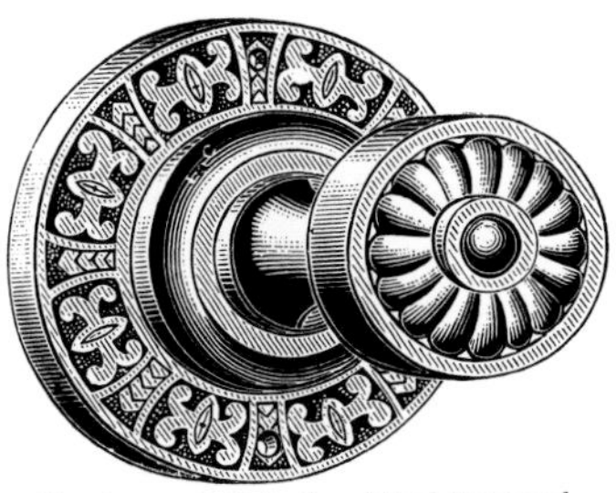

No. 8392.—Polished or Steel Bronzed.
Size, ... 2¾ ins.
PRICE, ... **21/** per doz.

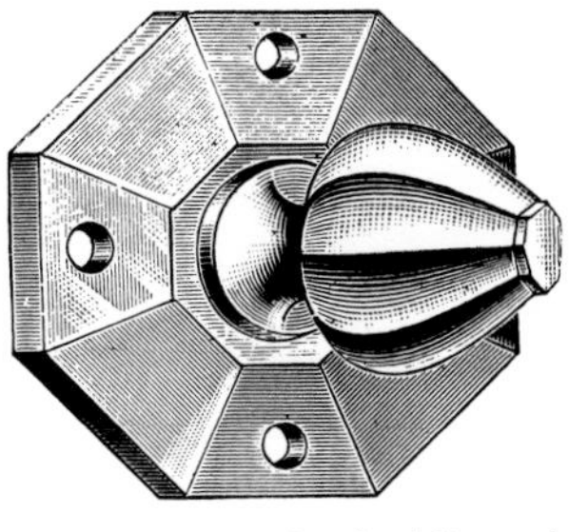

No. 8393.—Polished or Steel Bronzed.
Size, ... 3 ins.
PRICE, ... **27/** per doz.

CRANK BELL PULLS

LEVER BELL PULLS
Scale—one-third.

No. 8396.
Plain China, White
or Black, ... **3/** p. pair.
Gold Lines, ... **3/6** ,,

No. 8397.
White or Black China,
with Gold Lines, ... **4/6** p. pair.

No. 8399.
Polished Brass, ... **5/3** p. pair.
With Oak, Ebony, or
Cocoa Wood Fur-
niture, ... **6/** ,,

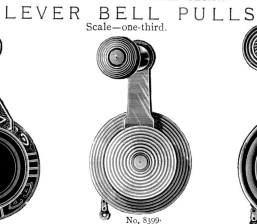

No. 8402.
Polished Brass, **7/6** p. pair.
Wood Furniture same
price.

No. 8403.
Polished Brass, ... **11/** p. pair.
Wood Furniture same
price.

SUNK BRASS BELL PULLS

No. 8406.
Sizes, ... 3½ 4 4½ 5 5½ 6 ins.
PRICES, Bronzed, **2/6 2/6 3/ 3/6 4/3 5/6** each.
Plain, or named "House," "Office," "Servants," "Visitors," &c., same price.

No. 8407.
Sizes, ... 4 4½ 5 ins.
PRICES, Polished, ... **2/6 3/3 3/9** each.

No. 8408.
Sizes, ... 4 4½ 5 ins.
PRICES, Polished, ... **2/9 3/6 4/** each.
Bell Pulls fitted with Wheel and Chain Action, **1/** each extra.

No. 8409.
Sizes,... ... ... 4 4½ 5 ins.
PRICES, Bright or Bronzed, **3/ 4/ 5/9** each.

QUADRANT BELL PULLS

No. 8415.
Polished Brass.
4 × 1 in., **15/3** p. doz.

No. 8417.
Bronzed Brass.
4½ × 1½ ins., **24/** p. doz.

No. 8418.
Bronzed.
4¾ × 1¾ ins., **27/** p. doz.

No. 8420.
Malleable Iron,
Berlin Black.
6½ × 2½ ins.,
18/ per doz.

No. 8421.
Polished or Bronzed.
4½ × 1 in., **1/9** each.
4½ × 1½ ,, **2/6** ,,
4¾ × 2 ,, **3/3** ,,
5 × 2¼ ,, **3/6** ,,

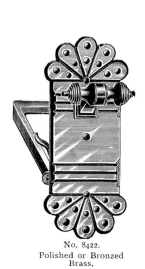

No. 8422.
Polished or Bronzed
Brass.
6¼ × 2⅜ ins., **5/** each.

No. 8424.—Polished.
5¼ × 2¼ ins., ... **4/9** each.
6½ × 2 ,, ... **6/** ,,
7 × 2¼ ,, ... **6/6** ,,
7½ × 2¼ ,, ... **7/6** ,,

No. 8426.
Polished or Bronzed.
6 × 2¼ ins., **6/** each.

GOTHIC BELL PULLS

No. 8430.—Malleable Iron, Berlin Blacked, 20 ins. long, **2/6** each.

No. 8431.—Polished Brass, 24 ins. long, **3/6**; Berlin Blacked, **4/6** each.

No. 8432.—Cast Iron, Japanned 24 ins. long, **3/6**; Bronzed, **4/6** each.

No. 8433.—Malleable Iron, Berlin Blacked, 24 ins. long, **3/3** each.

No. 8434.—Polished Brass, **10/6** each.

No. 8435.—Polished Brass, Copper Handle, 15 ins. long, **5/** each.

BRASS ELECTRIC BELL PUSHES

Flat Back Push.

No. 8600.

Cast Brass, Bronzed, Ebonite Backs.

Sizes, .. 2½ 3 4 ins.
Prices, ... 1/1½ 1/3 2/ each.
  „ ... 12/ 13/6 22/6 p. doz.

No. 8602.

Polished, Best Finish, Ebonite Backs, Tops Screw off.

Sizes, ... 2½ 3 3½ ins.
Prices, 1/7½ 1/9 2/3 each.
  „ 18/ 20/3 25/6 p. doz.

No. 8604.

Plain Polished Pattern, same prices.

No. 8603.

Polished, Ebonite Backs.

Sizes, ... 1¾ 2½ ins.
Prices, 1/3 1/9 each.
  „ 13/6 19/6 p. doz.

The "Chippendale."

No. 8606.

Cast Brass, Polished, Best Quality.

Sizes, ... 2½ 3 ins.
Prices, 3/ 3/6 each.
  „ 33/ 36/ p. doz.

No. 8601.

Polished Brass, Ebonite Back, "Press" on Plunger.

Sizes, 2½ 3 3½ 4 ins.
Prices, 1/4½ 1/6 2/3 2/9 each.
  „ 15/ 16/6 24/ 30/ p. doz.

No. 8607.

Cast Brass, Polished, Best Quality.

Size, ... 3½ ins.
Price, ... 3/ each.
  „ ... ... 34/6 p. doz.

No. 8608.

Cast Brass, Best Quality.

Sizes, ... 2½ 3 ins.
Prices, ... 2/9 3/ each.
  „ ... 30/ 33/ p. doz.

No. 8609.

Cast Brass, Best Quality, Platinum Points and Ivory Plungers.

Sizes, ... 3½ 4 ins.
Prices, ... 5/ 5/6 each.
  „ ... 54/ 60/ p. doz.

No. 8610.

Cast Brass, Best Quality, Platinum Points and Ivory Plungers.

Sizes, .. 3 3½ ins.
Prices, .. 5/ 5/6 each.
  „ ... 54/ 60/ p. doz.

No. 8611.

Cast Brass, Best Quality, Platinum Points and Ivory Plungers.

Sizes, ... 3 3½ ins.
Prices, ... 5/3 5/6 each.
  „ ... 57/ 60/ p. doz.

Side Lever Pull.

Bedside Pull.

Short Barrel Back.

No. 8615.

Cast Brass, Polished or Bronzed, Ebonite Backs.

Sizes, 2 2½ 3 3½ 4 ins.
Prices, 1/6 1/6 2/ 2/6 3/ each.
  „ 15/ 17/3 21/ 28/6 33/ p. doz.

Long Barrel Back.

No. 8616.

Cast Brass, Polished or Bronzed, Best Quality, Water Tight.

Sizes, 2 2½ 3 3½ 4 5 6 ins.
Prices, 3/ 3/3 3/6 4/3 5/ 6/9 9/ each.
  „ 33/ 36/ 39/ 48/ 57/ 72/ 99/ p. doz.

No. 8620.

Cast Polished Brass, Rubbing Contact, Best Quality.

Sizes, ... 3 ins.
Prices, ... 3/9 each.
  „ ... ... 42/ p. doz.

No. 8621.

Cast Polished Brass, Best Quality.

Size, ... 3 ins.
Price, ... 2/9 each.
  „ ... ... 30/ p. doz.

No. 8625.

Cast Brass, Bronzed or Bright, Ebonite Backs.

Size, ... 4 × 1¼ ins.
Price, ... 1/ each.
  „ ... 10/6 p. doz.

No. 8626.

Cast Brass, Polished, Letters Blacked, Ebonite Backs.

Size, ... 3½ × 1½ ins.
Price, ... 1/6 each.
  „ ... 15/9 p. doz.

Flat Back Push.

No. 8627.

Polished or Bronzed, Ebonite Backs.

Sizes, 1½ 2 2½ ins. wide·
Prices, 1/6 1/9 2/6 each.
  „ 17/3 20/3 28/6 p. doz.

Barrel Back Push.

No. 8629.

Polished or Bronzed, Best Quality.

Sizes, 1 1½ 2 2½ 3 4 ins. wide.
Prices, 2/3 3/3 4/ 4/6 5/6 10/6 each.
  „ 25/6 36/ 45/ 51/ 63/ 120/ p. doz.

Flat Back Push.

No. 8630.

Best Quality, Polished or Bronzed.

Size, ... 3¼ × 1¼ ins.
Price, ... 3/6 each.
  „ ... 39/ p. doz.

ELECTRIC BELL PUSHES

CHINA PUSHES

No. 8550.—Plain, White, Cream, or Black, Hard-wood } Each. /9 Per Doz. 7/6
Backs, G.S. Pointed Springs, 3 ins., ...
,, 8551.—White, Cream, or Black, with Gold Lines, 3 ins., 1/ 10/6
,, 8552.—Best Quality White, Cream, or Black, Gold Lines, } 1/6 17/3
Brass Backs, Platinum Pointed Springs, 3 ins.,
Ebonite Backs same price as Brass Backs.

No. 8556.—Reeded China, Cream or Black, Hard-wood } Each. 1/ Per Doz. 10/6
Backs, G.S. Pointed Springs, 3 ins., ...
,, 8557.—Ditto, with Red and Gold Lines, ... 1/9 20/3
Ebonite or Brass Backs, with Platinum Points, 6/ per doz. extra.

No. 8558.—Imitation Marble, Brown, Grey, &c., Oak Backs, 1/ Each. Per Doz. 10/6
Ebonite or Brass Backs, with Platinum Points, 6/ per doz. extra.

No. 8560.—Cream China, Oak Backs, G.S. Pointed } Each. 1/6 Per Doz. 16/6
Springs, ...
,, 8561.—Ditto, with Gold Decoration, ... 2/ 22/6
Ebonite or Brass Backs, with Platinum Points, 6/ per doz. extra.

A large assortment of Fancy China Pushes kept in Stock, samples on application.

WOOD PUSHES

Sizes, ... 2½ 3 ins.
No. 8570.—Oak, Cocus, or Walnut, ... 7/6 — p. doz
,, 8574.—Superior Quality, Oak, Cocus, Walnut, Best } 9/ 11/ ,,
G.S. Springs, ...

No. 8578.—Superior Quality, Ebony, Best [G.S. } 2 2½ 3 ins.
Springs, Double Platinum Pointed, } — 18/ 21/ p. doz.
Large Real Ivory Plungers, ...
,, 8579.—Finest Ivory throughout. ... ... 12/ 16/ 22/ each.

No. 8575.—Cocus, Oak, Walnut, or Rosewood, Best G.S. } 3 ins. 15/9 per doz.
Springs, Platinum Pointed, ...
,, 8576.—Ditto, Ebony, ... 17/6 ,,

No. 8580.—Superior Quality, Oak, Cocus, Walnut, } 2½ 3 3½ ins.
Best Polished G.S. Springs, Double } 18/ 21/ 26/ p. doz.
Platinum Pointed, Large Real Ivory
Plungers, ...

WALL ROSETTES

No. 8585.—2½ ins.. Cocus, Ebonized, } 7/6 p. doz.
Rosewood, or Walnut, ...
,, 8586.—3 inches, Superior Quality, } 12/ ,,
Ebony, Cocus, &c., ...

PULL AND PUSH

No. 8595.—Cocus, ... 3/ each.
,, 8596.—Ebony, ... 3/6 ,,

PEAR PRESSES

TO MATCH ROSETTES

No. 8590.—Cocus, Ebonized, Rosewood, } 10/6 p. doz
or Walnut, ...
,, 8591.—Superior Quality, Ebony, Cocus, &c., 18/ ,,

PULL BOXES

No. 8597.—Cocus, Top Screws } Each. Per Doz.
off, Direct Pull, } 2/ 22/6
Rubbing Contact,

ELECTRIC BELLS AND INDICATORS

ENGLISH MAKE

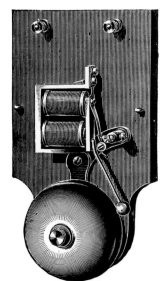

No. 8519.—Medium quality, perfect in every detail. Polished Teak Case, Metallic Base, Cast Bell-metal Gong, Improved Contact Pillar Platinum Contacts.

PRICES.

Sizes, ...	2½	3	3½	4	5	6 ins.	
No. 8519. Medium Quality,	4/6	5/3	7/6	9/9	—	—	each.
No. 8520. Superior Quality,	5/3	6/	9/	10/6	15/	21/	,,
No. 8521. Best Quality,	—	10/6	12/	15/	21/	30/	,,

Prices of cheap German Bells quoted if desired.

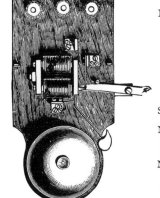

No. 8523.—Medium Quality Continuous-ringing or Burglar-alarm Bell.

PRICES.

Sizes, ...	3	3½	4	5	6 ins.	
No. 8523. Medium Quality,	9/9	12/	15/9	—	—	each.
No. 8524. Best Quality,	—	15/9	18/9	24/	37/6	,,

ORDINARY QUALITY INDICATORS

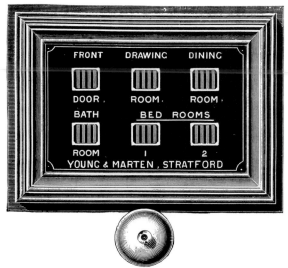

No. 8525.—Improved Pendulum Movements; Polished Walnut Case, with solid mouldings; Glass written Names of Rooms and Customers' Names in Black and Gold included.

PRICE, 3 Signals, ... 4/9 per signal.
  ,, 4 or 5 Signals, ... 4/3 ,,
  ,, 6 Signals, and above, ... 4/ ,,

Bells count as one Signal.

NOTE.—No extra charge for writing names of rooms.

BEST QUALITY INDICATORS

Handsome Solid Teak, Mahogany, or Walnut Cases; Best Quality Movements, and well fitted; Glass, with Gilt Border, and written Names of Rooms and Customers' Names in Gold.

	3 Signals.	4 to 9 Signals.	10 or more Signals.	
No. 8526.—PRICES, Pendulum Movement,	7/6	6/3	6/	per signal
,, 8527.— ,, Mechanical Replacement,	7/	6/	5/9	,,
,, 8528.— ,, Electrical ,,	8/6	7/6	7/3	,,

Bells attached count as one signal.

Unless otherwise ordered, Indicators are made with Bells fitted.

BELL BOARDS

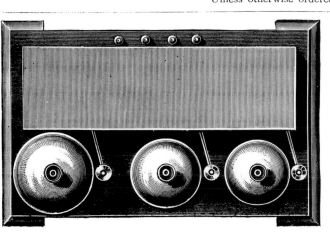

No. 8530.—PRICE, Superior Quality, Stout Solid Mahogany Cases, Platinum Contacts, Cast Bell-metal Gongs, in sets of 3 and above, ... 5/6 per bell.

No. 8532.—PRICE, with Pendulums fitted to each Bell to swing when Bell rings, ... 7/6 ,,

CAST-IRON BATHS AND FITTINGS.

OUR "MARVELLOUS" C. I. SIENNA BATH.

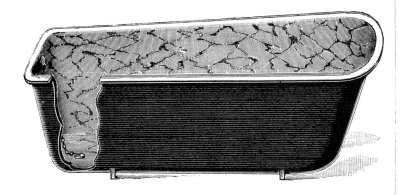

No. 982. SIENNA BATH, 5′ 6″, full size, no Brass Work ... **33/-** each.

No. 983. SIENNA BATH, 5′ 6″, full size, with Plug and Union
and Chain ... ... **36/9** ,,

No. 984. SIENNA BATH, 5′ 6″, full size, with Plug and Union,
Overflow and Chain ... ... **40/6** ,,

No. 992. IMPROVED C. I. BATH, FOR WOOD FIXING.

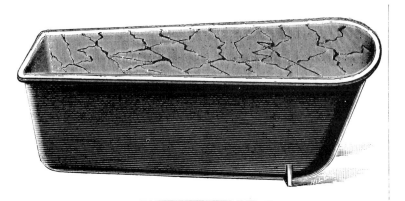

	Length	60″	66″	72″
Fine Cast, unpainted		**30/-**	**36/-**	**54/-** each.
Fine Cast and painted		**32/3**	**39/-**	**57/-** ,,
Third Finish, Enamelled or Best Japanned Sienna		**34/6**	**41/3**	**60/-** ,,
Special Medium Enamelled, Second Finish ...		**48/-**	**57/-**	**72/-** ,,
Best Extra Hard Enamelled, First Finish ...		**78/-**	**84/-**	**99/-** ,,

---

No. 993. IMPROVED C. I. ROMAN SHAPE BATH ON FEET.

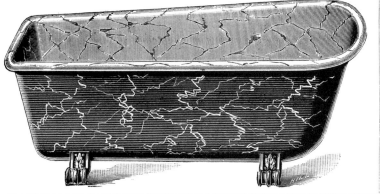

Constructed to stand without woodwork. Japanned Marble, Grained, or any co
outside to 3 best finishes.

	Length	60″	66″	72″
Fine Cast, unpainted		**48/9**	**54/9**	**72/9** each
Fine Cast, painted		**51/-**	**57/9**	**75/9** ,,
Third Finish, Enamelled or Japanned Sienna ...		**53/3**	**60/-**	**78/9** ,,
Special Medium Finish, Enamelled, Second Finish		**66/9**	**75/9**	**90/9** ,,
Best Extra Hard Enamelled, First Finish ...		**96/9**	**102/9**	**117/9** ,,

---

No. 991. THE "EME" SIMPLEX BATH, FOR WOOD FIXING.

REGISTERED.

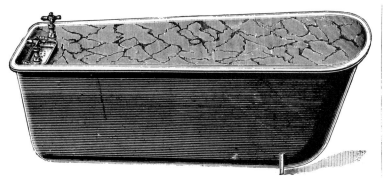

Consists of 66″ Bath, with one Soap Dish; two No. 275 High Pressure
Cocks "Hot" and "Cold"; one No. 66 Overflow; one No. 65 Bath Plug
Union; and Chain complete. This arrangement is far preferable to the "St
pipe" arrangement, inasmuch as there are *no wires to become loose or break.*
taps discharging themselves directly into the bath, *no leakage can possibly occur at*

Third Finish, Enamelled					**63/-** each.
Second ,, ,, ...					**78/9** ,,
First ,, ,, ...					**105/9** ,,

If with best Nickel-plated Fittings, **7/6** per set extra.
If Fittings are approved and stamped by New River Company, **7/6** per set ext
No. 67 Lever-Handle Bath Cocks, as shewn to No. 904 Bath, next page, may
alternated for No. 275 at same prices.

STRATFORD, Walthamstow and Leytonstone.

COMBINATION CAST-IRON BATHS AND FITTINGS.

No. 904.   THE "EME" SIMPLEX ROMAN SHAPE BATH.—(*Registered*).

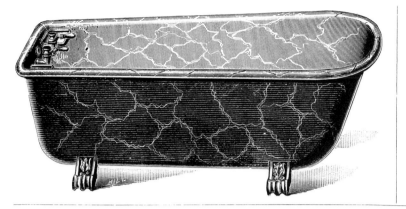

Consists of 66″ Bath, on feet, requiring no woodwork fixing, Japanned Marble, grained, or any color outside, with two Soap Dishes, two No. 67 Lever-handle Bath Cocks, "Hot" and "Cold"; one No. 66 Overflow; one No. 65 Bath Plug and Union; and Chain complete.   This arrangement is far preferable to the "Stand-pipe" arrangement, inasmuch as there are *no wires to become loose or break*.   The taps discharging themselves directly into the bath, *no leakage can possibly occur at foot.*

Third Finish, Enamelled	...	...	...	...	...	...	**84/–** each.
Second ,, ,,	..	...	..	...	..	...	**99/9** ,,
First ,, ,,	...	...	...	...	...	...	**126/9** ,,

If with best Nickel-plated Fittings, **7/6** per set extra.
If Fittings are approved and stamped by New River Company, **7/6** per set extra.
No. 275 High Pressure Bath Cocks, as shewn to No. 991 Bath, page 64, may be alternated for No. 67 at same prices.

No. 905.   THE "DESIDERATUM" NEW COMBINATION BATH,

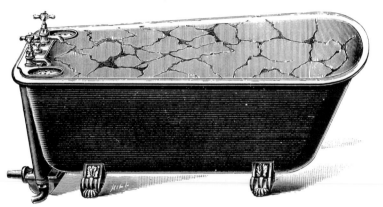

For woodwork fixing, consists of Bath, with flat edge, painted black outside, feet similar to Roman shape, "Hot" and "Cold" Water Cocks, two Soap Dishes, and Waste Trapped.

					Length	60″	66″	72″
Third Finish, Enamelled...	...	...	...			**79/6**	**86/3**	**105/–** each.
Second ,, ,,	...	...	...			**93/–**	**102/–**	**117/–** ,,
First ,, ,,	...	...	...			**123/–**	**129/–**	**144/–** ,,

No. 953.   THE "DESIDERATUM" NEW COMBINATION ROMAN SHAPE BATH,

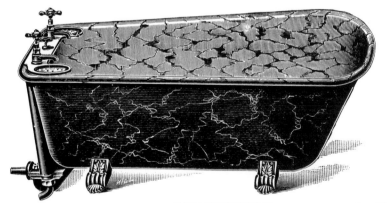

On feet, requiring no woodwork fixing, Japanned Marble outside, Roll Edge, ornamental feet, "Hot" and "Cold" Water Cocks, two Soap Dishes, and Waste Trapped.

					Length	60″	66″	72″
Third Finish, Enamelled...	...	...	...			**98/3**	**105/–**	**123/9** each.
Second ,, ,,	...	...	...			**111/9**	**120/9**	**135/9** ,,
First ,, ,,	...	...	...			**141/9**	**147/9**	**162/9** ,,

No. 1528.   THE "COMPACTUM" COMBINATION BATH,

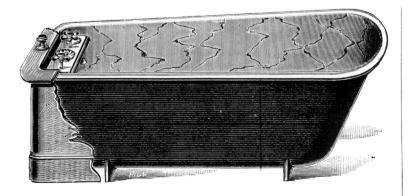

For woodwork fixing, consists of Bath, Japanned Sienna inside, and painted black outside, "Hot" and "Cold" Water Cocks, Porcelain Soap Tray, and Waste Trapped above floor line, easily accessible.

Length 5′ 6″	...	...	...	...	...	...	...	**81/–** each.

STRATFORD, Walthamstow and Leytonstone.

COMBINATION CAST-IRON BATHS AND FITTINGS.

The "Victoria," "Sultana," and "Hygeia" Baths are finished in a manner suitable for the best class of work. Amongst their many advantages, they combine our steamless and noiseless system, which occasions the occupants of adjoining rooms no annoyance, and also keeps the atmosphere of Bath-room free from dense vapour.

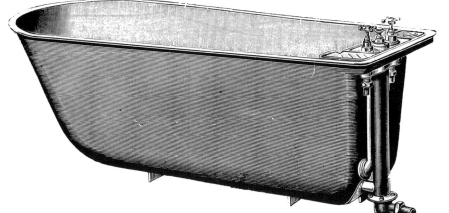

No. 1242. THE "VICTORIA" BATH, for Wood Enclosure.

Bath complete, with Hot and Cold Taps, Lift-up or Quadrant Waste, and Trap.

					Length	5' 0"	5' 6"	6' 0"	
Plain Painted	...	...	...	...		**111/-**	**114/-**	**132/-**	each.
3rd class Sienna	...	...	...	...		**117/-**	**123/-**	**141/-**	,,
2nd ,, Enamelled	...	...	...			**147/-**	**157/6**	**183/-**	,,
1st ,, ,,	...	...	...			**172/6**	**180/-**	**210/-**	,,
Porcelain Enamelled	...	...	...			**228/9**	**247/6**	**280/6**	,,

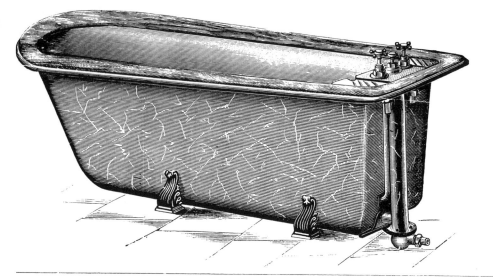

No. 1243. THE "SULTANA" BATH, Roman Shape, with Wood Capping.

Bath complete, with Walnut or Mahogany Capping, Hot, Cold and Waste, and Trap.

	Length	5' 0"	5' 6"	6' 0"	
3rd class Sienna, and Grained or Marbled outside ...		**181/6**	**192/-**	**211/6**	each.
2nd class Enamelled, and Grained or Marbled outside		**216/-**	**225/-**	**250/6**	,,
1st class Enamelled, and Grained or Marbled outside		**240/-**	**250/6**	**279/-**	,,
Porcelain Enamelled, and Grained or Marbled outside		**295/6**	**316/6**	**351/-**	,,

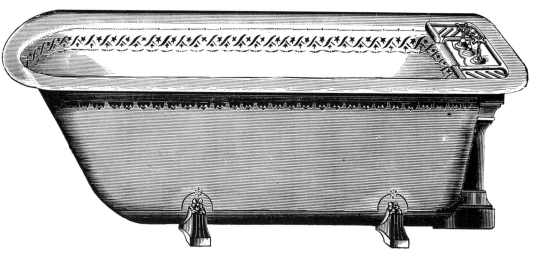

No. 1244. THE "HYGEIA" BATH,

Parallel sides.

THE PATENT "HYGEIA" BATH is made parallel sided, and can be had with bold curled iron edge, or with moulded Mahogany or Walnut capping, same as shewn on the "Sultana" Bath. In addition to the Improved China Soap Dishes, extending across the end of Bath, we supply these Baths with a moulded movable Shield, to conceal the supply pipes, &c., and thus, with other improvements, we produce an independent Bath with a completeness hitherto unobtainable.

		Length	5' 0"	5' 6"	5' 6" × 2' 3"	6' 0"	
No. 1244. BATH, with Iron curled edge, movable Shield, and Fittings complete, and Grained or Marbled outside	3rd class Sienna		**153/9**	**163/6**	**187/6**	**174/-**	each.
	2nd ,, Enamelled ...		**192/-**	**205/6**	**232/6**	**213/-**	,,
	1st ,, ,, ...		**223/6**	**235/6**	**265/6**	**274/6**	,,
	Porcelain		**300/-**	**318/-**	**363/-**	**342/-**	,,
No. 1244½. BATH, with moulded Walnut or Manogany Wood capping, movable Shield, and Fittings complete, and Grained or Marbled outside	3rd class Sienna		**187/6**	**202/6**	**226/6**	**219/-**	,,
	2nd ,, Enamelled ...		**225/9**	**243/-**	**270/-**	**258/-**	,,
	1st ,, ,, ...		**257/3**	**273/-**	**303/-**	**319/6**	,,
	Porcelain		**333/9**	**355/6**	**400/6**	**387/-**	,,

Nickel-plating Taps, **7/6** extra. Stencilling Borders and Lines inside and outside Bath, **15/-** extra.

STRATFORD, Walthamstow and Leytonstone.

COMBINATION BATHS.

No. 1245. HOSPITAL BATH.

This Bath is intended for use in Hospitals, &c., and when filled in an adjoining apartment is wheeled to the bedside of the patient. The Bath is made of strong charcoal iron, and is mounted on wheels having indiarubber tyres. An outlet tap is provided for emptying into waste grid.

Japanned inside and outside, any color ... Length 5' 0" — 150/- each; 5' 6" — 157/6 each.

If with covered end, 15/- each extra.

Wooden Platform between bottom of Bath and axles, 12/- each extra.

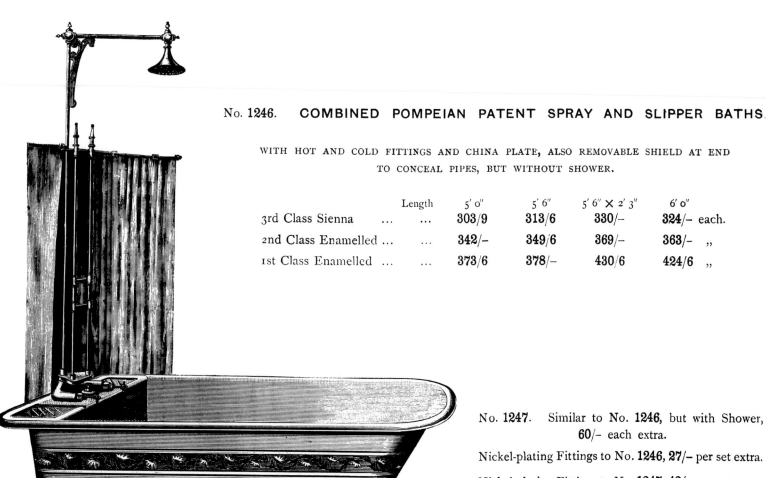

No. 1246. COMBINED POMPEIAN PATENT SPRAY AND SLIPPER BATHS.

WITH HOT AND COLD FITTINGS AND CHINA PLATE, ALSO REMOVABLE SHIELD AT END TO CONCEAL PIPES, BUT WITHOUT SHOWER.

	Length	5' 0"	5' 6"	5' 6" X 2' 3"	6' 0"
3rd Class Sienna		303/9	313/6	330/-	324/- each.
2nd Class Enamelled		342/-	349/6	369/-	363/- ,,
1st Class Enamelled		373/6	378/-	430/6	424/6 ,,

No. 1247. Similar to No. 1246, but with Shower, 60/- each extra.

Nickel-plating Fittings to No. 1246, 27/- per set extra.

Nickel-plating Fittings to No. 1247, 42/- per set extra.

COMBINATION BATHS.

No. 1248. IMPROVED "SITZ" BATH.   **No. 1269. HOT WATER TOWEL RAIL.**

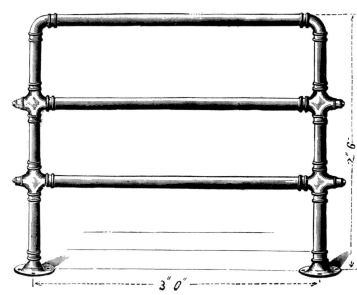

Improved "Sitz" Bath, 1st class Enamelled inside, and Grained or Marbled outside, any color; with all Fittings complete for fixing to supply and waste.

Cast-Brass Bath	...	..	...	...	...	...	**360/-** each.
Cast-Iron Bath	...	...	...	...	...	...	**255/-** ,,
Plating Fittings, extra	...	...	...	...	...	...	**15/-** set.

A cheaper form of this shape Bath is made in Zinc or Copper. Drawings, details, and prices upon application.

The Hot Water Towel Rail shewn above is a convenient acquisition in the bath-room or bedroom. Besides being useful for drying bath towels, &c., it will be obvious that a comfortable temperature may also be maintained, an improvement at certain times most desirable These Towel Rails are made of Brass, polished and lacquered, or they may be plated.

Price, in polished Brass	...	...	...	...	...	**132/-** each.
Nickel-plating..	...	...	...	...	...	**...24/-** each extra

No. 1249. COMBINATION BATH AND FITTINGS WITH WOODWORK.

Bath Framing made in Walnut or Mahogany, with double tile back and end, including Patent Steamless and Noiseless Victoria Taper-sided or Parallel Bath.

		No. 1249. Taper-sided Bath.			No. 1249½. Parallel Bath.			
		5′ 0″	5′ 6″	6′ 0″	5′ 0″	5′ 6″	5′ 6″ × 2′ 3″	6′ 0″
3rd class Sienna	... ...	498/9	513/9	547/6	505/6	521/3	545/3	558/- each.
2nd ,, Enamelled	... ...	525/-	543/9	584/3	535/6	555/9	582/9	597/9 ,,
1st ,, ,,	... ...	551/3	566/3	611/3	564/9	581/3	611/3	627/9 ,.

Cheaper Wood Enclosures and special designs made to order.

STRATFORD, Walthamstow and Leytonstone.

COMBINATION BATHS.

PATENT ORIENTAL BATH.

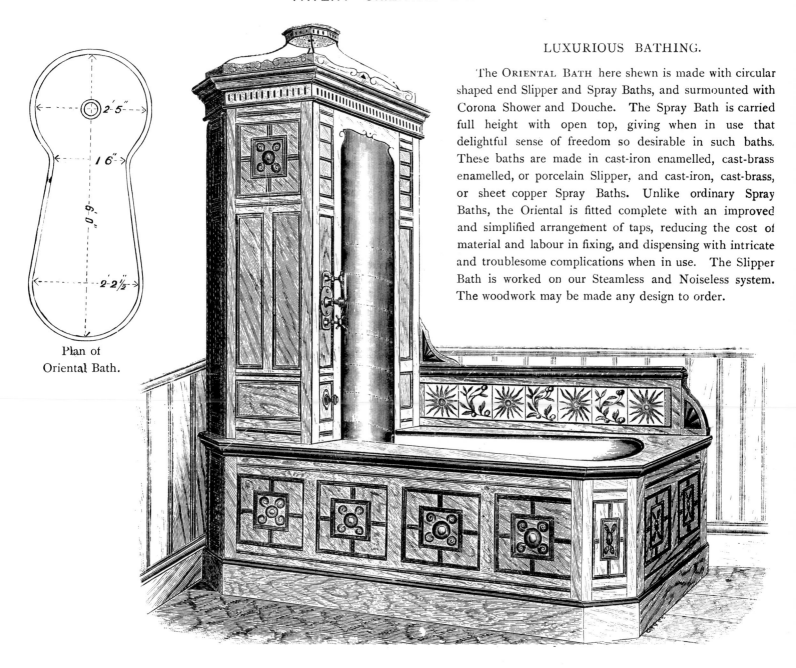

2' 5"

1' 6"

6' 0"

2' 2½"

Plan of
Oriental Bath.

LUXURIOUS BATHING.

The ORIENTAL BATH here shewn is made with circular shaped end Slipper and Spray Baths, and surmounted with Corona Shower and Douche. The Spray Bath is carried full height with open top, giving when in use that delightful sense of freedom so desirable in such baths. These baths are made in cast-iron enamelled, cast-brass enamelled, or porcelain Slipper, and cast-iron, cast-brass, or sheet copper Spray Baths. Unlike ordinary Spray Baths, the Oriental is fitted complete with an improved and simplified arrangement of taps, reducing the cost of material and labour in fixing, and dispensing with intricate and troublesome complications when in use. The Slipper Bath is worked on our Steamless and Noiseless system. The woodwork may be made any design to order.

No. **1530.** Cast-Iron Slipper and Spray Bath, first-class Enamelled, with all Fittings complete (no Lead Piping or Wood Enclosure) for Hot and Cold, Slipper, Spray, Shower, and Douche Baths ... ... **720/-** each.

No. **1531.** Cast-Iron Slipper and Copper Spray Bath, first-class Enamelled, with all Fittings, as above described ... ... **780/-** „

No. **1532.** Porcelain Slipper Bath (6' 0", parallel, best), Copper Spray Bath, first-class Enamelled, with all Fittings, as above described ... ... **855/-** „

No. **1533.** Wood Enclosure for above in high-class Cabinet Work, Walnut or Mahogany, and Tile Back, as drawn... ... **900/-** „

Cheaper Wood Enclosures and special designs made to order.

STRATFORD, Walthamstow and Leytonstone.

GAS BATHS.

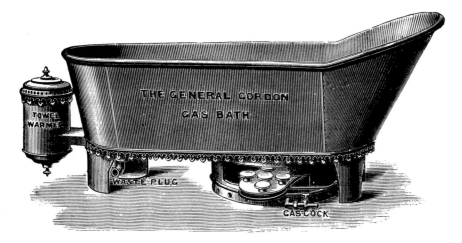

No. 994.

THE "GENERAL GORDON" GAS BATH.

(RIGHT HAND.)

Sides made of Best Sheet Iron, carefully tinned, and japanned inside White and outside dark Oak; the bottom entirely of hardened Copper. Fitted with Waste Plug and loose Bent Union for easy connection to waste pipe. Movable Towel Warmer   Powerful Atmospheric Burner

Prices complete, including Gas Tap—

5' o" long	...	...	...	...	112/6 each.
5' 6" long	...	...	...	...	127/6 ,,

The ornamental fret shewn round the bottom of the Bath is now usually omitted, as it is found to be inconvenient.

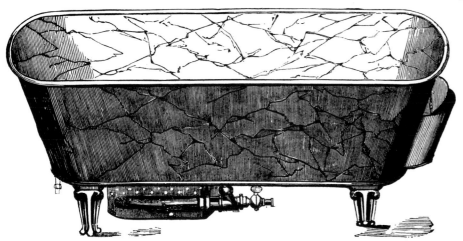

No. 995.

"EXCELSIOR" GAS BATH.

(LEFT HAND.)

☞ *Free from Smoke or Smell.*

This is a strong, well-made Bath, fitted with linen warmer, brass union, and plug and washer for emptying. Japanned Oak outside and White Marble inside.

The price is such as will be sure to command a large sale.

5' o" long	...	...	...	...	135/- each.
5' 6" long	...	...	...	...	157/6 ,,

With entire Copper Bottoms, made to order, 18/- extra.

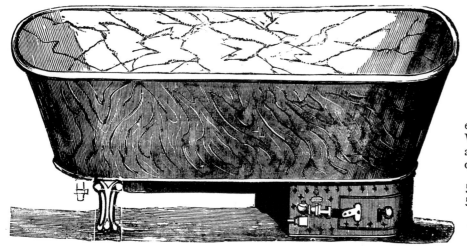

No. 998.

"UNIVERSAL" GAS BATH.

(RIGHT HAND.)

☞ *Free from Smoke or Smell.*

This is a stronger Bath than No. 995, made with entire Copper Bottom. Japanned Oak outside and White Marble inside, fitted with Registered Bath Furnace and Patent Gas and Air Burner, saving 50 per cent. in consumption of gas.

5' o" long	...	...	...	...	172/6 each.
5' 6" long	...	...	...	...	187/6 ,,

With Overflow, 4/6 extra.   Linen Airer, 18/- extra.

DIRECTIONS FOR LIGHTING.

Swing out the Burner or Burners. Turn on the Gas; then wait a few seconds before applying the Light. This is very important as it gives time for the Gas and Air to mix together, thus causing a Blue Flame without any smoke. Then turn the Lighted Burner or Burners under the Bath.

If by any means the Gas should light at the Air Socket, thus causing a White Flame, turn off the Tap immediately and re-light according to preceding directions.

N.B.—On no account Light the Gas before the Water is put into the Bath, and see that Waste Pipe is Shut-off.

All Gas Baths are made handed. Orders should state which hand is required. In all cases where this is omitted Baths will be forwarded as shewn in drawing.

STRATFORD, Walthamstow and Leytonstone.

GAS BATHS.

BATHS AND GEYSERS COMBINED.

No. 1007. THE "QUEEN" GAS BATH, COMPLETE WITH "CHAMPION" GEYSER.

The Bath is japanned White Marble inside, and Green Marble outside, with wide roll edge.

The "Geyser" is made entirely of Copper, and polished: but can be had to match Bath at same prices.

No. 1006 is same as 1007, except that the top edge is narrower

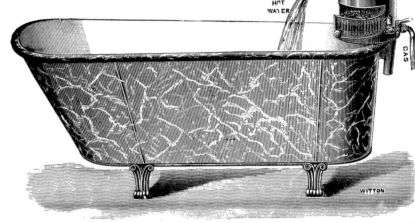

	Length inside. ft. in.	Length over all. ft. in.	Gives Hot Bath in	Gal-lons.	Price No. 1006.	Price No. 1007.
No. 1006A ...	5 0	5 6	25 min.	20	157/6	187/6 each
,, 1006B ...	5 3	6 0	20 ,,	25	187/6	217/6 ,,
,, 1006C ...	5 6	6 6	15 ,,	30	215/-	240/- ,,

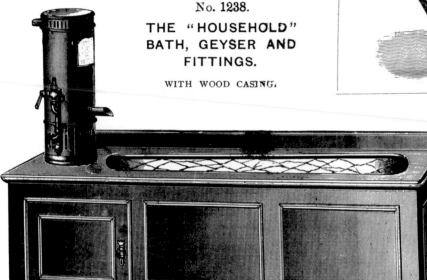

No. 1238.
THE "HOUSEHOLD" BATH, GEYSER AND FITTINGS.
WITH WOOD CASING.

	Bath Inside. ft. in.	Geyser gives Hot Water per Minute.	Price complete.
No. 1238A ...	5 0 ...	1 to 1½ galls. ...	390/- per set.
,, 1238B ...	5 3 ...	2 ,, 3 ,, ...	450/- ,,
,, 1238C ...	5 6 ...	3 ,, 5 ,, ...	495/- ,,

Bath of Galvanized Iron, with double-beaded top 2½" wide, japanned White Marble inside and Colored Marble outside, Copper Standard quick waste and overflow with Brass Unions, the Standard supporting a Tray upon which the Geyser is placed. This arrangement is complete in itself, and includes all the Cocks and Unions necessary for easy connection to gas, water and waste Pipes. The Copper Standard for waste and overflow is a very great improvement upon the old plan.

No. 1239.
THE "SALISBURY" BATH AND GEYSER.
TO STAND WITHOUT WOOD-WORK.

	Bath Inside. ft. in.	Length over all. ft. in.	Geyser gives Hot Water per Minute.	Price complete.
No. 1239A ...	5 0 ...	5 9 ...	1½ galls. ...	270/- per set.
,, 1239B ...	5 3 ...	6 3 ...	2 ,, ...	315/- ,,
,, 1239C ...	5 6 ...	6 9 ...	3 ,, ...	405/- ,,
,, 1239D ...	6 0 ...	7 6 ...	4 ,, ...	480/- ,,

The capacity of all Geysers is computed in Summer; in Winter a longer period will be required to attain same result.

STRATFORD, Walthamstow and Leytonstone.

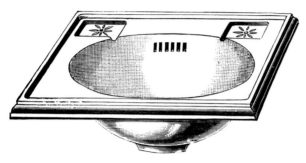

No. 2741. OBLONG LAVATORY.
26¼″ × 18½″. Basin, 19¼″ × 13¼″.
White... **30/-** each. Marbled... **36/-** each. Decorated... **42/-** each. White & Gold... **67/6** each.

No. 2742. OBLONG LAVATORY.
27½″ × 21″, Basin, 20½″ × 14½″.
White... **39/-** each. Marbled... **45/-** each. Decorated... **51/-** each. White & Gold... **78/-** each.

No. 2743. OBLONG LAVATORY.
28½″ × 22½″. Basin, 21½″ × 15½″.
White... **45/-** each. Marbled... **51/-** each. Decorated... **60/-** each. White & Gold... **96/-** each.

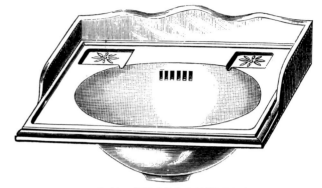

No. 2744. OBLONG LAVATORY.
26¼″ × 18½″, with Skirtings. Basin, 19¼″ × 13¼″.
White... **36/-** each. Marbled... **42/-** each. Decorated... **52/6** each. White & Gold... **78/-** each.

No. 2745. OBLONG LAVATORY,
27½″ × 21″, with Skirtings. Basin, 20½″ × 14½″.
White .. **46/6** each. Marbled... **51/-** each. Decorated... **63/-** each. White & Gold... **96/-** each.

No. 2746. OBLONG LAVATORY.
28½″ × 22½″, with Skirtings. Basin, 21½″ × 15½″.
White... **54/-** each. Marbled... **63/-** each. Decorated... **72/-** each. White & Gold... **108/-** each.

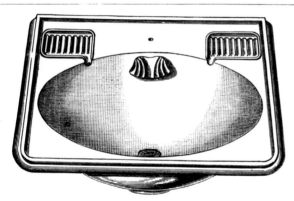

No. 2747. OBLONG LAVATORY.
27″ × 19″. Basin, 19½″ × 13¼″.
White... **30/-** each. Marbled... **36/-** each. Decorated... **42/-** each. White & Gold... **67/6** each.

No. 2748. OBLONG LAVATORY,
27″ × 20½″. Basin, 20½″ × 14½″.
White... **39/-** each. Marbled... **45/-** each. Decorated... **51/-** each. White & Gold... **78/-** each.

No. 2749. OBLONG LAVATORY.
28″ × 22″. Basin, 21½″ × 15½″.
White... **45/-** each. Marbled... **51/-** each. Decorated... **60/-** each. White & Gold... **96/-** each.

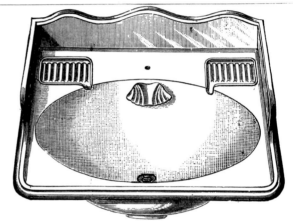

No. 2750. OBLONG LAVATORY.
27″ × 19″, with Skirtings. Basin, 19½″ × 13¼″.
White... **36/-** each. Marbled... **42/-** each. Decorated... **51/-** each. White & Gold... **78/-** each.

No. 2751. OBLONG LAVATORY.
27″ × 20½″, with Skirtings. Basin, 20½″ × 14½″.
White... **46/6** each. Marbled... **51/-** each. Decorated... **60/-** each. White & Gold... **96/-** each.

No. 2752. OBLONG LAVATORY.
28″ × 22″, with Skirtings. Basin, 21½″ × 15½″.
White... **54/-** each. Marbled... **63/-** each. Decorated... **75/-** each. White & Gold... **108/-** each

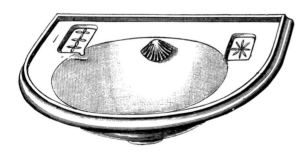

No. 2753. ROUND FRONT LAVATORY.
27″ × 19½″. Basin, 16¾″ × 13½″.
White... **39/-** each. Marbled... **43/6** each. Decorated... **51/-** each. White & Gold... **75/-** each.

No. 2754. ROUND FRONT LAVATORY.
30″ × 23″. Basin, 19½″ × 15½″.
White... **46/6** each. Marbled... **52/6** each. Decorated... **58/6** each. White & Gold... **87/-** each.

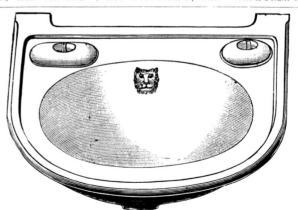

No. 2755. ROUND FRONT LAVATORY.
29½″ × 28½″. Basin, 23¼″ × 16½″.
White... **60/-** each. Marbled .. **70/6** each. Decorated... **76/6** each. White & Gold... **111/-** each.

Any of the above LAVATORIES can be supplied with Holes for Taps.

STRATFORD, Walthamstow and Leytonstone.

EARTHENWARE SANITARY GOODS.
PATENT RECESSED LAVATORY BASINS.

These Lavatories have been designed to overcome the following objections raised against Lavatories as generally made. In having difficulty to get the arms well into the basin, and also of the water running from the arms to the floor, or on to the person. These objections are entirely obviated by the new form of Lavatory, which enables those using same to approach very close to the basin proper, and the recessed formation prevents the water falling on to the person or floor, and so adding greatly to the comfort and convenience of the user.

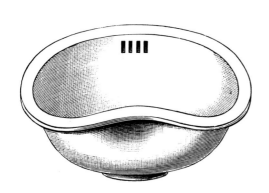

No. 2761. PATENT RECESSED, PLUG AND SHAMPOOING BASIN.
19″ × 15½″.

White	...	...	15/- each.	Marbled	...	...	19/6 each.
Decorated	...	...	22/6 ,,	White and Gold	...	31/6 ,,

No. 2762. PATENT RECESSED, PLUG AND SHAMPOOING BASIN.
21″ × 17½″.

White	...	...	18/- each.	Marbled	...	...	23/3 each.
Decorated	...	...	25/6 ,,	White and Gold	...	38/3 ,,

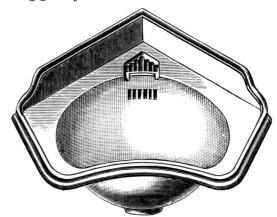

No. 2763. ANGULAR RECESSED LAVATORY, *WITHOUT* SKIRTINGS.
Side 18″. Back to Front, 20½″. Basin, 16½″ × 12″.
White... 28/6 each. Marbled... 33/- each. Decorated... 40/6 each. White & Gold... 57/- each.
No. 2764 Same sizes as 2763, but *with* Skirtings.
White... 33/- each. Marbled... 37/6 each. Decorated... 46/6 each. White & Gold... 64/6 each.

No. 2765. ANGULAR RECESSED LAVATORY, *WITHOUT* SKIRTINGS.
Side, 20″. Back to Front, 24″. Basin, 18½″ × 14″.
White... 33/- each. Marbled... 36/- each. Decorated... 45/- each. White & Gold... 64/6 each.
No. 2766. Same sizes as 2765, but *with* Skirtings.
White... 37/6 each. Marbled... 42/- each. Decorated... 52/6 each. White & Gold... 75/- each.

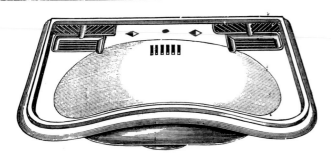

No. 2767. OBLONG RECESSED LAVATORY.
25″ × 19″. Basin 19¼″ × 12½″.

White	...	...	33/- each.	Marbled	...	...	37/6 each.
Decorated	...	...	45/- ,,	White and Gold	...	67/6 ,,

No. 2768. OBLONG RECESSED LAVATORY.
27″ × 23″. Basin 21″ × 14½″.

White	...	...	45/- each.	Marbled	...	...	51/- each.
Decorated	...	...	57/- ,,	White and Gold	...	84/- ,,

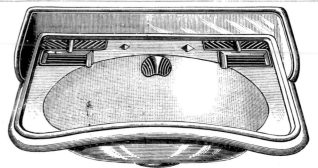

No. 2769. OBLONG RECESSED LAVATORY, WITH SKIRTINGS.
25″ × 19″. Basin 19¼″ × 12½″.

White	...	...	39/- each.	Marbled	...	...	45/- each.
Decorated	...	...	54/- ,,	White and Gold	...	81/- ,,

No. 2770. OBLONG RECESSED LAVATORY, WITH SKIRTINGS.
27″ × 23″. Basin, 21″ × 14½″.

White	...	...	54/- each.	Marbled	...	...	61/6 each.
Decorated	...	...	69/- ,,	White and Gold	...	99/- ,,

ARTISTIC CAST-IRON STANDS, specially constructed to suit the RECESSED BASINS are shewn on pages 58 to 62.

SPECIAL SHAPE PLUG BASINS.

No. 2771. ANTI-SPLASH PLUG BASIN.
17″ outside, 12″ inside.

White.	Marbled.	Gold Lines.
10/6 each.	12/- each.	24/- each.

No. 2772. OVAL PLUG BASIN.

	White.	Marbled.	Gold Lines.
18″ × 15″ × 5″	13/6 each.	18/- each.	30/- each.
19″ × 15″ × 5″	15/- ,,	19/6 ,,	31/6 ,,
20″ × 15″ × 5½″	17/3 ,,	21/- ,,	33/- ,,
22″ × 16″ × 6″	20/3 ,,	25/6 ,,	40/6 ,,
26″ × 17″ × 6″	26/3 ,,	31/6 ,,	52/6 ,,

If without Head Supply.
First two sizes ... ... 1/1½ less.
Other sizes ... ... 1/6 ,,

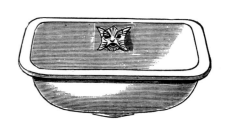

No. 2773. OBLONG PLUG BASIN.
17″ × 14″.

White.	Marbled.	Gold Lines.
12/- each.	14/3 each.	26/6 each.

If without Head Supply, 1/6 less.

PATENT LAVATORY STANDS AND BASINS.

No. 2801. ANGULAR LAVATORY STAND,

In Walnut or Mahogany, with angular Basin and Taps complete.

No. 2802. LAVATORY STAND,

In Pitch Pine or Ash, Tiled Back, Basin and Taps complete.

BASIN			22″ × 18″	27″ × 20″	30″ × 22″
Walnut or Mahogany	...	...	225/-	247/6	285/- each.
Ash or Pitch Pine	...	...	217/6	240/-	270/- ,,

BASIN	...	18″ × 18″	22″ × 18″	27″ × 20″	30″ × 22″
Ash or Pitch Pine	...	150/-	187/6	210/-	247/6 each.

No. 2803. ANGULAR LAVATORY STAND,

In Mahogany or American Walnut, with Patent Basin and Taps complete.

No. 2804. LAVATORY STAND,

In Mahogany or American Walnut, Tiled Back and Shelf, and fitted with PATENT BASIN with Vertical Spray.

BASIN	...	22″ × 18″	27″ × 20″	30″ × 22′
Mahogany or American Walnut	...	247/6	262/6	300/- each.

BASIN	...	...	27″ × 20″	30″ × 22″
Mahogany or American Walnut	...	...	315/-	352/6 each

If without Vertical Spray, 39/- each *less*.

Nos. 2801-2 or 3, Fitted with VERTICAL SPRAY to Lavatory, 39/- each extra. Plating Taps and Waste, 4/6 per Lavatory extra.

STRATFORD, Walthamstow and Leytonstone.

PATENT LAVATORIES, WITH SHOWER & CONCEALED URINAL.

No. 2807. CAST BRASS BRACKETS AND EARTHENWARE LAVATORY.

Combined Hot and Cold Taps and Swivel Shower.
Frieze in Walnut or Mahogany.

No. 2808. CAST BRASS BRACKETS & EARTHENWARE LAVATORY.

Combined Hot and Cold Taps and Swivel Shower.
Frieze in Walnut or Mahogany.

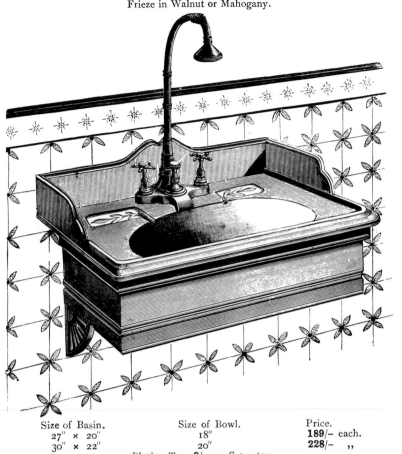

Size of Basin.	Size of Bowl.	Price.
27″ × 20″	18″	189/- each.
30″ × 22″	20″	228/- ,,
	Plating Taps 9/- per Set extra.	

Size of Basin.	Size of Bowl.	Price.
27″ × 20″	17″ × 11″	189/- each.
30″ × 22″	17″ × 13½″	228/- ,,
	Plating Taps 9/- per Set extra.	

No. 2809. FOLDING LAVATORY.

In Walnut, Mahogany or Teak, with Zinc Removable Receiver, with
Basin, Tap and Soap Dishes complete.

No. 2810. CONCEALED URINAL.

For Offices, Banks, &c., Automatic action when top handle is pushed,
doors open and basin is flushed; reverse action closes doors and tap.

Price 120/- each.
Combined Hot Tap 15/- extra.

In Walnut, Mahogany or Oak, with Ivoryware Basin, plated
mountings and trap complete ... ... 97/6 each.

STRATFORD, Walthamstow and Leytonstone.

No. 2781. ANGULAR LAVATORY AND BRACKET.

REGISTERED DESIGN.

No. 2782. ANGULAR LAVATORY AND BRACKET.

REGISTERED DESIGN.

No. 2783. ANGULAR LAVATORY AND STAND.

REGISTERED DESIGN.

No. 2784. ANGULAR LAVATORY AND STAND.

REGISTERED DESIGN.

STRATFORD, Walthamstow and Leytonstone.

No. 2785. MIRROR, WITH FRAME.

REGISTERED DESIGN.

No. 2786. MIRROR, WITH FRAME.

REGISTERED DESIGN.

No. 2787. LAVATORY AND STAND.

REGISTERED DESIGN.

No. 2788. LAVATORY AND STAND. (Patent Recessed Basin.)

REGISTERED DESIGN.

No. 2789. LAVATORY AND STAND. (Patent Recessed Basin and Tiled Back.)

REGISTERED DESIGN.

"PALATINE" SERIES OF SANITARY LAVATORIES.

No. 2794. LAVATORY, STAND AND MIRROR.

Cast Iron Stand, with Tile Back and Mirror, with Earthenware Lavatory as shewn (27″ × 19″), and with improved Hot and Cold Water Taps, Plug and Chain, complete.

No. 2795. LAVATORY, STAND AND MIRROR.

Cast Iron Stand, with Tile Back and Mirror, with Patent recessed Earthenware Lavatory as shewn (25″ × 19″), and with improved Hot and Cold Water Taps, Plug and Chain, complete.

REGISTERED DESIGN.

BASIN ...	White.	Marbled.	White and Gold.
FINE CAST, with one Coat of Paint	110/6	115/6	141/6 each.
ENAMEL PAINTED, in two Colors, BEST FINISH	148/3	153/-	178/3 ,,
ENAMELLED, Oak, Rosewood, Walnut or Marble, BEST FINISH ...	152/3	157/6	182/3 ,,

REGISTERED DESIGN.

BASIN ...	White.	Marbled.	White and Gold.
FINE CAST, with one Coat of Paint	120/-	126/-	160/- each.
ENAMEL PAINTED, in two Colors, BEST FINISH	157/6	162/9	198/- ,,
ENAMELLED, Oak, Rosewood, Walnut or Marble, BEST FINISH ...	162/9	167/9	202/6 ,,

If with White Metal or Nickel-plated Fittings, add to above prices 10/6 per set.

STRATFORD, Walthamstow and Leytonstone.

PATENT LAVATORIES AND MIRRORS COMPLETE.

No. 2805. LAVATORY STAND, with **D**-shaped Basin, Taps, Fancy Tiled Back, Bracket Shelves and Bevelled-edge Mirror.

No. 2806. HANDSOME LAVATORY STAND, in American Walnut or Mahogany.

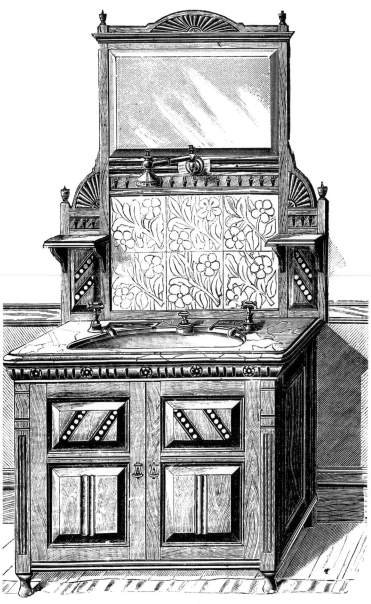

	22″ × 18″	27″ × 20″	30″ × 22″
Walnut or Mahogany	307/6	360/-	390/- each.
If in Ash or Pitch Pine ...	298/6	347/6	377/6 ,,

If with Plated Fittings **4/6** extra.

If with Bracket Shower as No. 2806, **25/6** extra.

If with Vertical Spray as No. 2804, **39/-** extra.

High Tiled Back, Bevelled-edge Mirror, with 20-inch **D**-shaped Basin, Hot and Cold Taps, $1\frac{1}{4}″$ New England or **D** Fossil Marble Slab (36 inches by 24 inches), with moulded edges and soap-sinkings complete.

Price, as described, **600/-** each.

If with Bracket Shower (as shewn), **25/6** extra.

If with Vertical Spray, as No. 2804, **39/-** extra.

STRATFORD, Walthamstow and Leytonstone.

CLOSET CISTERN PULLS, CLOSET HANDLES, COTTAGE VALVES, &c.

No. 318. PULL.

Galvanized Chain, 30" long. -/6 each.

No. 319. PULL.

Galvanized Chain, 30" long, Beech handle. -/9 each.

No. 317½. GALVANIZED DISH AND HANDLE.

1/3 each.

No 313. ROUND DISH AND GRIP.

With China Grip, 7/6 each.
With Glass Grip, 9/- each.

No. 320. PULL.

30" Brass Chain and Ivory China Handle. 1/3 each.

No. 311. PULL.

30" Brass Chain and Ivory China Handle, 1/6 each.

No. 374. PULL.

30" Brass Chain and Hand-painted Handle, assorted patterns. 3/9 each.

No. 383. PULL, GUIDE AND ROD.

Ivory China Handle and Brass Block, 5/3 each.
If with Mahogany Block, 7/6 each.

No. 382. PULL, GUIDE AND ROD.

Ivory China Handle and Imitation Mahogany Block, 3/9 each.

No. 386. BRASS PIPE CLIP.

To suit 1¼" Lead Pipe ... 6/9 per doz.
„ 1½" „ ... ... 7/6 „
Other sizes to order.

No. 376. COTTAGE VALVE.

With Brass Dish and Handle, ¾" Valve ... 9/- set.
Without Dish and Rod „ ... 5/6 „

No. 377. CLOSET VALVE, FRAME, AND REGULATOR.

No. 312. SUNK DISH AND HANDLE ON ADJUSTABLE IRON FRAME SUPPORT, WITH CRANK.

With Ebony Grip, 9/9 each.
With Glass Grip 12/9 „

No. 213. INDICATOR BOLT.

ENGAGED

FOR WATER CLOSETS AND OFFICE DOORS.

Will suit either hand by reversing the Tablet ... ... 5/3 each.

¾" 1" 1¼" Valves.
24/- 27/- 33/- each.
With Dish and Rod, 4/6 each extra.

CAST IRON BRACKETS FOR CLOSET CISTERNS.

No. 1455. BRACKET. **No. 1456. BRACKET.** **No. 1457. BRACKET.** **No. 1458. BRACKET.** **No. 1469. BRACKET.**

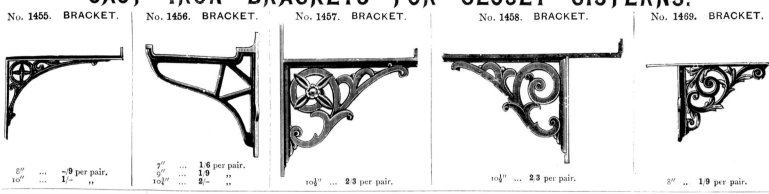

8″ ... -/9 per pair.	
10″ ... 1/- ,,	

7″ ... 1/6 per pair.	
9″ ... 1/9 ,,	
10¾″ ... 2/- ,,	

10½″ ... 2/3 per pair.

10½″ ... 2/3 per pair.

8″ .. 1/9 per pair.

SEATS AND BRACKETS FOR PEDESTAL CLOSETS.

No. 1459. BRACKET. **No. 397. SINGLE FLAP CLOSET SEAT.** **No. 398. DOUBLE FLAP CLOSET SEAT.**

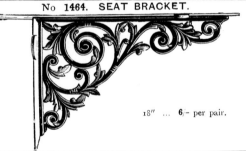

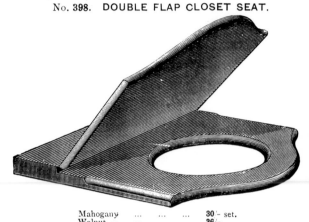

No. 397. 20½″ wide, 8″ back portion, 18″ hinged flap.

No. 398. Same sizes.

	1″	1¼″ thick.
Deal	12/- ...	13/6 each.
Pitch Pine ...	15/-	18/- ,,
Mahogany ...	15/-	18/- ,,
Walnut	18/-	21/- ,,

Mahogany	30/- set.
Walnut	36/- ,,

No. 417. WROUGHT ROD AND CAST IRON WEIGHTS.
Self-Tipping Levers ... ... 9/- per pair.

10½″ ... 2/9 per pair.

No. 1460. SEAT BRACKET. **No 1464. SEAT BRACKET.** **No. 1465. SEAT BRACKET.**

16″ ... 4/6 per pair.

18″ ... 6/- per pair.

15″ ... 6/9 per pair.

No. 1466. PEDESTAL BRACKET. **No. 1467. PEDESTAL BRACKET.** **No. 1468. PEDESTAL BRACKET.**

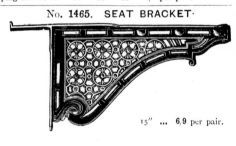

REGISTERED DESIGN.

16″ ... 8/3 per pair.

18″ ... 9/- per pair.

18″ ... 10/6 per pair.

EARTHENWARE SANITARY GOODS.
PEDESTAL CLOSETS,
FOR USE AS CLOSET, URINAL OR SLOP SINK.

No 391. THE "TRENT" PEDESTAL WASH-OUT CLOSET.

Oval Basin, 16″ × 14½″.   Height, 17″, with **S** or **P** Trap.

Cane and White (not printed)	…	…	…	…	…	**22/6** each.
All White or Ivory (not printed)	…	…	…	…	…	**30/-** ,,
White, and printed inside and out, as drawn …	…	…	…	**37/6** ,,

No. 392. THE "TURBINE" PEDESTAL WASH-OUT CLOSET.

THE DESIGN ON THIS CLOSET IS EMBOSSED OR RAISED.

Oval Basin, 16½″ × 14½″.   Height, 17½″, with **S** or **P** Trap.

Cane and White …	…	…	…	…	…	…	**33/9** each.
All White or Ivory	…	…	…	…	…	…	**45/-** ,,

No. 393. THE "RAPIDUS" PEDESTAL WASH-DOWN CLOSET

Oval Basin, 16″ × 14½″.   Height, 17½″, with **S** Trap.

All White or Ivory	…	…	…	…	…	**30/-** each.
White and printed	…	…	…	…	…	**37/6** ,,

No. 390. THE "KENSINGTON" PEDESTAL WASH-OUT CLOSET.

THE DESIGN ON THIS CLOSET IS EMBOSSED OR RAISED.

Oval Basin, 16½″ × 13″.   Height, 17½″, with **S** or **P** Trap.

Cane and White …	…	…	…	…	…	…	**36/-** each.
All White or Ivory	…	…	…	…	…	…	**48/-** ,,

N.B.—When ordering, please give Number or Name of Engraving, and state if **S** or **P** Traps are required.

EARTHENWARE SANITARY GOODS.

PEDESTAL CLOSETS FOR USE AS CLOSET, URINAL OR SLOP-SINK.

Special Cheap Set.

THE "TRENT" COMBINATION CLOSET.

No. 240. The "Trent" £ s. d.
Syphon Cistern, 2 gallons 0 13 6 each.
No. 1456. The "Trent"
Syphon Cistern Brackets 0 1 6 per pair.
No. 311. The "Trent"
Syphon Cistern Pull ... 0 1 6 each.
No. 391. The "Trent"
Cane and White Closet 1 2 6 ,,
No. 472. The "Trent"
Cane and White Paper
Box ... ... 0 4 6 ,,
No. 397. The "Trent"
Polished Mahogany Seat,
1″ thick ... ... 0 15 0 ,,
No. 1460. The "Trent"
Seat Brackets ... ... 0 4 6 per pair.

Per Complete Set ... **£3 3 0**
(No fall pipe.)

Superior Set, as drawn.

THE "TRENT" COMBINATION CLOSET.

No. 240. The "Trent" £ s. d.
Syphon Cistern, 3 gallons 0 18 0 each.
No. 1456, The "Trent"
Syphon Cistern Brackets 0 2 0 per pair.
No. 311. The "Trent"
Syphon Cistern Pull ... 0 1 6 each.
No. 391. The "Trent"
Iris on White Closet ... 1 17 6 ,,
No. 472. The "Trent"
Iris on White Paper Box 0 9 0 ,,
No. 397. The "Trent"
Polished Mahogany Seat,
1″ thick ... ... 0 15 0 ,,
No. 1460. The "Trent"
Seat Brackets ... ... 0 4 6 per pair.

Per Complete Set ... **£4 7 6**
(No fall pipe.)

THE "IRIS" TRENT COMBINATION SANITARY CLOSET SET.

Very superior Set.

THE "TURBINE" COMBINATION CLOSET.

No. 272. The "Turbine" £ s. d.
Syphon Cistern ... ... 1 0 3 each.

No. 1458. The "Turbine"
Syphon Cistern Brackets 0 2 3 per pair.

No. 382. The "Turbine"
Pull on Block ... ... 0 7 6 each.

No. 392. The "Turbine"
Ivory Closet ... ... 2 5 0 ,,

No. 473. The "Turbine"
Ivory Closet Paper Box 0 9 0 ,,

No. 397. The "Turbine"
Polished Mahogany Seat,
1¼″ thick... ... ... 0 18 0 ,,

No. 1467. The "Turbine"
Pedestal Seat Brackets... 0 9 0 per pair

Per Complete Set ... **£5 11 0**
(No fall pipe.)

"RAPIDUS" SET and "KENSINGTON" SET can be calculated from opposite page and foregoing, or quoted upon application.

PAPER BOXES FOR PEDESTAL CLOSETS.

No. 471. "RAPIDUS" PAPER BOX.

White or Ivory.   White and Printed.

6/9 each.   **9/–** each.

No. 473. "TURBINE" PAPER BOX.

Cane and White.   White or Ivory.

6/9 each.   **9/–** each.

No. 472. "IRIS" TRENT PAPER BOX.

Cane and White, not printed.   White or Ivory, not printed.   "Iris" printed on White or Ivory.

4/6 each.   **6/9** each.   **9/–** each.

No. 474 "KENSINGTON" PAPER BOX.

Cane and White.   White or Ivory.

7/6 each.   **9/9** each.

STRATFORD, Walthamstow and Leytonstone.

EARTHENWARE SANITARY GOODS.

PEDESTAL CLOSETS FOR USE AS CLOSET, URINAL OR SLOP-SINK.

No. 394.   THE "BURTON" WASH-DOWN CLOSET.

No. 395.   THE "BRIGHTON" EXCELSIOR CLOSET.

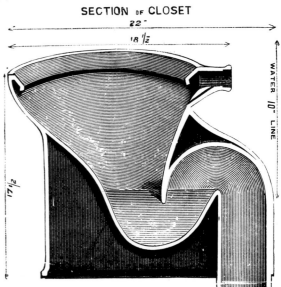

PLAIN PATTERN.   TARVER PATTERN.

The "Burton" Closet is made in one piece of Earthenware, and is designed to supply the demand for a self-contained closet. The rim being Sharpe's Patent Rim, causes the water to flush all parts of the Basin, and the water standing in bottom of closet prevents the outlet from soiling, thus securing a clean basin.

This Closet can be supplied in either **S** or **P** Trap.

It is recommended that a 3-*gallon* Syphon Cistern should be fixed to this Closet.

Cane and White	...	...	...	...	**24/-** each.
Cane and Printed	...	...	...	..	**30/-** ,,
All White	...	...	...	...	**33/-** ,,
,, and Printed Inside	...	...	...	**39/-** ,,
,, and Two Gold Lines	...	...	**45/-** ,,

Traps with Ventilating Pipe, **1/-** extra.

This Closet is also made in two pieces, *i.e.* the "Household."

Height 16¼", Basin 15¼" × 14¼".

		White.	Blue.	Marbled.	Decorated.	White & Gold.
Plain Pattern	...	**57/-**	**63/-**	**66/-**	**67/6**	**90/-** each
Tarver ,,	...	**63/-**	**69/-**	**72/-**	**75/-**	**93/-** ,,

No. 396.   THE "PRIMROSE" CLOSET.

(Registered No. 106177.)

SECTION OF CLOSET

The "Primrose" Closet is made in one piece of Earthenware, and is what is usually termed a Wash-down Closet. The Rim being Sharpe's Patent Rim, causes the water to flush all parts of the Basin, and the water standing in bottom of Closet (*see* section above) prevents the outlet from soiling, thus securing a clean Basin.

The Closet is of an ornamental raised pattern, and if fixed with a hinged seat, combines a Water Closet, Slop Sink, and Urinal. This Closet can be supplied in either **S** or **P** Trap.

White outside and inside	... ...	**45/-** each.
,, ,, ,, Printed	... ...	**49/6** ,,
Majolica outside and White inside	... ...	**54/-** each.
,, ,, ,, ,, Printed	...	**60/-** ,,

N.B.—When ordering, please give Number or Name of Engraving, and state if **S** or **P** Traps are required.

STRATFORD, Walthamstow and Leytonstone.

WATER CLOSETS.

No. 1892. JENNINGS' PATENT VALVE CLOSET AND TRAP.

In one piece of Earthenware.

Elevation.

Sectional elevation showing the Plunger raised and contents passing away, also arrangement of Ventilating Pipe.

Complete with Regulating Supply Valve and Ball-trapped Overflow Plug.

In White Ware Glazed, with Earthenware Sunk Handle Dish	110/3	each.
,, with Printed Basin and Dish to correspond	141/9	,,
,, with Enamelled Blue Basin and Dish to correspond, and Ivory Handle	181/3	,,
,, ,, ,, ,, with Handsome Gilt Scroll and Ivory Handle from	212/9	,,

No. 1893. JENNINGS' PATENT COMBINED SELF-ACTION SELF-FLUSHING CLOSET AND URINAL.

Suitable for Public Houses, Factories, Railway Stations, &c.

This apparatus will commend itself to all who have ever been under the unpleasant necessity of visiting a W.C. as ordinarily in use at Public Houses ; and for Factories and for use of Steerage Passengers and Seamen on board Ship (above water line), they are equally desirable.

THEY COMPEL CLEANLINESS AND DECENCY.

Fig. 1.—When the seat is released, the counterbalance weights bring it to a vertical position, the movement ensuring an abundant flush of Water, and, if used as a Urinal or Slop Sink, the seat will not be fouled.

Fig. 2.—Shows the seat depressed. This action also causes the basin and trap to be flushed before use as a W.C., a very important advantage.

The Basin, with Flushing Rim or Fan, is of strong Porcelain-enamelled Cast-Iron, with Inspection Cover to Trap ; the working parts are strongly made, and the absence of complicated parts renders any casing unnecessary, so that the outside of apparatus may be cleansed and repainted as desired.

Price complete, as shown, with Birch Seat	110/3	per set.
,, ,, with Polished Mahogany or Oak Seat	126/-	,,

In fixing : bed outlet of Trap to Soil Pipe in a little red putty, and lay on Service Pipe to Union **S**, no carpenter's work being required.

No. 1894. JENNINGS' PATENT "TRAPLESS" VALVE WATER CLOSETS.

The cheapest, most efficient and compact Closets ever produced.

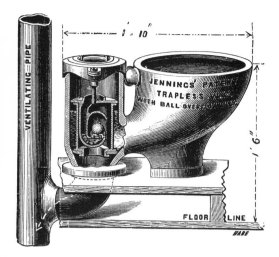 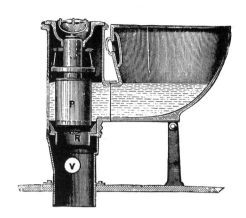 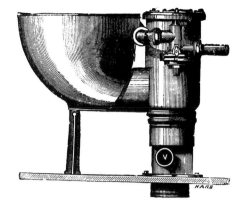

NOTE.—In fixing this Closet, the soil-pipe should be so arranged as to be 12 inches to the left of centre of Closet space, and 13 inches from back wall, in all cases well ventilated ; and the height of Cistern over Closet should be stated when ordering. The "All Earthenware Trapless Closet" may be had of same height if desired. Therefore, when ordering, please say if the soil-pipe will be arranged under floor as usual, or above as shown.

PRICES.

	Iron Cylinder and Earthenware Basin.			In one piece of Earthenware.
With White Basin	94/6 each.	...	...	110/3 each.
,, Printed Basin	126/– ,,	...	...	141/9 ,,
,, Enamelled Blue Basin, with Cast Brass-sunk Dish and Cut-glass Handle...	165/– ,,	...	...	180/– ,,
,, ,, Basin with Gilt Scroll, Silver-plated Cast Brass-sunk Dish and Amber Cut-glass or Ivory Handle, from	198/– ,,	...	...	213/– ,,

Best French-polished Mahogany Seats, Enclosures, Paper Hoods, &c., in Stock and made to Order.

Showing Apparatus with Seat raised for use as Urinal.

No. 1895. JENNINGS' "SERVANTS AND COTTAGE" W.C.

White Earthenware Flushing Rim Basin, in Vitrified Glazed Stoneware Pedestal Casing, with Earthenware or Drawn Lead Syphon Trap.

These Closets are recommended as a cheap and suitable arrangement for Servants' use, Area Closets, or small workshops, as they are strong, simple, and effective, and the absence of the ordinary wood enclosure prevents accumulation of rubbish or leakage from being overlooked.

Complete as shown, including Hopper Closet and Earthenware Trap, Varnished Pine Hinged Seat and Skirting, **52/6** per set.

If with Hard Wood Birch Seat in place of Pine do., **7/6** each extra.

If with Drawn Lead Trap, S. Q. or P., in place of Earthenware, **12/–** each extra.

Each form of Apparatus throws one and a half pints of earth each time the closet is used. When ordering Apparatus, state whether it is proposed to fix the same over a vault, or whether over a tank or pail.

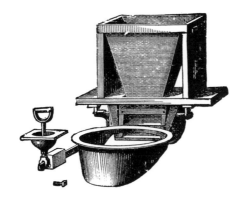
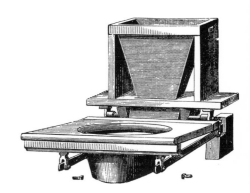

APPARATUS No. 2851.

"PULL-OUT,"

With Galvanized Iron Rim, and Iron Handle,

37/6 per Set.

If supplied with Deal Seat, on Bearers, fixed ready for placing in position (as shewn with No. 2854),

12/- per Set extra.

APPARATUS No. 2852.

"PULL-UP" (New Patent)

With Galvanized Iron Rim and Iron Handle,

51/- per Set.

If supplied with Deal Seat or Bearers, fixed ready for placing in position (as shewn with No. 2854),

18/9 per Set extra.

APPARATUS No. 2853.

"SELF-ACTING" (New Patent),

With Galvanized Iron Rim and Deal Seat,

63/- per Set.

If supplied with Deal Seat, on Bearers, fixed ready for placing in position (as shewn with No. 2854),

15/9 per Set extra.

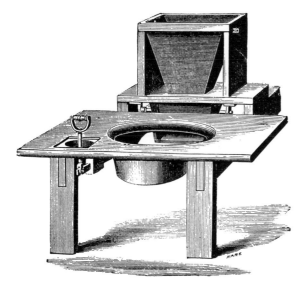
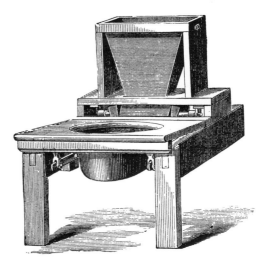

APPARATUS No. 2854.

"PULL-UP" (New Patent),

With Galvanised Iron Rim, Iron Handle and Deal Seat, on Bearers, fixed ready for placing in position,
69/9 per Set.

If supplied without Seat and Bearers,
18/9 per Set less.

APPARATUS No. 2855.

"SELF-ACTING" (New Patent),

With White Earthenware Rim and Deal Seat, on Bearers, fixed ready for placing in position,
84/9 per Set.

If supplied without Bearers,
14/3 per Set less.

STRATFORD, Walthamstow and Leytonstone.

PATENT EARTH CLOSETS (MOULE'S SYSTEM).
APPARATUS FOR USE IN CLOSETS.

Each form of Apparatus throws one and a half pints of earth each time the closet is used. When ordering Apparatus, state whether it is proposed to fix the same over a vault, or whether over a tank or pail.

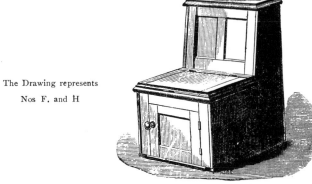

The Drawing represents
Nos F. and H

Commodes about 3' 0" high, 1' 10" wide, and 2' 3" from back to front.

No. 2856. APPARATUS.
"PULL UP."

With White Earthenware Rim, Galvanized Iron Valve beneath the rim, best Handle and Teak or Mahogany seat, 3' 0" wide, on bearers fixed ready for placing in position ... ... **180/-** per set.

No. 2857. COMMODES OR PORTABLE EARTH CLOSET.

No. 2857A. COMMODE, "PULL OUT" in plain Deal (Unvarnished), with Iron Handle and Iron Rim ...	**75/-**	each.
No. 2857B. COMMODE, "PULL UP" (new patent), in plain Deal (Unvarnished), with Iron Handle and Iron Rim	**90/-**	,,
No. 2857C. COMMODE, "SELF-ACTING" (new patent) in plain Deal (Unvarnished), with Iron Rim ...	**100/6**	,,
No. 2857D. COMMODE, "PULL-UP," (new patent), in plain Deal, (Varnished), with Brass Handle and Earthenware Rim	**114/-**	,,
No. 2857E. COMMODE, "SELF-ACTING" (new patent), in plain Deal, (Varnished), with Earthenware Rim...	**123/9**	,,
No. 2857F. COMMODE, "PULL-UP" (new patent), in panelled Deal, (Varnished), with best Brass Handle and Earthenware Rim	**150/-**	,,
No. 2857G. COMMODE, "SELF-ACTING" (new patent), in panelled Deal (Varnished), with Earthenware Rim	**162/-**	,,
No. 2857H. COMMODE, "PULL-UP" (new patent), in panelled Teak or Mahogany (French Polished), of the very best make	**247/6**	,,
No. 2857J. COMMODE, "SELF-ACTING" in Teak or Mahogany (French Polished), of the very best make	**262/6**	,,

Each Commode is furnished with a Pail and Cover, excepting Nos. A, B, and C, included in the above prices.

RECEPTACLES FOR USE IN EARTH CLOSETS.
(Extra to all the foregoing Nos. 2851 to 2856).

No. 2858. PAIL.

Holds 12 charges, and is the most convenient size for carrying up and down stairs. It is fitted either with or without Cover, and is made to take out from either the front, back, or side. The Riser must be 1' 4" high.

Without Cover ... **7/6** each. With Cover ... **9/-** each.

No. 2859. W.O PAIL.

Holds 20 charges, and is fitted either with or without Cover. It is made to take out either from the front, back or side. The Riser must be 1' 7½" high with a 3½" Step.

13/6 each.

No. 2860. TANK.

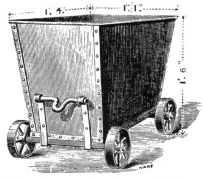

Made to be removed from the front of the Closet.

No. 2861. TANK.
Same size as No. 2860, but made to be removed from back of the Closet.

No. 2862. TANK.

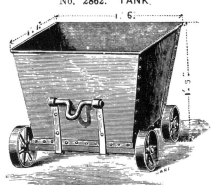

Made to be removed from side of Closet.
Nos. 2860 to 2862.

Without Wheels, holds 44 charges.	With Wheels, holds 36 charges.
33/- each.	**39/-** each.

The Riser must be 1' 10¾" high with a 6¾" step.

No. 2863. SELF-ACTING CINDER SIFTER.

Amongst the many advantages of this novel and ingenious invention the most noticeable is the almost entire

ABSENCE OF TROUBLE AND DIRT.

The arrangement of Sifters being self-acting, it is merely necessary to empty the cinders into the hopper, and as they descend they are entirely separated, the ashes passing into the top drawer and the cinders into the lower one.

45/- each.

Although designed for use in conjunction with the Earth Closet System, this Cinder Sifter will be found invaluable for any household.

STRATFORD, Walthamstow and Leytonstone.

No. E M 44   No. E M 45   No. E M 46   No. E M 47   No. E M 48

No. E M 49   No. E M 50

DINNERS

No. E M 51   No. E M 52   No. E M 59   No. E M 60   No. E M 61

No. E M 53   No. E M 54

No. E M 55   No. E M 56

No. E M 62

No. E M 63   No. E M 65   No. E M 67   No. E M 69   No. E M 71   No. E M 73

No. E M 64   No. E M 66   No. E M 68   No. E M 70   No. E M 72   No. E M 74

No. E M 57   No. E M 58

THE ABOVE WERE DESIGNED IN THE STUDIO OF YOUNG & MARTEN, LTD., STRATFORD.   PRICES ARE GIVEN ON PAGE 28.

STRATFORD, WALTHAMSTOW AND LEYTONSTONE.

YOUNG & MARTEN, LTD., NEW DESIGNS OF BRILLIANT-CUT GLASS.

No. B C 1 No. B C 2 No. B C 3 No. B C 4 No. B C 5 No. B C 6 No. B C 7

No. B C 8 No. B C 9 No. B C 10 No. B C 11

No. B C 12 No. B C 13 No. B C 14 No. B C 15 No. B C 16

No. B C 17 No. B C 18 No. B. C. 22 No. B C 23 No. B C 24

No. B C 19

No. B C 20 No. B C 21

THE ABOVE WERE DESIGNED IN THE STUDIO OF YOUNG & MARTEN, LTD., STRATFORD.   PRICES ARE GIVEN ON PAGE 28.

160

No. B C 25   No. B C 26   No. B C 27   No. B C 28   No. B C 29

No. B C 30   No. B C 31   No. B C 32

No. B C 33   No. B C 35   No. B C 36   No. B C 37   No. B C 38   No. B C 40   No. B C 39

THE RED LION

BAR

No. B C 41   No. B C 42   No. B C 43

WHISKIES

THE ABOVE WERE DESIGNED IN THE STUDIO OF YOUNG & MARTEN, LTD., STRATFORD.   PRICES ARE GIVEN ON PAGE 28.

161

ENAMELLED SHEET, FANCY AND COLORED GLASS.

ENAMELLED SHEET—Stock Patterns.

No. G455.

No G456.

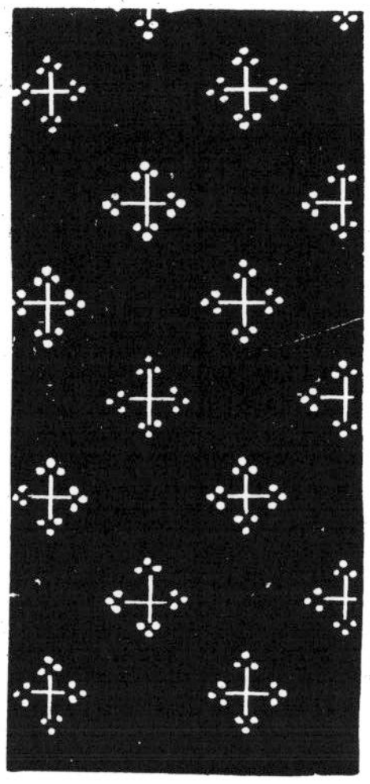

No. G457.

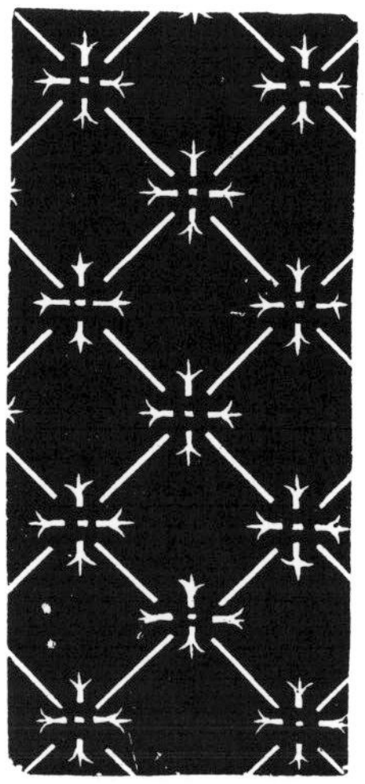

No. G458.

No. G459.

No. G460.

For Orders of 100 Feet and Over.

	Original Sheets.	Cut Sizes. Squares under 2 feet.	Squares under 5 feet.	Squares under 10 superficial feet.
Patterns Nos. G455 to G460— Enamelled, 15 oz.	-/3⅛	-/3⅛	-/3¾	-/4⅛ per foot
,, 21 oz.	-/3¾	-/3¾	-/5⅜	-/6 ,,

ENGRAVED GLASS FOR DOOR PANELS.

No. G451.

No. G452.

No. G453.

No. G454

Nos G451 to G454, with Border.

	21 oz.	26 oz.	32 oz.
Price, Glass included	1/0½	1/3	1/10½ per foot

We stock No. G452 without the border, which is always sent for this design unless specially ordered with border.
38 × 10 in., 40 × 11 in., 42 × 12 in., in 21-oz. Sheet.
Price .. .. 1/0½ per foot.

YOUNG & MARTEN, Merchants and Manufacturers,

WHOLESALE TRADE PRICES OF HEATING STOVES.

No. 813. IMPROVED SHOP STOVE.

Suitable for Heating Small Shops and Workrooms.

	Width.	Depth.	Height.	
No. 813 AA	7¼ in.	7¼ in.	12½ in.	4/3 each
,, 813 A	8½ in.	8½ in.	17½ in.	5/3 ,,
,, 813 B	9½ in.	9½ in.	19½ in.	7/3 ,,
,, 813 C	10½ in.	10½ in.	22½ in.	9/3 ,,
,, 813 D	11½ in.	11½ in.	23½ in.	11/3 ,,
,, 813 E	12½ in.	12½ in.	26 in.	13/3 ,,

The three largest sizes can be fitted with Brick linings at 1/6 each extra.

No. 808. THE "QUEEN" OFFICE STOVE.

The "QUEEN" pattern is a general favourite, and is highly commended for bedroom, office, shop or cabin, as, in addition to its use as a warming stove, it may be transformed into a Cooking Stove by simply removing the elegant ornamental top, which stands directly over the two fire covers. This stove is fitted with fire-brick lining, and the sliding doors in front assist in kindling or deadening the fire as required.

It is supplied with Cup-lifter and Poker.

Extreme Sizes.

No. 808 A, 17in. wide, 23½in. high, 12in. deep, 10/- ea.
,, 808 B, 18½ ,, 25 ,, 13 ,, 14/- ,,

Bottom Plate projects 5 inches.

No. 812. THE "ROSE" HALL STOVE

Registered Design.

This is an artistic design of a Warming Stove, well suited for Dining Halls, Schools or Offices.

	Height.	Depth.	Width.	
No. 812 A	25 in.	20 in.	18 in.	22/- each
,, 812 B	30 in.	25 in.	21 in.	28/- ,,
,, 812 C	35 in.	25 in.	25 in.	45/- ,,

No. 789. THE "ELEGANT" SLOW COMBUSTION HEATING STOVE.

Is of a very attractive and pleasing design.

VERY STRONG AND DURABLE.

REQUIRES VERY LITTLE ATTENTION, AND BURNS ALMOST EVERYTHING.

Most suitable for Halls, Schoolrooms, and Public Buildings.

	Height.	Diameter.	Heating Power.
No. 789 A ..	25 in. ..	10½ × 10½ in. ..	6,000 cubit feet
,, 789 B ..	32 in. ..	13 × 13 in. ..	12,000 ,,
,, 789 C ..	36 in. ..	15 × 15 in. ..	18,000 ,,

PRICES, INCLUDING IRON TRAYS.

No. 789 A ..	Blacked, 47/6 ..	Ground and Berlin Blacked, 62/6
,, 789 B ..	,, 65/- ..	,, ,, ,, 82/6
,, 789 C ..	,, 85/- ..	,, ,, ,, 102/6

No. 1838. THE "MELROSE" OPEN FIRE HEATING STOVE.

	Height.	Width.	Depth.
Extreme Measurements	44½	25¼	20½ in.

When with Fender add 7½ in. to depth.

Open Fire as shown, plain blacked	£4	0	0
Open Fire with Tile instead of top Panel in front	£4	2	6

If with plain Fender, 2/- less. If without Fender, 4/- less.

STRATFORD, Walthamstow and Leytonstone.

PORTABLE AND SELF-SETTING RANGES

THE "LARBERT" COOKING RANGE

No. 1770 The "Larbert," with Hot Closet.

HOT-PLATE,

27 ins. high × 17 ins. deep.

———

COMPACT AND PERFECT,

STRONG, SURE,

ECONOMICAL AND EFFICIENT.

———

The 42-inch size only fitted with two Hot Closets, as drawn to No. 1780; the others have a Closet, as shown to No. 1770.

No. 1780 The "Larbert," with Open and Close Fire and Hot Closets.

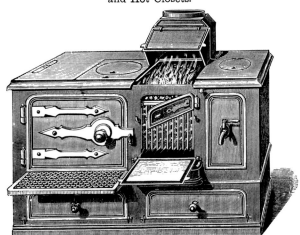

Sizes,	24 to 30	32 to 36	38 to 42 inches.
PRICES—Ranges with Hot Closet, extra to Prices of Nos. 1757 and 1758 (see preceding page),	12/	15/	18/ each.
„ „ „ Open and Close Fire,	4/6	5/3	6/ „ extra.

The 20-inch size cannot be supplied with either Hot Closet or Open Fire Hood.

THE "HOUSEHOLDER" PORTABLE COOKING RANGE

No. 2928—Oven and Boiler.

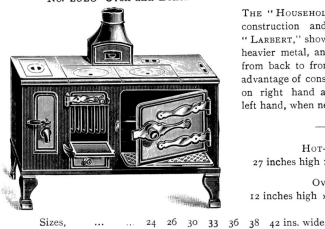

THE "HOUSEHOLDER" is similar in construction and action to the "LARBERT," shown above, but is of heavier metal, and hot-plate deeper from back to front; it has also the advantage of construction with oven on right hand as well as on the left hand, when needed.

———

HOT-PLATE,

27 inches high × 19 inches deep.

OVENS,

12 inches high × 13¾ inches deep.

No. 2929—Double Oven.

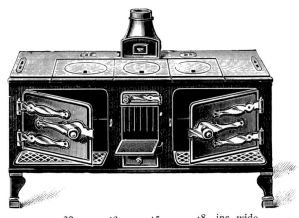

Sizes,	24	26	30	33	36	38	42 ins. wide.
Oven, Inside,	10	12	14	14	14	16	16 „ „
PRICES, No. 2927, Oven and Sham,	45/	48/	60/	63/	66/	72/	90/ each.
PRICES, No. 2928, Oven and Boiler,	—	63/	66/	75/	81/	102/	„

Sizes,	39	42	45	48 ins. wide.
Ovens, Inside,	10 & 10	12 & 10	14 & 10	14 & 12 „ „
PRICES, No. 2929, Double Ovens,	111/	120/	132/	141/ each.

Sizes,	24 to 30	33 to 36	38 to 48 inches wide.
PRICES—Ranges with Hot Closets, extra to Prices of Nos. 2927, 2928, and 2929,	12/	15/	18/ each.
„ „ „ Open and Close Fire,	4/6	5/3	6/ „ extra.
„ „ „ Skirtings fitted,	10/6	12/	15/ per set extra.

Smoke Pipe and Smoke Plate, for all sizes up to 36 inches, **3/9 per set**; above 36 inches, **4/6 per set.**

STRATFORD, E., WALTHAMSTOW, N.E., AND LEYTONSTONE, E., LONDON

PORTABLE AND SELF-SETTING RANGES

No. 1297 THE "DELIGHT" COOKING RANGE

With Hot Closet and Open and Close Fire.

THE

"DELIGHT"

IN THIS FORM HAS

THE ADVANTAGE

OF THE

HOT CLOSET,

WHICH IS

EQUIVALENT TO

ANOTHER OVEN.

(Reg. No. 64,477.)

SELF-SETTING

AND

COMPACT.

———

NO FLUES TO BUILD.

———

WILL ACT WELL

ANYWHERE.

———

WE GUARANTEE

EVERY "DELIGHT"

A SUCCESS.

Hot-plate, 27 inches high × 16 inches deep.

Sizes made,									24	26	28	30	32	34	36	38	42 inches wide.
Oven, Inside,									10	12	12	14	12	14	14	16	16 ,, ,,
PRICES—No. 1296, Oven and Sham, with Hot Closet,									57/	60/	64/6	69/	75/	78/	81/	99/	108/ each.

Sizes made,										28	30	32	34	36	38	42 inches wide.
Oven, Inside,										10	12	12	14	14	16	16 ,, ,,
PRICES—No. 1297, Oven and Boiler, with Hot Closet, as drawn,										72/	75/	81/	84/	90/	111/	120/ each.

Wrought Pressure Boiler for Bath, **54/ each extra** on Oven and Sham prices.

The "Delight" Range fitted with "Patent Raising Bottom Grate," **6/ each extra.**

Smoke Pipe and Smoke Plate for all sizes up to 36 inches, **3/9 per set**; above 36 inches, **4/6 per set.**

THE FOLLOWING ARE FROM MANY TESTIMONIALS WE HAVE RECEIVED :—

Mr. READ writes :—I am perfectly satisfied with the 36-inch Open and Close Fire "Delight" Kitchener in every way. It fulfils its duty better than any Kitchener that has ever come under my notice, and I should be glad to show it in use to anyone who wished for a perfect stove.

Mr. WIRE writes :—Having used the "Delight" Range for many years, I have had many more than one hundred fixed in different places with the utmost satisfaction. Many of my tenants having them in use where the chimney has smoked, have also testified they are a "Delight" indeed.

STRATFORD, E., WALTHAMSTOW, N.E., AND LEYTONSTONE, E., LONDON

YOUNG & MARTEN, Ltd., Merchants and Manufacturers,

THE "CROWN" PORTABLE GAS-HEATED WASHING COPPERS.

Outer case galvanized sheet steel, fitted with well-tinned copper pan and improved atmospheric burner and tap, complete with all the necessary piping, elbows, and hood for conducting waste steam and gas fumes.

No. 6/31	10 gallons	12	14	16	18	20 gallons
	40/-	45/-	50/-	56/-	64/-	72/- each

Brass Draw-off Cock from 5/- extra

"ATLANTIC" TUBING.

No. F5962. — Warranted Gas-tight, with ⅜-inch Brass Couplings.

Stock Colors—Green or Maroon.

PRICE.

In lengths of 4 to 12 feet .. 6d. per ft.
100 feet boxes .. .. 5¼d. ,,
2-feet and 3-feet lengths are charged as 4 feet.

THE NEW PATENT RUBBER END TUBING.

No. F5961.—Similar to Atlantic Tubing, but with Flexible Rubber Ends, making an instantaneous Gas-tight joint.

In lengths of 4 feet to 12 eet .. .. 5¼d. per oot
100 feet boxes .. .. 4½d. ,,

THE "SYPHON" CLARK'S PATENT HYGIENIC GAS-HEATING STOVES.

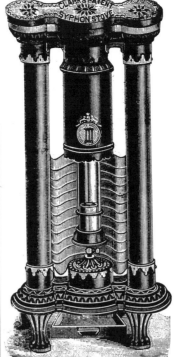

No. 5/6785

PRICE £5 0 0
,, with Polished } Copper Columns } 5 7 6

DIMENSIONS.

Height .. .. 42 inches
Width .. .. 21 ,,
Depth .. .. 14 ,,

For Heating and Lighting. Consumes 10 feet of Gas per hour when full on. Suitable for Entrance Halls, Conservatories, Large Rooms, Shops, or Space 16 by 16 feet.

No. 2/6786

PRICE £3 15 0
,, with Polished } Copper Columns } 4 0 0

DIMENSIONS.—Height, 40 inches Width, 18 inches; Depth, 12 inches.
For Heating and Lighting. Consumes 8 feet of Gas per hour when full on. Suitable for Halls, Conservatories, Shops, Bedrooms, or Space 14 by 14 feet.

No. 8/6787

Smaller size than No. 2/6786

PRICE £2 15 0
,, with Polished } Copper Columns } 3 0 0

DIMENSIONS.—Height, 33 inches; Width, 15 inches; Depth, 10 inches.
For Heating and Lighting. Consumes 6 feet of Gas per hour when full on. Suitable for Apartments 12 by 12 feet.

No. 1/6788

PRICE £1 18 0
with Polished } Copper Column } 2 3 0

DIMENSIONS.

Height .. .. 33 inches
Width .. .. 10½ ,,
Depth .. .. 10½ ,,

For Heating and Lighting. Consumes 6 feet of Gas per hour when full on. Suitable for Offices, Landings, Passages, Small Conservatories, or Space 10 by 10 feet.

THE "LEEDS" PATENT FLOOR WARMING GAS STOVES.

The consumption of gas by these Stoves is extremely moderate. A three or our-tile Stove, with five burners, will use from 12 to 14 feet per hour, which, with gas at 3/- per 1000 feet, amounts to a cost of only about 5d. per day ot 10 hours' constant burning, or say ½d. per hour.

Gas connection can be made rom either side. Rich tinted and jewelled glass in canopies.

They are now made in three sizes and styles as noted below.

No. 6803 Four-tile Stove.

No.	Sizes.	Dimensions over all.			Heating Capacity.	PRICES, Fine Cast and Stove Blacked.	PRICES, Ground and Berlin Blacked.
		Width.	Height.	Depth.			
6801	Two-tile Stove	16½ ins.	24 ins.	12 ins.	Two-tile for Room 15 ft. square	51/- each	60/- each
6802	Three-tile ,,	22½ ,,	27 ,,	16½ ,,	Three-tile ,, 18 ,,	78/- ,,	87/- ,,
6803	Four-tile ,,	28½ ,,	27 ,,	16½ ,,	Four-tile ,, 21 ,,	105/- ,,	114/- ,,

---

STRATFORD, Walthamstow and Leytonstone.

YOUNG & MARTEN, Ltd., Merchants and Manufacturers,

COPPERS, COPPER FITTINGS, PORTABLE WASHING COPPERS & MISCELLANEOUS CASTINGS.

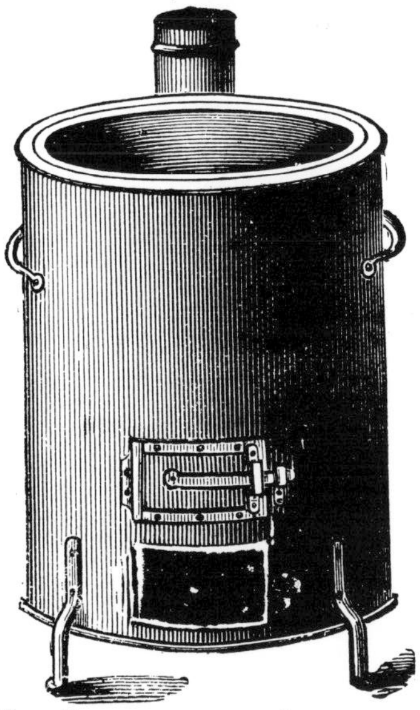

No. C1025.

PORTABLE COPPER.

Wrought Iron

Casing and Furnace Pan,

with Elbow

and 2-ft. Flue Pipe.

Capacity	6	8	10	12	16	20	25 gallons.
With Galvanized Pan	23/3	27/9	31/10½	37/10½	48/-	60/-	72/- each.
With Copper Pan	33/9	41/3	48/9	58/7½	75/-	93/9	114/9 ,,

No. C1024.

THE "HOUSEHOLD" Portable Copper.

For Restaurant and Domestic Uses.

No Feet to get Broken off.

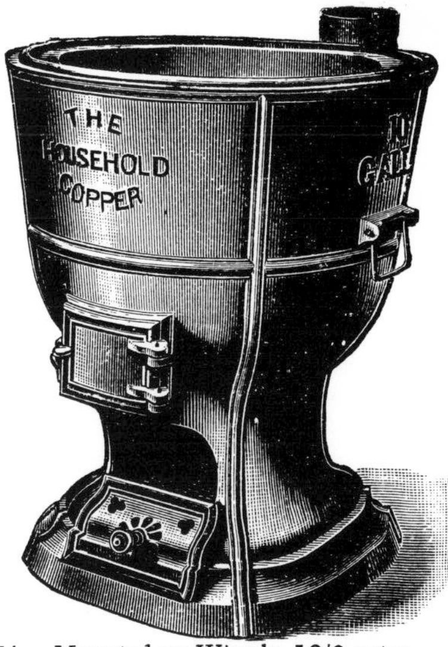

	galls. imp. measure.			
Size to hold	8	10	12	14
With Galvanized Pan ..	43/6	48/-	54/-	63/-

	galls. imp. measure.			
Size to hold	16	18	20	25
With Galvanized Pan ..	67/6	72/-	78/9	86/3

With Copper Pan, 10 gallons, 81/- Mounted on Wheels, 18/9 extra

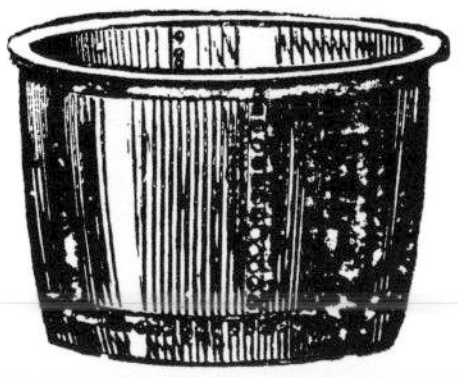

No. C1161. **WASHING COPPERS.**

6 to 200 gallons .. .. .. 1/6 per lb.

Average weight, 1 lb. 8 oz. per gallon.

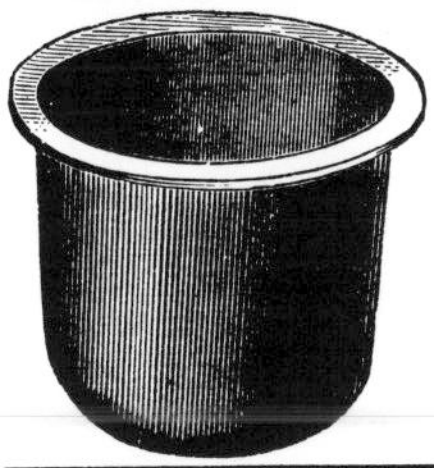

No. C1163.

STRONG GALVANIZED FURNACE PANS.

6 to 12 gallons	..	7½d. per gallon
14 to 20 ,,	..	8¼d. ,,
25 to 40 ,,	..	10½d. ,,
45 to 100 ,,	..	1/1½ ,,

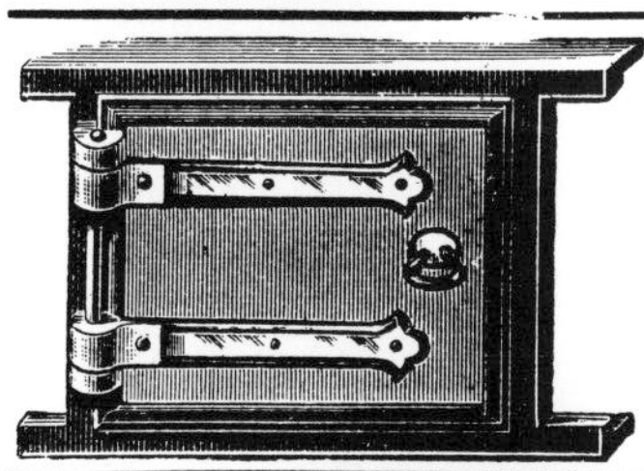

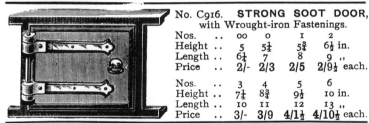

No. C916. **STRONG SOOT DOOR,** with Wrought-iron Fastenings.

Nos. ..	00	0	1	2	
Height ..	5	5¼	5¾	6½	in.
Length ..	6¼	7	8	9	,,
Price ..	2/-	2/3	2/5	2/9½	each.
Nos. ..	3	4	5	6	
Height ..	7¼	8¾	9½	10	in.
Length ..	10	11	12	13	,,
Price ..	3/-	3/9	4/1½	4/10½	each.

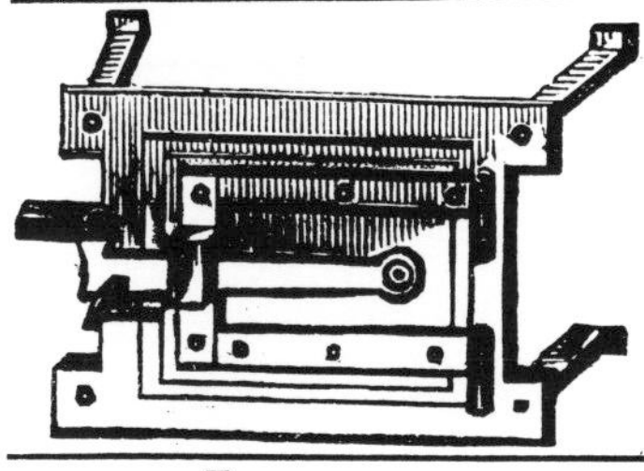

No. C1164.

COPPER DOOR AND FRAME.

Size Nos. ..	1	2	3	
Ordinary ..	1/-	1/3	2/0¾	each.
Medium ..	1/6	2/3	3/-	,,
Heavy ..	3/-	4/1½	4/6	
Size Nos. ..	4	5	6	
Ordinary ..	2/9¾	—	—	each.
Medium ..	4/6	—	—	,,
Heavy ..	6/-	8/3	9/-	,,

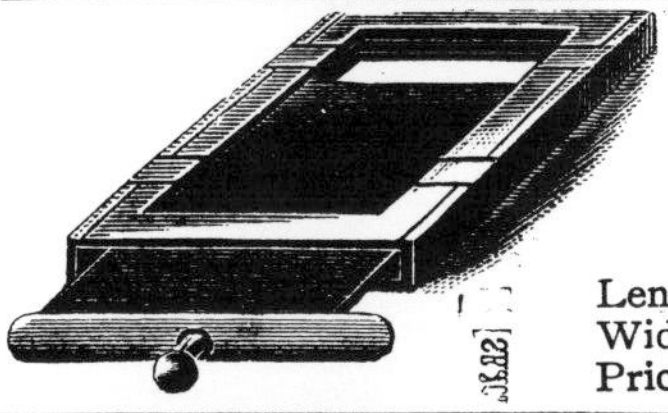

No. C925.

DAMPERS AND FRAMES.

Length	6	7¼	8¼	9½	11	12½	14½	in.
Width	5	6¼	7	8	9	10	11½	,,
Price	11¼d.	1/3	1/8¼	2/0¾	2/5¼	2/9¾	4/1½	ea.

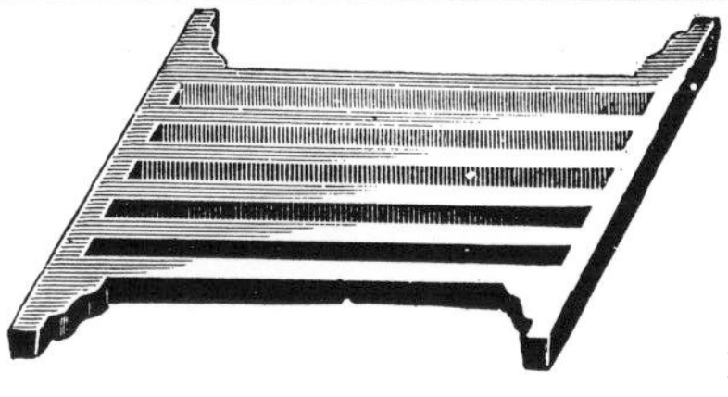

No. C1165. **COPPER GRATES.**

Size Nos.	1	2	3	
Ordinary	-/6¾	-/11¼	1/1½	each.
Heavy	1/1½	1/6	1/10½	,,
Bearing Bars	-/4½	-/6	-/9	,,
Nos.	4	5	6	
Ordinary	1/6	—	—	each
Heavy	2/7½	3/9	4/6	,,
Bearing Bars	1/-	1/3	2/-	p. pair.

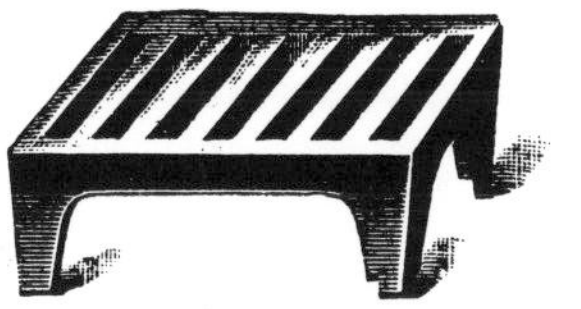

No. C1158. **FALSE BOTTOMS.**

6×4 in.	7×5 in.	8×6 in.	9×5 in.	10×6 in.
9d.	1/-	1/6	1/6	1/10½ each

And any size 6 to 10 ins. long by 4 to 7 ins. wide

Small quantities, 3d. per lb. Quantities of 1 cwt. and upwards, 12/9 per cwt.

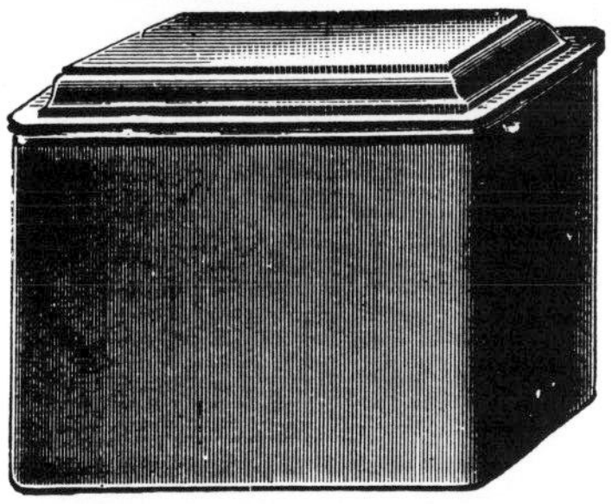

No. C920.

SUPPLY CISTERN & COVER.

Length	12	13	15	18 inches
Width	6	7	8	8½ ,,
Depth	10	10	10½	11½ ,,
Price	4/3	5/3	7/3	9/9 each

No. C1128. **AIR GRATINGS.**

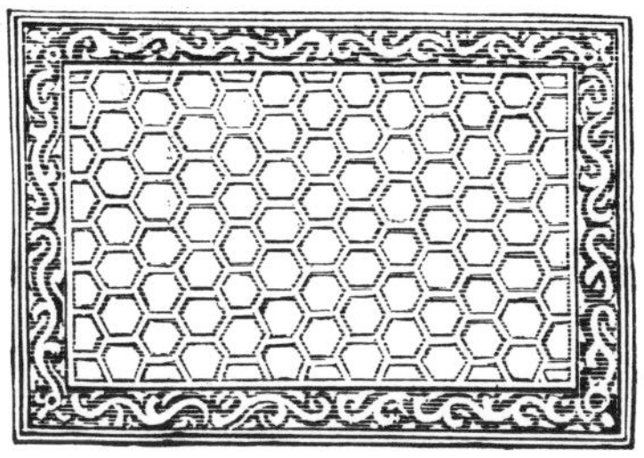

9 × 6 in.	..	9d. each
12 × 6 ,,	..	1/1½ ,,
9 × 9 ,,	..	1/3[illegible] ,,
12 × 9 ,,	..	1/4½ ,,
12 × 12 ,,	..	2/3 ,,
15 × 12 ,,	..	2/3 ,,
15 × 15 ,,	..	2/9 ,,
24 × 12 ,,	..	3/9 ,,
18 × 18 ,,	..	3/9 ,,
24 × 18 ,,	..	5/3 ,,
36 × 9½ ,,	..	4/1½ ,,

We can make this design to any size and thickness. When made ¾ in. thick it is suitable for an Area Grating for light wear.

No. C1134. **VENTILATORS or STEP RISERS.**

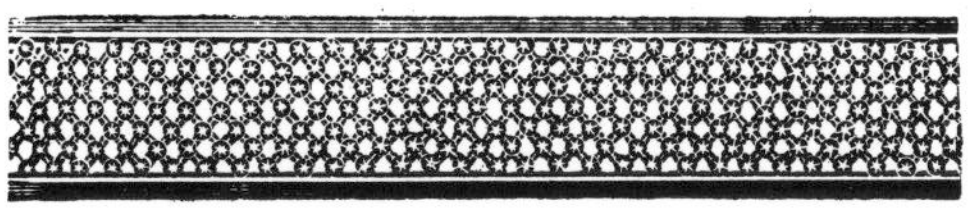

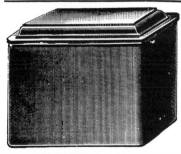

Stock Sizes.

24 to 54 inches long by 3 to 6 inches wide.

3	3½	4	4½	5	6 inches wide.
4½d.	5¼d.	6d.	6¾d.	7½d.	9d. per foot run.

STRATFORD, Walthamstow and Leytonstone.

CAST-IRON LAMP PILLARS

Painted One Coat.

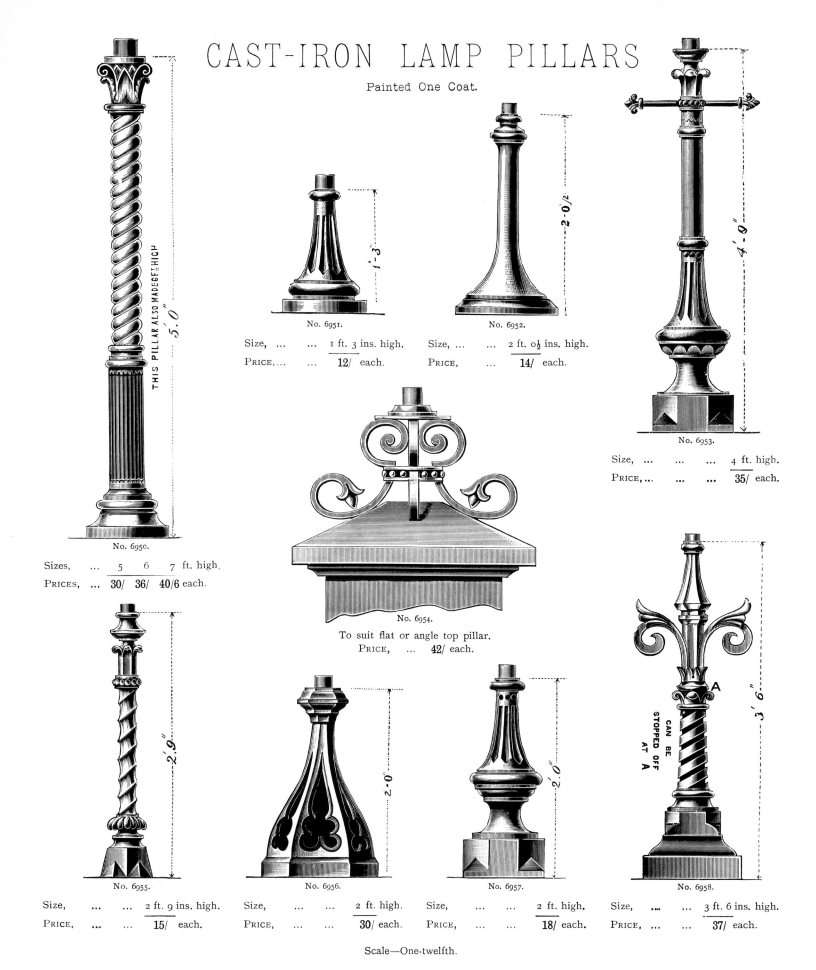

THIS PILLAR ALSO MADE 6 FT. HIGH

5' 0"

No. 6950.

| Sizes, | ... | 5 | 6 | 7 | ft. high. |
| Prices, | ... | 30/ | 36/ | 40/6 | each. |

1'-3"

No. 6951.

| Size, | ... | ... | 1 ft. 3 ins. high. |
| Price, | ... | ... | 12/ each. |

2'-0½"

No. 6952.

| Size, | ... | ... | 2 ft. 0½ ins. high. |
| Price, | ... | ... | 14/ each. |

4'-0"

No. 6953.

| Size, | ... | ... | ... | 4 ft. high. |
| Price, | ... | ... | ... | 35/ each. |

No. 6954.

To suit flat or angle top pillar.
Price, ... 42/ each.

2'.9"

No. 6955.

| Size, | ... | ... | 2 ft. 9 ins. high. |
| Price, | ... | ... | 15/ each. |

2'-0"

No. 6956.

| Size, | ... | ... | 2 ft. high. |
| Price, | ... | ... | 30/ each. |

2'.0"

No. 6957.

| Size, | ... | ... | 2 ft. high. |
| Price, | ... | ... | 18/ each. |

CAN BE STOPPED OFF AT A

A

3'.6"

No. 6958.

| Size, | ... | ... | 3 ft. 6 ins. high. |
| Price, | ... | ... | 37/ each. |

Scale—One-twelfth.

CAST-IRON LAMP PILLARS

Painted One Coat.

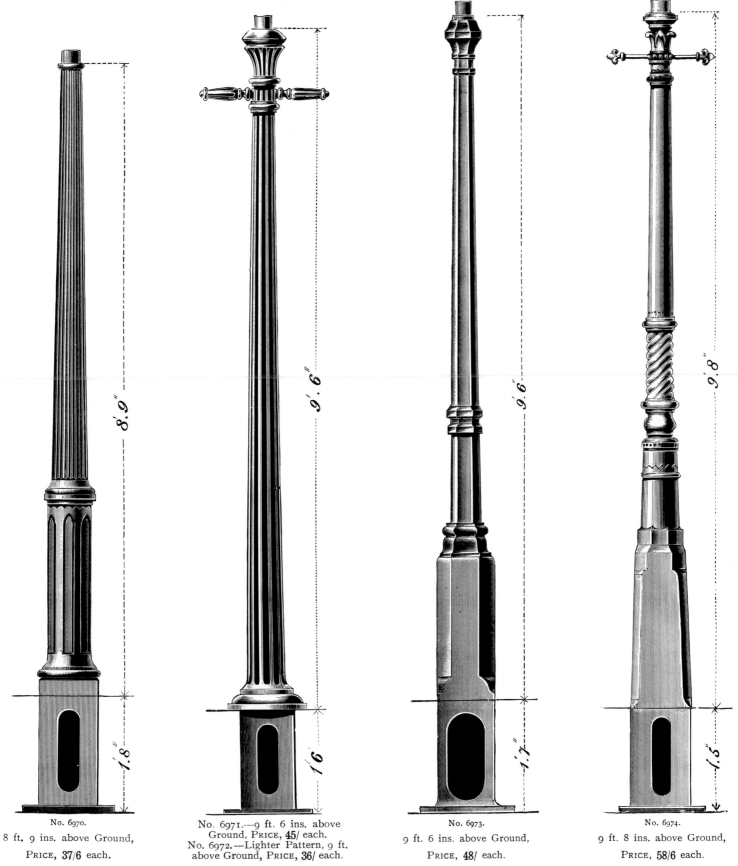

No. 6970.
8 ft. 9 ins. above Ground,
PRICE, 37/6 each.

No. 6971.—9 ft. 6 ins. above
Ground, PRICE, 45/ each.
No. 6972.—Lighter Pattern, 9 ft.
above Ground, PRICE, 36/ each.

No. 6973.
9 ft. 6 ins. above Ground,
PRICE, 48/ each.

No. 6974.
9 ft. 8 ins. above Ground,
PRICE, 58/6 each.

Scale—¾ in. = 1 ft.   **Special prices quoted for large quantities.**

STRATFORD, E., WALTHAMSTOW, N.E., AND LEYTONSTONE, E. LONDON

CAST-IRON LAMP PILLARS

Painted One Coat.

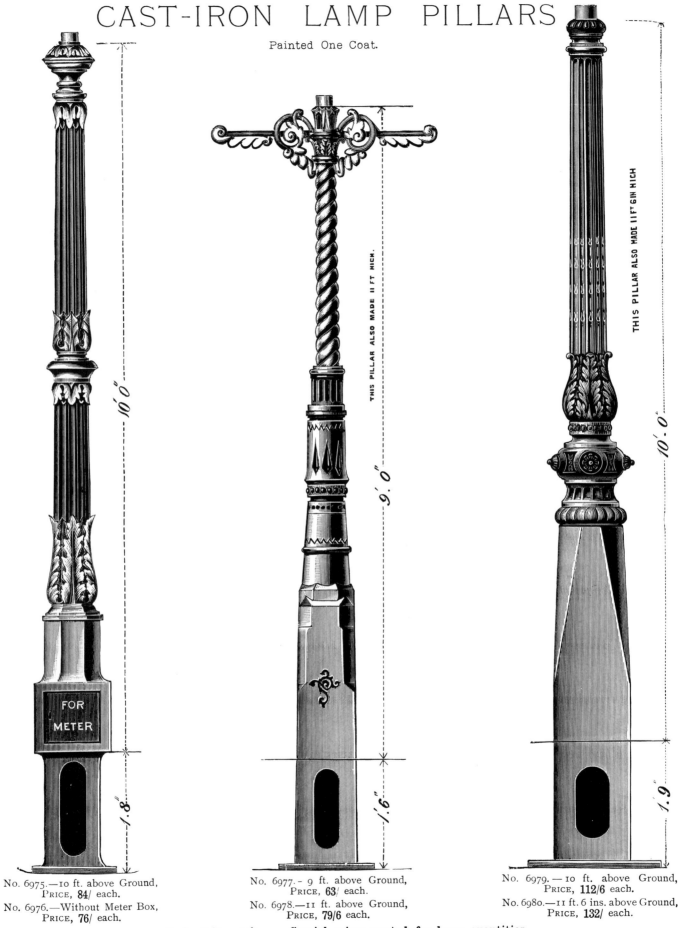

THIS PILLAR ALSO MADE 11 FT HIGH.

THIS PILLAR ALSO MADE 11 FT 6 IN HIGH

FOR METER

No. 6975.—10 ft. above Ground, PRICE, **84/** each.

No. 6976.—Without Meter Box, PRICE, **76/** each.

No. 6977.— 9 ft. above Ground, PRICE, **63/** each.

No. 6978.—11 ft. above Ground, PRICE, **79/6** each.

No. 6979.— 10 ft. above Ground, PRICE, **112/6** each.

No. 6980.—11 ft. 6 ins. above Ground, PRICE, **132/** each.

Scale—¾ in. = 1 ft.   **Special prices quoted for large quantities.**

STRATFORD, E., WALTHAMSTOW, N.E., AND LEYTONSTONE, E., LONDON

WROUGHT AND CAST IRON LAMP BRACKETS

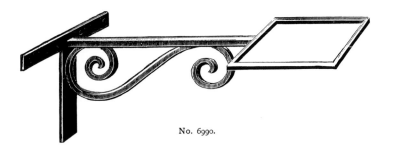

No. 6990.

Wrought Bracket, with Frame to carry 14-in. Lamp.
PRICE, ... **12/9 each.**

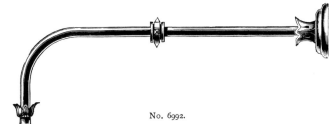

No. 6992.

| 1-in. Tube, | ... | ... | ... | PRICE, **10/6** each. |
| 1¼-in. ,, | ... | ... | ... | ,, **12/6** ,, |

No. 6991.

Wrought-iron Cradle, to Carry 14-in. Lamp.
PRICE, ... **8/3 each.**

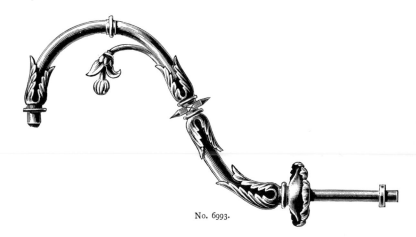

No. 6993.

| 1¼-in. Tube, 3 ft. 6 in. Projection, | ... | PRICE, **25/6** each. |
| 1½-in. ,, 4 ,, 0 ,, ,, | ... | ,, **39/** ,, |

LAMP-LIGHTER'S SPIRIT TORCH

No. 6037.

Brass, with Copper Lining, ... PRICE, **9/** each.

No. 6994.

| 1-in. Tube, | ... | ... | ... | ... | PRICE, **28/6** each. |
| 1¼-in. ,, | ... | ... | ... | ... | ,, **33/** ,, |

When ordering Lamp Brackets, please give thickness of wall for length of bolt, projection from fixing point to centre of Lamp, and height between fixing point and pavement.

YOUNG & MARTEN, Ltd., Merchants and Manufacturers,

PATENT COAL PLATE, PAVEMENT LIGHTS,
AND PAVEMENT GUTTERS

YOUNG & MARTEN'S PATENT AUTOMATIC-LOCKING COAL PLATE

Design No. C 7101.   Patent No. 13403.

Complete, as when fixed.

Design No. C 7101.   Patent No. 13403.

SECTION.
Showing Stud and Automatic Grip in position,
ready to close and lock.

— ADVANTAGES. —

SELF-LOCKING.

BURGLAR PROOF.

NON-SLIPPING.

CANNOT BE OPENED FROM OUTSIDE.

STRONGLY MADE.

Design No. C 7101.   Patent No 13403.

SECTION.
Showing Automatic Grip near Locking Point.

Design No. C 7101.   Patent No. 13403.

SECTION.
Showing Automatic Grip and Eccentric Overbalance
of Weight, securely locked.

Size of Plate, 12 inches diameter; over rim, 14 inches diameter.   PRICE, including Plate, Rim, Locking Gear, and Chain, 5/3 per set.

EXPLANATORY.—It will be seen from illustration showing the section that on flange at one side of plate is a stout lug cast on, which fits into slot in rim. At other side is locking lever, hung from underside of plate, having an easy movement—one which, as plate is lowered to its position in rim by its own eccentric weight, automatically grips the under portion of outer rim, and thus the plate is secured to the latter **by an immovable Lock and Bolt.** To open or release plate, a chain is provided, accessible from *inside* only ; a slight pull detaches the grip, and the Coal Plate itself can then be raised from *inside*.

NOTE.—This Patent Coal Plate is offered to the public as a means of relieving householders and owners of property from responsibilities arising from the removal of an ordinary lift-off coal plate, either by children or unauthorised persons.   By the use of this Patent Plate accidents are avoided, also possible litigation necessarily following.   The invention being within the legal regulation, according to Act of Parliament, whereby a heavy penalty can be enforced: "*If any occupier or occupiers do or shall leave open, or not sufficiently or substantially cover or keep covered and* SECURED, *to the satisfaction of the local authorities, any coal plate.*"

PAVEMENT LIGHTS

No. C 7102 Pavement Light.

No. C 7103
Convex Lens.

No. C 7104.
Semi-prism Lens.

A valuable method of utilizing cellar room as offices, workshops, &c., without the use of gas.   We have patterns for the following over-all sizes :—

LENGTHS.
1 ft. 1¼ ins., 1 ft. 5¾ ins., 1 ft. 10½ ins., 2 ft. 2¾ ins., 2 ft. 7¼ ins., 2 ft. 11¾ ins., 3 ft. 4¼ ins., 3 ft. 8¾ ins., 4 ft. 1¼ ins., 4 ft. 5¾ ins., 4 ft. 10¼ ins., 5 ft. 2¾ ins.,
5 ft. 7¼ ins., 6 ft. 6 ins., 6 ft. 4¼ ins.

WIDTHS.
11 ins., 1 ft. 2¾ ins., 1 ft. 6¼ ins., 1 ft. 9¾ ins., 2 ft. 1¼ ins., 2 ft. 4¾ ins., 2 ft. 8¼ ins., 2 ft. 11¾ ins., 3 ft. 3¼ ins., 3 ft. 6¾ ins., 3 ft. 10¼ ins., 4 ft. 1¾ ins., 4 ft. 5¼ ins.
NOTE.—Either of the lengths enumerated can be worked in conjunction with either of the widths stated.

PRICES.—Pavement Light, glazed with ¾-inch thick Rough Cast Plate, at **4/6** per foot super. (then called No. C 7105).
  ,,   Ditto, ditto, No. C 7103 Convex Lenses, at **7/6** per foot super. (then called No. C 7106).
  ,,   Ditto, ditto, No. C 7103 Convex Lenses, alternately with No. C 7104 Semi-prism Lenses, **10/6** per foot super. (then called No. C 7107).
  ,,   No. C 7103 Convex Lenses, 4 × 3 ins., **5¼d.** each.   No. C 7104 Semi-prism Lenses, 4 × 3 ins., **10½d.** each.

No. C 4032 PAVEMENT GUTTERS

PRICE, in 6 feet lengths, **2/1½** per foot ; in 2, 3 & 4 feet lengths, **2/3** per foot.

End Pieces, with Inlets for Round Rain-water Pipe, 3 to 6 in. diameter, **3/9** each.

End Pieces, with Inlets for Square or Rectangular Pipe, **4/6** each.

STRATFORD, Walthamstow and Leytonstone.

YOUNG & MARTEN, Ltd., Merchants and Manufacturers,

GATES AND RAILINGS.

No. C1092. GATE AND RAILING—"BUTTERFLY" PATTERN.

Railing Metal, unfitted .. .. 13/6 per cwt.

9-in. Iron Coping { V Pattern .. 1/3 per foot. / O G " .. 1/6 "

Wrought Horizontal Bars .. 12/- per cwt.

SPECIAL.

Price for Castings fitted ready for erection for a house of 16 ft. frontage:—

Gate, 34 in. × 48 in., fitted with Lock or Latch, Clip, Bearer and pair of Standards with Braces..	£1 4 0
Panels and Wrought Bars	0 15 0
Without Coping, per set	£1 19 0
As above, but with 9 in. V Coping, per set	£2 14 0

	Panelling	Panelling and Coping.
Extra beyond 16 ft. frontage	1/3 per ft.	2/6 per ft.

No. C1107. GATE AND RAILING—"STRING RING" PATTERN.

Railing Metal, unfitted .. 14/- per cwt.

9-in. Iron Coping { V Pattern 1/3 per ft. / O G " 1/6 "

Wrought Horizontal Bars 12/- per cwt.

SPECIAL.

Price for Castings, fitted ready for erection, for a house of 16 ft. frontage :—

Gate 34 in. × 46 in., fitted with Lock or Latch, Clip, Bearer and pair of Standards with Braces	£1 4 0
Panels and Wrought Bars ..	1 1 0
Without Coping, per set ..	£2 5 0
As above, but with 9 in. V Coping, per set	£3 0 0

	Panelling.	Panelling and Coping.
Extra beyond 16 ft. frontage	1/9 per ft.	3/- per ft.

No. C1280. "QUEEN ANNE" VILLA GATE AND RAILING.

Railing Metal, unfitted .. .. 15/9 per cwt.

9-in. O G. Iron Coping .. .. 1/6 per foot.

SPECIAL.

Price for Castings, fitted ready for erection, for a house of 16 ft. frontage :—

Gate 38 in. × 47 in., fitted with Lock, Clip, Bearer and pair of Standards with Braces	£2 3 6
Panelling 22 in. high..	1 16 0
Without Coping, per set	£3 19 6
As above, with 9 in. O G Coping ..	£4 17 6

	Panelling	Panelling and Coping.
Extra beyond 16 ft. frontage..	3/- per ft.	4/6 per ft.

NOTE.—We can supply any Gate shown, fitted with Latch in place of Lock, at same rates. The Latch is strongly recommended, as it is not affected by the weather.

STRATFORD, Walthamstow and Leytonstone.

YOUNG & MARTEN, Ltd., Merchants and Manufacturers,
GATES AND RAILINGS.

No. C1555.

"WOLSELEY" GATE AND RAILING.

SPECIAL.

Price or Castings, fitted ready for erection for a house of 16 ft. frontage :—

Gate, fitted with Latch, pair Standards and Braces, fitted with Hanging Clip and Bearer	£1 10 0
Panelling, 29 in. high	£1 12 6
Per set, without Coping	£3 2 6
As above, but including 9 in. O.G Coping ..	£4 1 6

	Panelling Per ft.	Panelling and Coping. Per ft.
Extra beyond 16 ft. frontage ..	2/6	4/-

No. C3962.

GATE AND RAILING.

REGISTERED DESIGN, No. 275307.

THE "SUBURBAN" PATTERN.

New Design.

SPECIAL.

Price for Castings, fitted ready for erection for a house of 16 ft. frontage :—

Gate, 33 in. × 52½ in. high, fitted with Latch and Gothic Knobs, pair Standards and Braces, fitted with Hanging Clip and Bearer	£1 16 0
Panelling, 26 in. high	£1 4 0
Per set, without Coping	£3 0 0
The same, but including 9 in. O.G. Coping	£3 18 0

	Panelling. Per ft.	Panelling and Coping Per ft.
Extra beyond 16 ft. frontage	2/-	3/6

No. C4271.

GATE AND RAILING.

Registered Design, No. 336,859

THE "MARYLAND" PATTERN.

SPECIAL.

Price for Castings fitted ready for erection for a house of 16 ft. frontage :—

Gate, 36 in. wide by 51 in. high, fitted with Latch, Clip, Bearer, and pair of Standards with Braces	£1 7 6
Panelling, 29 in. high	£1 1 0
Without Coping, per set..	£2 8 6
As above, but with 9 in. O.G. Coping, per set ..	£3 8 6

	Panelling. Per ft.	Panelling and Coping. Per ft.
Extra beyond 16 ft. frontage	1/9	3/5

STRATFORD, Walthamstow and Leytonstone.

No. C4187.

"Easton" Gate and Railing.

Price for Castings fitted ready for erection for a house of 16 ft. frontage :—

Gate, 38 in. × 44 in., fitted with Latch and Furniture and Hanging Clip, pair of Standards and Braces	£1 7 6	
Panelling, 18 in. high	1 6 6	
Without Coping, per set	2 14 0	
As above, but with 9 in. Iron V Coping	3 12 0	

	Panelling, per foot.	Panelling and Coping, per foot.
Extra beyond 16 ft. frontage	2/7	3/6

No. C2000.

Gate and Railing.

Price for Castings fitted ready for erection for a house of 16 ft. frontage :—

Gate 31 in. × 36 in., fitted with Latch, Clip, Bearer, and pair of Standards with Braces ..	£1 19 0	
Panelling, 23½ in. high	1 8 6	
Without Coping, per set ..	3 7 6	
As above, but with 9 in. Coping, per set ..	4 5 6	

	Panelling. Per ft.	Panelling and Coping. Per ft.
Extra beyond 16 ft. frontage	2/4½	3/10½

No. C1097.

Close Pattern Gate & Railing

Price for Castings fitted ready for erection for a house of 16 ft. frontage :—

Gate, 34 in. × 48½ in., fitted with Lock, Clip, Bearer, and pair of Standards with Braces ..	£1 17 6	
Panelling, 30 in. high	1 14 6	
Without Coping, per set	3 12 0	
As above, but with 9 in. Coping, per set ..	4 11 6	

	Panelling Per ft.	Panelling and Coping Per ft.
Extra beyond 16 ft. frontage	2/9	4/3

GATES AND RAILINGS.

No. C1170. "QUEEN ANNE" GATE AND RAILING. Registered Design.

Price for Castings fitted ready for erection for a house of 16 ft. frontage:—

Gate, 36¾ in. × 51¼ in., fitted with Lock, Clip, Bearer, and pair of Standards with Braces .. £2 9 6

Panelling, 22 in. high 1 7 0

Without Coping, per set .. 3 16 6

As above, but with 9 in. O.G. Coping, per set 4 14 6

	Panelling. Per ft.	Panelling and Coping Per ft.
Extra beyond 16 ft. frontage ..	2/3	3/9

No. C1028. "NELSON," PATTERN.

PRICE for Castings fitted ready for erection for a house of 16 feet frontage—

Gate, 38½ × 57 ins., fitted with Lock, Clip, Bearer, and pair of Standards with Braces.. £2 1 3

Panelling, 27 ins. high 1 17 6

Without Coping, per set 3 18 9

As above, but with 9 in. O.G. Coping, per set 4 17 6

Extra beyond 16 feet frontage—

Panelling .. .. 3/- per ft.

" and Coping .. .. 4/6 "

No. C1093. No. C1094.

No. C1093 and No. C1094

"ARCH" PATTERN GATE & RAILING.

Price for Castings, fitted ready for erection for a house of 16 ft. frontage :—

Gate, 31 in. × 46 in. fitted with Lock, Clip, Bearer and pair of Standards with Braces .. .. } £1 16 0

Panelling 30 in. high 1 10 0

With Coping, per set 3 6 0

The same with 9 in O.G. Coping ,, 4 5 6

	Panelling.	Panelling and Coping
	2/3 per ft.	3/9 per ft.
No. C1093..	4/6 ,,	6/- ,,

STRATFORD, Walthamstow and Leytonstone.

No. C3762 (Registered Design).   2 ft. 2 in. high.

Price for Castings, fitted ready for erection, for a house of 16 ft. frontage :—

Gate, 35½ in. × 50 in., fitted with Lock, Clip, Bearer and pair of Standards and Braces £2 8 0

Panelling 26 in. high.. .. .. .. 1 16 0

Without Coping, per set £4 4 0

As above, but with 9 in. O G Coping per set £5 3 6

	Panelling.	Panelling and Coping.
Extra beyond 16 ft. frontage,	2/10½ per ft.	4/4½ per ft.

No. C3763 (Registered Design).   1 ft. 10 in. high.

Price for Castings, fitted ready for erection, for a house of 16 ft. frontage :—

Gate, 37 in. × 60 in., fitted with Lock, Clip, Bearer and pair of Standards with Braces £3 3 0

Panelling 22 in. high.. .. .. .. 2 2 0

Without Coping, per set £5 5 0

As above, but with 9 in. O G Coping, per set £6 4 6

	Panelling	Panelling and Coping.
Extra beyond 16 ft. frontage..	3/4½ per ft.	4/10½ per ft.

Extra if with 2 Pilasters as shewn instead of Standards 27/- per gate set.

No C3764 (Registered Design).   2 ft. 6 in. high

Price for Castings, fitted ready for erection, for a house of 16 ft. frontage :—

Gate, 33 in. × 54 in., fitted with Lock, Clip, Bearer and pair of heavy Pillars as shewn .. £3 18 0

Panelling 30 in. high 2 2 0

Without Coping, per set £6 0 0

As above, but with 9 in. O G Coping, per set .. £6 19 6

	Panelling.	Panelling and Coping.
Extra beyond 16 ft. frontage ..	3/4½ per ft.	4/10½ per ft.

CUTTING AND LAYING RAILINGS TO PLAN 10 °/o EXTRA.

STRATFORD, Walthamstow and Leytonstone.

YOUNG & MARTEN, Ltd., Merchants and Manufacturers,
GATES AND RAILINGS.
BETTER CLASS.

No. C1176. **HEAVY PATTERN "VILLA" GATE AND RAILING.** Registered Design.

SPECIAL.

Price for Castings fitted ready for erection for a house of 20 ft. frontage :—

	£		
Gate, 38 in. × 55 in., fitted with Lock, Clip, Bearer and pair of Standards with Braces	£3	16	6
Panelling, 36 in. high	4	8	0
Without Coping, per set ..	8	4	6
As above, but with 9 in. Coping, per set	9	12	6

	Panelling. Per ft.	Panelling. and Coping. Per ft.
Extra beyond 20 ft frontage	5/6	7/-

Carriage Entrance Gates to suit this design, 8 ft. 4¼ ins. wide opening.

Price .. £15 0 0 per pair. No Pillars.

No. C3342. **"BLENHEIM" PATTERN.**

Price for Castings fitted ready for erection for a house of 16 ft. frontage :—

	£		
Gate 42 × 60 in., fitted with Lock, Clip, Bearer, and pair of Standards with Braces	£3	18	0
Panelling, 30 in. high	2	8	0
Without Coping, per set	£6	6	0
As above, but with 9-in. O.G. Coping, per set	7	7	0

Extra beyond 16 ft. frontage :—

Panelling	4/- per ft.
,, and Coping	5/9 ,,

SIZES TO WHICH WALLS MAY BE BUILT.

No.	Height of Wall from Step to Top of Coping.		Width of Gate Space for Gate and two Standards.		Width of Gate Space for two Gates, two Standards, and Double-hanging Pilaster.		Width of Gate Space for Gate and two Pilasters.		No.	Height of Wall from Step to Top of Coping.		Width of Gate Space for Gate and two Standards.		Width of Gate Space for two Gates, two Standards, and Double-hanging Pilasters.		Width of Gate Space for Gate and two Pilasters.	
	Ft.	Ins.	Ft.	Ins.	Ft.	Ins.	Ft.	Ins.		Ft.	Ins.	Ft.	Ins.	Ft.	Ins.	Ft.	Ins.
C 1091	2	3¾	3	8	7	8	4	1	C 3763	1	11	3	11	8	6	5	9
C 1092	2	0¼	3	4	7	9	5	4	C 1109*	2	1	3	10	8	0	5	1
C 1107	1	7½	3	8	7	10	5	9	C 3873	2	0	3	6	8	0	5	6
C 1094	1	5½	3	7	8	0	5	8	C 3342	2	6	4	3	—		—	
C 2000	1	11	3	4½	7	10¼	—		C 3872	2	0	4	0	—		—	
C 1170	1	9¾	4	1	8	9	6	3	C 1174	1	6½	4	0	8	8	—	
C 1097	1	7	3	7	7	9	5	2	C 1176	1	7	4	1	8	9	6	3
C 1169	2	0	3	5	7	7	5	4	C 3764	2	0	4	0	—		—	
C 1280	1	10¾	3	11	8	9	—		C 3961	1	10	3	9	8	0	—	
C 1028	1	11	3	4	7	5	5	3	C 3962	1	9¾	3	4½	7	9	5	6
C 3762	2	0	3	8	8	0	5	6	C 3963	2	3	3	10	8	4		

* This is for Railing 23 inches high.

EXTRAS.—Division Fencing, consisting of two wrought-iron horizontal bars ¾-inch diameter, and cast-iron standard with plate base supplied thus :—

6 ft. Set, two Horizontal Bars, and one Standard	6/- per set.
10 ,, ,, ,, ,, ,, ...	7/6 ,,
15 ft. Set, two Horizontal Bars, and two Standards ..	11/3 per set.
20 ,, ,, ,, ,, three ,, ...	15/- ,,

Ramps, Circled Corners, Corner Standards, Angle Pieces, and alterations from specified details are extra to any pattern Railing

We shall be pleased to estimate to plans deviating in any details from foregoing description.

FIXING RAILING AT SITE.

Having a staff of Experienced Men, we undertake to fix any of the foregoing Patterns within 20 miles of our Warehouse at Low Rates. We invite enquiries for Supplying and Fixing Railing Complete.

STRATFORD, Walthamstow and Leytonstone.

YOUNG & MARTEN, Ltd., Merchants and Manufacturers,

CARRIAGE ENTRANCE GATES.

No. C3875
"String Ring" Pattern.

Size, 8 ft. wide by 3 ft. 10 in. high, fitted with Striking Plate, Drop Bolt and Lock, and including Hangings for Brick Piers.. .. ..£5 12 6

The same, but 4 ft. 7 in. high, as drawn 6 7 6

No. C3876
"Queen Anne" Pattern.

Size, 8 ft. wide by 4 ft. 3 in. high, fitted with Striking Plate, Drop Bolt and Lock, and including Hangings for Brick Piers.. .. ..£7 2 6

The same, but 5 ft. high, as drawn 8 12 6

No. C4271. ORNAMENTAL WROUGHT-IRON ENTRANCE GATES.

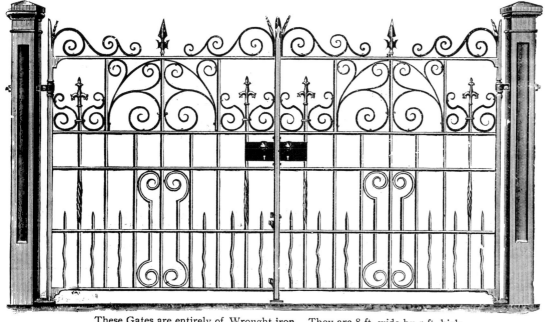

PRICES.

Pair Gates only, with best Brass Warded Lock, Sham and Hangings for Stone Piers.. .. .. .£15 0 0

Ditto, with pair of Cast-iron Pillars, 5 in. square, to fix on Stone, including Lewis Bolts.. .. .. .. 21 10 0

These Gates are entirely of Wrought-iron. They are 8 ft. wide by 5 ft. high.

STRATFORD, Walthamstow and Leytonstone.

YOUNG & MARTEN, Ltd., Merchants and Manufacturers,
WROUGHT IRON GATES AND RAILINGS.

NOTE.—In all cases where heights are given of wrought Railings these heights are overall, above ground or coping when fixed. The same remark applies to Gates, sufficient space being allowed at bottom to clear ground when being opened.

No. C3735. ORNAMENTAL GAME-PROOF HURDLES AND GATES. For the protection of Flower Gardens, Lawns &c.

All painted one coat before leaving works.

All necessary Bolts and Nuts are included in the prices under.

In 6 ft. Hurdles, End Uprights $1\frac{1}{4}$ in. $\times \frac{1}{4}$ in., Horizontals 1 in. $\times \frac{1}{4}$ in., Verticals $\frac{1}{4}$ in. diameter and placed $1\frac{1}{4}$ in. apart between. All Hurdles under 4 ft. high have only Three Horizontal Bars.

	Height above ground	30	36	42	48 inches
Hurdles		6/-	6/3	6/9	7/3 per yard

	Up to 3 ft. high.	Up to 4 ft. high.	
Hand Gates to match, 3 ft. wide, with Latch and Catch, and hung to Strong Wrought Iron Standards	37/6	40/6	each complete
„ „ hung to Square Cast Iron Pillars with Self-fixing Bases	57/6	63/-	„ „

No. C3333. EXTRA STRONG ORNAMENTAL HURDLES AND GATES.

All painted one coat before leaving works

All necessary Bolts and Nuts are included in the prices under

End Uprights and Horizontal Bars $1\frac{1}{4}$ in. $\times \frac{5}{16}$ in. Uprights $\frac{3}{8}$ in. diameter at $2\frac{1}{2}$ in. centres.

	Height above ground	30	36	42	48	inches
Hurdles (Those 30 in. and 36 in. high have only 2 Horizontals)	Price	6/6	6/9	7/6	8/3	per yard

		Up to 3 ft. high.	Up to 4 ft. high.	
Hand Gates to match, 3 ft. wide, with Latch and Catch, and hung to Strong Wrought Iron Standards		39/6	42/6	each
Hand Gates „ „ „ „ Cast Iron Pillars (self-fixing bases)		58/6	65/6	„
Pair of Gates „ 8 „ with Brass Warded Lock, „ „ „ „		121/6	132/-	per pair

No. C3328. WROUGHT IRON GATES AND RAILINGS.

Wrought Iron Railing, 22 inches high. Horizontals $1\frac{1}{4}$ in. $\times \frac{5}{16}$ in. Uprights $\frac{1}{2}$ in. square. Scrolls $\frac{1}{2}$ in. $\times \frac{1}{4}$ in. .. .. .. 4/9 per foot run
Hand Gates to match, 4 ft. high $\times$ 3 ft. wide, with Latch and Catch, and hung to $1\frac{1}{4}$ in. $\times \frac{1}{4}$ in. Wrought Standards for stone, with Backstay .. .. 54/- each

STRATFORD, Walthamstow and Leytonstone.

WROUGHT IRON GARDEN BORDER AND DIVISION RAILINGS AND CONTINUOUS UNCLIMBABLE RAILING.

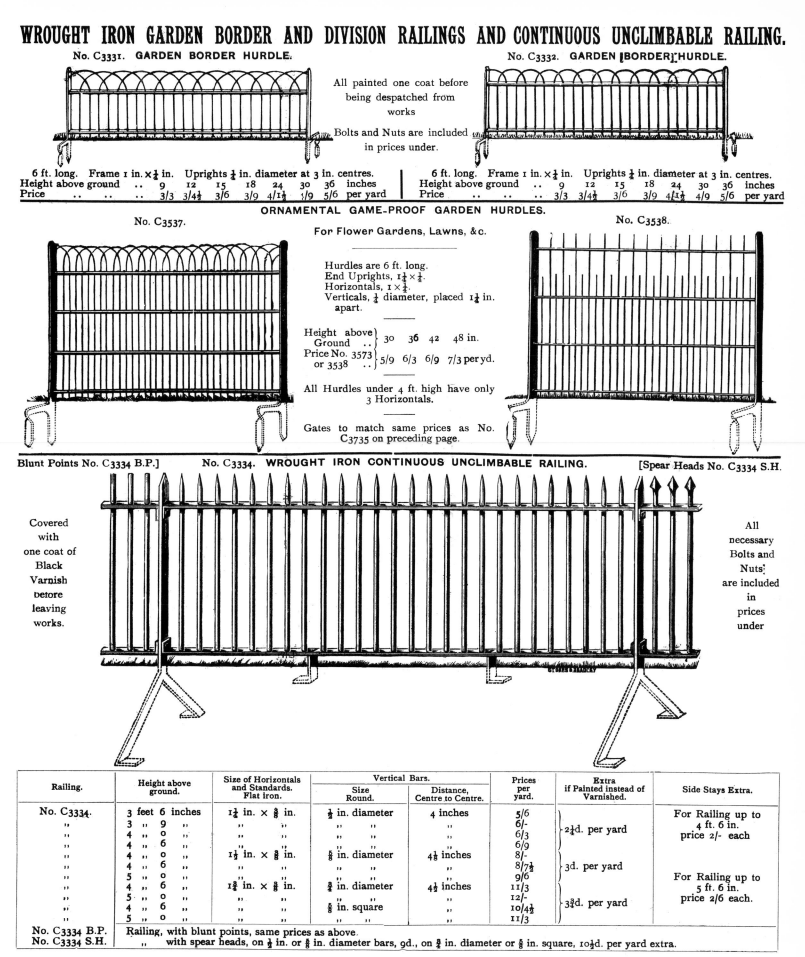

No. C3331. GARDEN BORDER HURDLE.

No. C3332. GARDEN [BORDER] HURDLE.

All painted one coat before being despatched from works

Bolts and Nuts are included in prices under.

6 ft. long. Frame 1 in. × ½ in. Uprights ¼ in. diameter at 3 in. centres.

Height above ground	..	9	12	15	18	24	30	36	inches
Price	.. ..	3/3	3/4½	3/6	3/9	4/1½	1/9	5/6	per yard

6 ft. long. Frame 1 in. × ½ in. Uprights ¼ in. diameter at 3 in. centres.

Height above ground	..	9	12	15	18	24	30	36	inches
Price	..	3/3	3/4½	3/6	3/9	4/1½	4/9	5/6	per yard

ORNAMENTAL GAME-PROOF GARDEN HURDLES.

No. C3537.

No. C3538.

For Flower Gardens, Lawns, &c.

Hurdles are 6 ft. long.
End Uprights, 1¼ × ¼.
Horizontals, 1 × ¼.
Verticals, ¼ diameter, placed 1¼ in. apart.

Height above Ground ..	30	36	42	48	in.
Price No. 3573 or 3538 ..	5/9	6/3	6/9	7/3	per yd.

All Hurdles under 4 ft. high have only 3 Horizontals.

Gates to match same prices as No. C3735 on preceding page.

Blunt Points No. C3334 B.P.]   No. C3334. WROUGHT IRON CONTINUOUS UNCLIMBABLE RAILING.   [Spear Heads No. C3334 S.H.

Covered with one coat of Black Varnish before leaving works.

All necessary Bolts and Nuts are included in prices under

Railing.	Height above ground.	Size of Horizontals and Standards. Flat iron.	Vertical Bars.		Prices per yard.	Extra if Painted instead of Varnished.	Side Stays Extra.
			Size Round.	Distance, Centre to Centre.			
No. C3334.	3 feet 6 inches	1¼ in. × ⅜ in.	½ in. diameter	4 inches	5/6		For Railing up to 4 ft. 6 in. price 2/- each
,,	3 ,, 9 ,,	,, ,,	,, ,,	,,	6/-	2¼d. per yard	
,,	4 ,, 0 ,,	,, ,,	,, ,,	,,	6/3		
,,	4 ,, 6 ,,	,, ,,	,, ,,	,,	6/9		
,,	4 ,, 0 ,,	1½ in. × ⅜ in.	⅝ in. diameter	4⅛ inches	8/-		
,,	4 ,, 6 ,,	,, ,,	,, ,,	,,	8/7½	3d. per yard	
,,	5 ,, 0 ,,	,, ,,	,, ,,	,,	9/6		
,,	4 ,, 6 ,,	1¼ in. × ⅜ in.	¾ in. diameter	4½ inches	11/3		For Railing up to 5 ft. 6 in. price 2/6 each.
,,	5 ,, 0 ,,	,, ,,	,, ,,	,,	12/-	3¾d. per yard	
,,	4 ,, 6 ,,	,, ,,	⅝ in. square	,,	10/4½		
,,	5 ,, 0 ,,	,, ,,	,, ,,	,,	11/3		
No. C3334 B.P.	Railing, with blunt points, same prices as above.						
No. C3334 S.H.	,, with spear heads, on ½ in. or ⅝ in. diameter bars, 9d., on ¾ in. diameter or ⅝ in. square, 10½d. per yard extra.						

STRATFORD, Walthamstow and Leytonstone.

WROUGHT IRON VERTICAL HAND GATES.

NOTE.—In all cases where heights are given of wrought railings these heights are *overall*, above ground or coping, when fixed. The same remark applies to gates, sufficient space being allowed at bottom to clear ground when being opened.

No. C3964.　　　　　　　　　　　No. C3965.

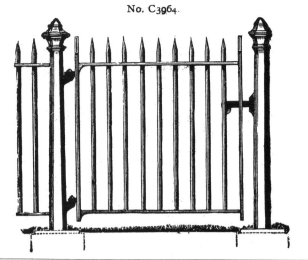

No.	Width.		Height above Ground.		Size of Round Vertical Bars	Distance Centre to Centre.	Price, with Hangings for Wood or Stone.	Price, hung to Cast-iron Pillars, to fix on Stone, including Bolts.	Price, hung to Cast-iron Pillars, with Self-fixing Bases.
	FT.	INS.	FT.	INS.		INS.			
	3	6	3	6	½ in. diam.	4	£1 19 6	£3 18 0	£4 7 0
	3	6	4	0	½ ,,	4	2 1 0	4 2 6	4 10 0
	3	6	4	6	½ ,,	4	2 2 6	4 4 0	4 13 0
C3964	3	6	4	0	⅝ ,,	4	2 3 6	4 4 0	4 13 0
	3	6	4	6	⅝ ,,	4	2 5 0	4 6 3	4 16 0
	3	6	5	0	⅝ ,,	4	2 6 6	4 10 0	4 18 0
	3	6	4	6	¾ ,,	4½	2 15 6	5 2 0	5 12 6
	3	6	5	0	¾ ,,	4½	2 17 0	5 11 0	6 0 0
	3	6	5	6	¾ ,,	4½	3 0 0	5 14 0	6 10 6

No. C3965.—Extra on above prices, 6/- each.　　　　If with Brass Warded Lock, 9/- each extra.

WROUGHT IRON GARDEN GATES.

No. C3966.　　　　　　　　　　　No. C3967.

No.	Width.		Height abov Ground.		Size of Round Vertical Bars.	Distance Centre to Centre.	Price, with Hangings for Wood or Stone.	Price, hung to Cast-iron Pillars, to fix on Stone, including Bolts.	Price, hung to Cast-iron Pillars, with Self-fixing Bases.
	FT.	INS.	FT.	INS.					
	3	6	3	6	½ in. diam.	4 ins. at top	£2 5 0	£4 1 0	£4 13 0
C3966	3	6	4	0	½ ,,	4 ,,	2 8 0	4 4 0	4 18 0
	3	6	4	0	⅝ ,,	4 ,,	2 11 0	4 8 0	5 11 0
	3	6	3	6	½ ,,	3 ins.	2 5 0	4 1 0	4 13 0
C3967	3	6	4	0	½ ,,	3 ,,	2 8 0	4 4 0	4 18 0
	3	6	4	0	⅝ ,,	3 ,,	2 11 0	4 8 0	5 11 0

If with Best Brass Warded Lock, 9/- each extra.

STRATFORD, Walthamstow and Leytonstone.

YOUNG & MARTEN, Ltd., Merchants and Manufacturers,

WROUGHT-IRON UNCLIMBABLE VERTICAL GATES.

NOTE.—In all cases where heights are given of Wrought-railings, these heights are **overall**, above ground or coping, when fixed. The same remark applies to Gates, sufficient space being allowed at bottom to clear ground when being opened,

No. C3968.

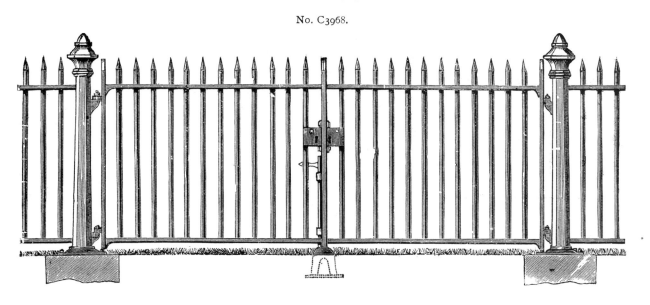

Gate stops, 10/- extra.

Sizes.	Price, with Hangings for Wood or Stone, per pair.			Price, Hung to Cast-iron Pillars, with Bases for Stone. per pair.			Price, Hung to Cast-iron Pillars with Self-fixing Bases, per pair.		
3 ft. 6 ins. high; Uprights, ½ in. diameter, at 4 in. Centres	£4	2	6	£6	0	0	£6	12	0
4 „ 0 „ „ „ ½ „ „ „ 4 „ „	4	7	6	6	7	6	6	19	6
4 „ 6 „ „ „ ½ „ „ „ 4 „ „	4	12	6	6	13	6	7	7	0
4 „ 0 „ „ „ 9/16 „ „ „ 4 „ „	4	16	0	6	18	0	7	11	6
4 „ 6 „ „ „ 5/8 „ „ „ 4 „ „	5	0	6	7	2	6	7	19	0
5 „ 0 „ „ „ 5/8 „ „ „ 4 „ „	5	5	0	7	10	0	8	3	6
4 „ 6 „ „ „ 3/4 „ „ „ 5/8 in. square, at 4½ in. Centres	6	0	0	9	0	0	10	0	0
5 „ 0 „ „ „ 3/4 „ „ „ 5/8 „ „ „ 4½ „ „	6	9	0	9	15	0	10	10	0
5 „ 6 „ „ „ 3/4 „ „ „ 5/8 „ „ „ 4½ „ „	6	18	0	10	0	0	11	0	0

If fitted with Brass Warded Lock and Sham, 18/9 per pair extra.

No. C4033.   Extra Strong.

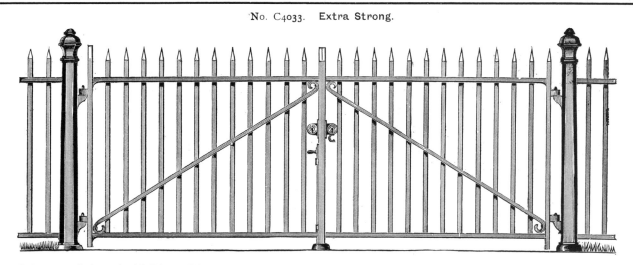

This pattern, being strongly braced with Diagonal Bars, is much strengthened, and is recommended where Vertical Gates are required for constant usage. Specification same as No. C3968 above shown, 21/- per pair extra.

STRATFORD, Walthamstow and Leytonstone.

VERANDAHS.

No. C4043.—CAST IRON PORCH OR DOOR HOOD.

This Porch or Door Hood is 5 ft. wide × 2 ft. 6 ins. × 3 ft. 6 ins., consisting of two side brackets front beam, bars to receive glass and to batt into wall at back, cresting, and finials. No glass included.

PRICE, marked ready for erection .. .. 63/- per set.

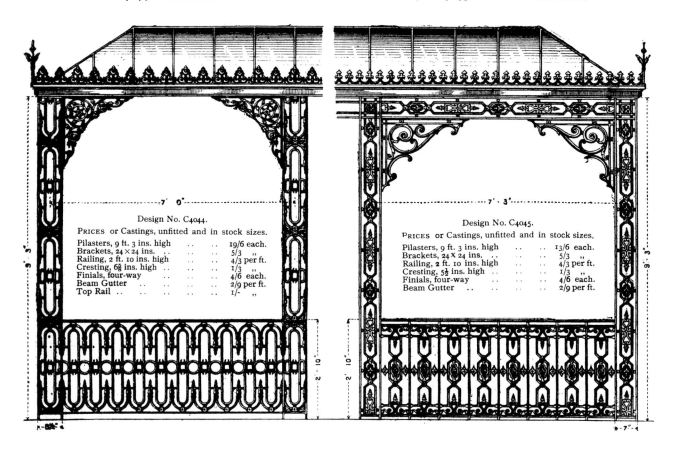

No. C4044.—VERANDAH.

No. C4045.—VERANDAH.

Design No. C4044.

PRICES or Castings, unfitted and in stock sizes.

Pilasters, 9 ft. 3 ins. high	.. ..	19/6 each.
Brackets, 24 × 24 ins. ..	.. ..	5/3 ,,
Railing, 2 ft. 10 ins. high	.. ..	4/3 per ft.
Cresting, 6¾ ins. high ..	.. ..	1/3 ,,
Finials, four-way	.. ..	4/6 each.
Beam Gutter	.. ..	2/9 per ft.
Top Rail	.. ..	1/- ,,

Design No. C4045.

PRICES or Castings, unfitted and in stock sizes.

Pilasters, 9 ft. 3 ins. high	.. ..	13/6 each.
Brackets, 24 × 24 ins. ..	.. ..	5/3 ,,
Railing, 2 ft. 10 ins. high	.. ..	4/3 per ft.
Cresting, 5½ ins. high ..	.. ..	1/3 ,,
Finials, four-way	.. ..	4/6 each.
Beam Gutter	.. ..	2/9 per ft.

For drawings and details of better and more elaborate Verandahs, *See* General Catalogue "Castings Section." We give the price of the parts of above separately in order that purchasers may determine the approximate cost in any desired form; it will be observed that the Castings priced above are unfitted, *i.e.*, not drilled or finished for connecting together, neither is roof nor glass included. We shall at any time be pleased to quote to customers plan for above or other designs complete and ready for erection.

STRATFORD, Walthamstow and Leytonstone.

No. C 3811 Spiral Stair.

With Wrought Hand Rail.

Right or Left Hand Wheeling.

All fitted ready for erection.

Diam. A to B.	Rise per Step.	No. of Baulsters on each Step.	Price per Step.
3 ft. 6 in	8 to 9 in	1	12/9
4 ,, 0 ,,	8 ,, 9 ,,	1	13/6
4 ,, 6 ,.	8 ,, 9 ,,	2	16/6
5 ,, 0 ,,	8 ,, 9 ,,	2	18/-
5 ,, 6 ,,	8 ,, 9 ,,	2	19/6
6 ,, 0 ,,	8 ,, 9 ,,	2	21/-

No. C 3812 Straight Stair.

With Hand Rail each side.

All fitted ready for erection.

Width.	Rise per Step.	Price, per Step.
2 ft 6 in.	7 to 8 in.	18/9
3 ,, 0 ,,	7 ,, 8 ,,	19/6
3 ,, 6 ,,	7 ,, 8 ,,	21/-
4 ,, 0 ,,	7 ,, 8 ,,	24/-

No. C 3813 Straight Stair.

With Hand Rail each side.

All fitted ready for erection.

Width.	Rise per Step.	Price, per Step.
3 ft. 0 in.	6 to 8 in.	36/-
3 ,, 6 ,,	6 ,, 8 ,,	39/-
4 ,, 0 ,,	6 ,, 8 ,,	45/-
4 ,, 6 ,,	6 ,, 8 ,,	48/-
5 ,, 0 ,,	6 ,, 8 ,,	51/-
5 ,, 6 ,,	6 ,, 8 ,	54/-
6 ,, 0 ,,	6 ,, 8 ,,	57/-

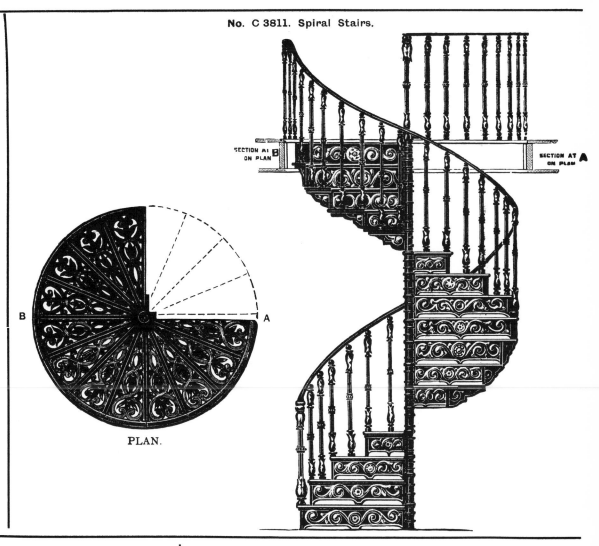

No. C 3811. Spiral Stairs.

SECTION A¹ ON PLAN B

SECTION AT A ON PLAN

PLAN.

No. C 3812 Straight Stair.

No. C 3813 Straight Stair.

Step back to front, either 10 or 12 inches.

MISCELLANEOUS CASTINGS.

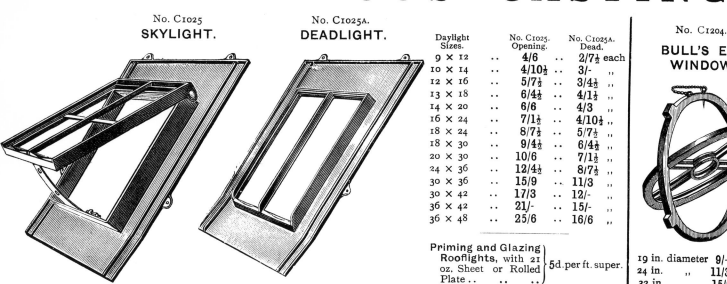

No. C1025
SKYLIGHT.

No. C1025A.
DEADLIGHT.

Daylight Sizes.	No. C1025. Opening.	No. C1025A. Dead.
9 × 12	4/6	2/7½ each
10 × 14	4/10½	3/- ,,
12 × 16	5/7½	3/4½ ,,
13 × 18	6/4½	4/1½ ,,
14 × 20	6/6	4/3 ,,
16 × 24	7/1½	4/10½ ,,
18 × 24	8/7½	5/7½ ,,
18 × 30	9/4½	6/4½ ,,
20 × 30	10/6	7/1½ ,,
24 × 36	12/4½	8/7½ ,,
30 × 36	15/9	11/3 ,,
30 × 42	17/3	12/- ,,
36 × 42	21/-	15/- ,,
36 × 48	25/6	16/6 ,,

Priming and Glazing Rooflights, with 21 oz. Sheet or Rolled Plate .. .. .. } 5d. per ft. super.

No. C1204.
BULL'S EYE WINDOW.

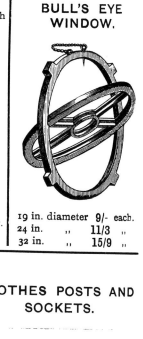

19 in. diameter	9/-	each
24 in. ,,	11/3	,,
32 in. ,,	15/9	,,

No. C2208.

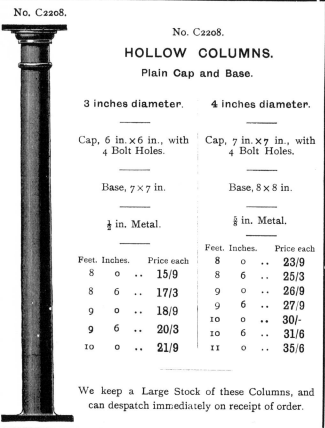

No. C2208.
HOLLOW COLUMNS.
Plain Cap and Base.

3 inches diameter.

Cap, 6 in. × 6 in., with 4 Bolt Holes.

Base, 7 × 7 in.

½ in. Metal.

Feet.	Inches.	Price each
8	0	15/9
8	6	17/3
9	0	18/9
9	6	20/3
10	0	21/9

4 inches diameter.

Cap, 7 in. × 7 in., with 4 Bolt Holes.

Base, 8 × 8 in.

⅝ in. Metal.

Feet.	Inches.	Price each
8	0	23/9
8	6	25/3
9	0	26/9
9	6	27/9
10	0	30/-
10	6	31/6
11	0	35/6

We keep a Large Stock of these Columns, and can despatch immediately on receipt of order.

Ornamental Bay Window Columns.

No. C1133.   No. C4080.

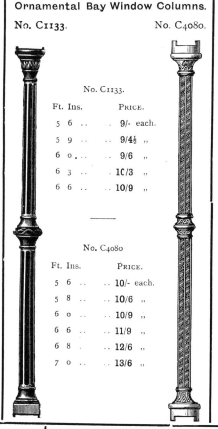

No. C1133.

Ft.	Ins.	PRICE.
5	6	9/- each.
5	9	9/4½ ,,
6	0	9/6 ,,
6	3	10/3 ,,
6	6	10/9 ,,

No. C4080.

Ft.	Ins.	PRICE.
5	6	10/- each.
5	8	10/6 ,,
6	0	10/9 ,,
6	6	11/9 ,,
6	8	12/6 ,,
7	0	13/6 ,,

No. C3273

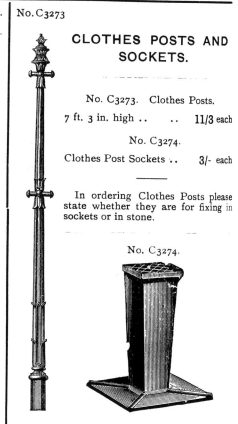

CLOTHES POSTS AND SOCKETS.

No. C3273. Clothes Posts.

7 ft. 3 in. high .. .. 11/3 each

No. C3274

Clothes Post Sockets .. 3/- each

In ordering Clothes Posts please state whether they are for fixing in sockets or in stone.

No. C3274.

No. C1159.

PARTITION BRACKETS.

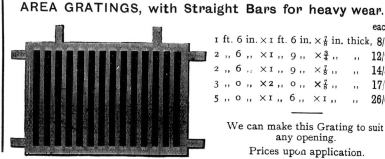

12 × 24	13 × 30	14 × 36	14 × 42	14 × 48
2/3	2/9	3/6	4/-	4/3 each

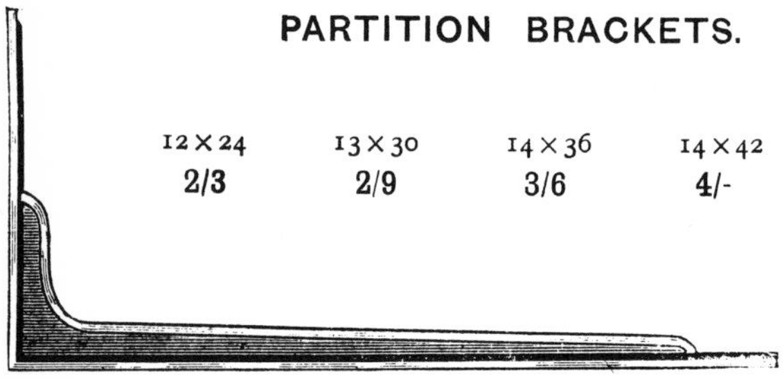

No. C1132.

AREA GRATINGS, with Straight Bars for heavy wear.

	each
1 ft. 6 in. × 1 ft. 6 in. × ⅞ in. thick,	8/3
2 ,, 6 ,, × 1 ,, 9 ,, × ¾ ,, ,,	12/9
2 ,, 6 ,, × 1 ,, 9 ,, × ⅞ ,, ,,	14/3
3 ,, 0 ,, × 2 ,, 0 ,, × ⅞ ,, ,,	17/-
5 ,, 0 ,, × 1 ,, 6 ,, × 1 ,, ,,	26/6

We can make this Grating to suit any opening.

Prices upon application.

STRATFORD, Walthamstow, Leytonstone, Millwall, & Brentford.

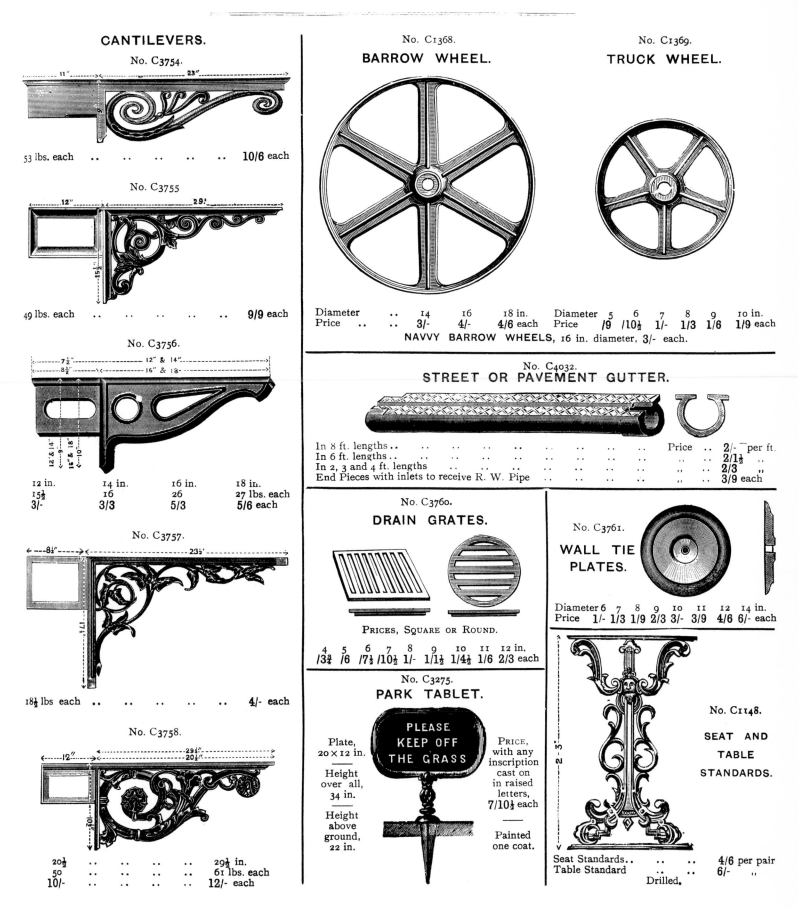

CANTILEVERS.

No. C3754.

11" 23"

53 lbs. each .. .. 10/6 each

No. C3755

12" 29"

15½"

49 lbs. each .. .. 9/9 each

No. C3756.

7½" 12" & 14"
8½" 16" & 18"

12 & 14" 9
16" & 18" 10"

12 in.	14 in.	16 in.	18 in.
15½	16	26	27 lbs. each
3/-	3/3	5/3	5/6 each

No. C3757.

8½" 23½"

17½"

18½ lbs each .. .. 4/- each

No. C3758.

12" 29¼"
20¼"

10"

20½				29¼ in.
50				61 lbs. each
10/-				12/- each

No. C1368.
BARROW WHEEL.

No. C1369.
TRUCK WHEEL.

Diameter	..	14	16	18 in.	Diameter	5	6	7	8	9	10 in.
Price	..	3/-	4/-	4/6 each	Price	/9	/10½	1/-	1/3	1/6	1/9 each

NAVVY BARROW WHEELS, 16 in. diameter, 3/- each.

No. C4032.
STREET OR PAVEMENT GUTTER.

In 8 ft. lengths .. .. Price .. 2/- per ft.
In 6 ft. lengths .. .. ,, .. 2/1½ ,,
In 2, 3 and 4 ft. lengths .. .. ,, .. 2/3 ,,
End Pieces with inlets to receive R. W. Pipe .. .. ,, .. 3/9 each

No. C3760.
DRAIN GRATES.

PRICES, SQUARE OR ROUND.

4	5	6	7	8	9	10	11	12 in.
/3¾	/6	/7½	/10½	1/-	1/1½	1/4½	1/6	2/3 each

No. C3761.
WALL TIE PLATES.

Diameter	6	7	8	9	10	11	12	14 in.
Price	1/-	1/3	1/9	2/3	3/-	3/9	4/6	6/- each

No. C3275.
PARK TABLET.

Plate, 20 × 12 in.

PLEASE KEEP OFF THE GRASS

Height over all, 34 in.

Height above ground, 22 in.

PRICE, with any inscription cast on in raised letters, 7/10½ each

Painted one coat.

No. C1148.
SEAT AND TABLE STANDARDS.

2' 3"

Seat Standards.. .. .. .. 4/6 per pair
Table Standard .. .. .. 6/- ,,
Drilled.

 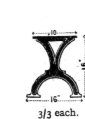 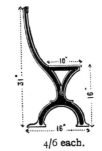 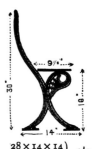 
 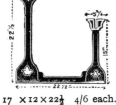 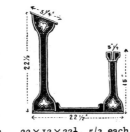  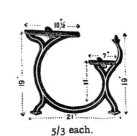 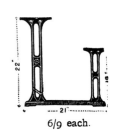
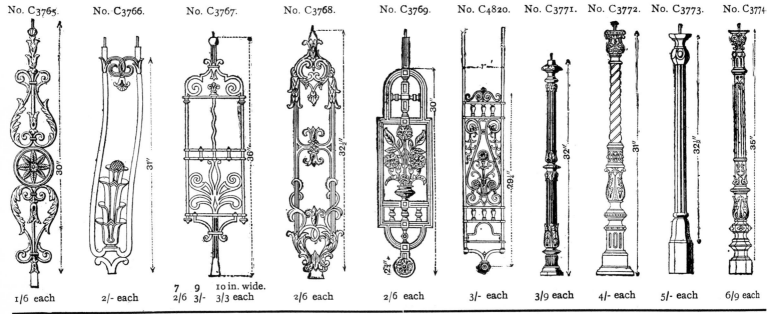

YOUNG & MARTEN, Ltd., Merchants and Manufacturers,

GARDEN AND PARK CHAIRS.

No. C3747.

Pair of Standards and Centre Support, **16/6**
Bolts and Nuts for do., **3/-** extra.

PRICES OF COMPLETE SEATS,

Including ironwork, painted one coat Green or Chocolate, and relieved with Gold and woodwork (Pitch Pine), varnished two coats.

No. C3748.

				5 ft.		6 ft. long	
No. C3747	..	..		51/-	..	57/6 each
No. C3748	..	..		33/9	..	37/6 ,,

Castings only .. .. .. **9/9** per pair
Bolts and Nuts, **1/3** per pair of Castings extra.

No. C3752.

SUITABLE

FOR

LAWNS.

35 in. high.

Painted .. 12/- each
Bronzed .. 15/- ,,

No. C3749. THE "LOUIS" CIRCULAR GARDEN CHAIR.

6 ft. 6 in.

long.

Price,

144/- each

No. C3749.

This is one of the **Very Finest Seats** that can be produced. The designing and modelling can bear criticism and will be appreciated where a thoroughly artistic thing is required.

No. C3753.

41 in. high.

Painted .. 18/- each
Bronzed .. 22/9 ,,

No. C3750.

THE "IVY" GARDEN CHAIR.

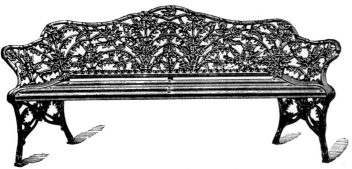

This is a well-known favourite Pattern.

4 ft. 9 in. long .. .. **63/-** each

No. C3751.

THE "LOUIS" STRAIGHT GARDEN CHAIR.

This is a splendid Specimen of good Designing and Modelling.

6 ft. 6 in. long .. .. **78/-** each

The Ironwork of the 'Louis" Circular, The "Ivy," and The "Louis" Straight Chairs is painted one coat of Green or Chocolate, and relieved with Gold. The woodwork is of the best Pitch Pine, and varnished two coats.

STRATFORD, Walthamstow, Leytonstone, Millwall, & Brentford.

YOUNG & MARTEN, Ltd., Merchants and Manufacturers,

PORTABLE GREENHOUSES AND GARDEN LIGHTS, STRONG, CHEAP, AND EASY TO ERECT.

No. T1560. GARDEN LIGHT.

Sizes of Lights, 6 feet long by 4 feet wide, framework made of 2 inches by 3 inches square sash stile, and properly rabbeted as necessary for the glass, with good 2-inch sash bars and iron bar. The Glazed Lights are brass sprigged and bedded in best oiled putty. These Frames are put on rail at the following prices :—

Unglazed Lights.		Glazed Lights, 21 oz., and painted 3 coats.	
4 ft. 6 in. × 3 ft. 6 in. ..	5/6 each	4 ft. 6 in. × 3 ft. 6 in. ..	15/- each
6 ft. × 4 ft.	7/- ,,	6 ft. × 4 ft.	17/6 ,,

No. T3170. PIT LIGHT FRAMES.

These Frames are made of good yellow deal, 23 inches high at back and 11 inches high in front. Made of 1-inch tongued and grooved boards; painted two coats of oil paint before sent out. The Lights are glazed with 21-ounce glass, bedded and sprigged, and fitted with handles.

One Light Frame, 4 × 3 ft. ..	£1 2 6	Two Light Frames, 8 × 6 ft.	£3 8 9
,, ,, 4 × 4 ,, ..	1 7 6	,, ,, 10 × 6 ,,	3 18 0
,, ,, 5 × 4 ,, ..	1 12 6	Three ,, 12 × 6 ,,	4 13 9
,, ,, 6 × 4 ,, ..	1 18 9	,, ,, 14 × 6 ,,	5 12 6
,, ,, 8 × 4 ,, ..	2 10 0	Four ,, 16 × 6 ,,	7 3 9
		Five ,, 20 × 6 ,,	8 2 6

Can be made any size to order.

No. T2265. SPAN-ROOF GREENHOUSE.
TENANT'S FIXTURE.

The "Amateur's Ideal Greenhouse." Strong and Cheap and Easy to erect, being built in sections and marked. The framework is substantially constructed of red deal, the lower part being filled in with good, sound, well-seasoned, tongued and grooved matchboards. The House is fitted with door complete, with rim lock and brass furniture, painted one coat of good oil color, supplied with all necessary ironwork and stages for each side, and good 21-oz. cut glass throughout.

Long.	Wide.	High.	To eaves.	Packed on rail.
10 ft.	7 ft.	7 ft. 6 in.	4 ft. 6 in.	£11 5 0 each.
12 ft.	8 ft.	8 ft. 0 in.	5 ft. 0 in.	12 15 0 ,,
15 ft.	9 ft.	8 ft. 6 in.	5 ft. 0 in.	15 15 0 ,,
20 ft.	10 ft.	9 ft. 0 in.	5 ft. 6 in.	20 17 6 ,,
25 ft.	10 ft.	9 ft. 0 in.	5 ft. 6 in.	29 10 3 ,,

No. T4280.—SPECIAL LINE.—AMATEUR SPAN-ROOF GREENHOUSE.

These Greenhouses are made up in Sections, the Ends and Sides being complete, and only requiring to be screwed together at corners and the Roof Bars easily fixed on.

CAN BE EASILY ERECTED BY ANY HANDY MAN OR GARDENER.

SPECIFICATION.—Made of Well-seasoned Yellow Deal. Framework morticed and tenoned together (not nailed as is usual). Tongued and grooved Match Board Base. Half Glass Marginal Door in End with Rim Lock and Brass Furniture. Ventilating Sash in Roof opened with Japanned Set Opener. Sashes at side opened with Japanned Casement Stay. Painted one coat of genuine White Lead Paint. Sufficient Glass for glazing same. *The two larger sized Houses fitted with a Wrought Iron Tie Rod and King Rod, which prevent the House from ever getting out of shape.*

Delivered by our Vans within 5 miles of Works or packed and put on Rail.

Long.	Wide.	High at Ridge.	High at Eaves.	Price.
10 ft.	7 ft.	7 ft. 6 in.	4 ft. 6 in.	£7 10 0
12 ft.	8 ft.	8 ft. 0 in.	5 ft. 0 in.	9 0 0
15 ft.	9 ft.	8 ft. 6 in.	5 ft. 0 in.	12 0 0

No. T2266. LEAN-TO GREENHOUSE.
TENANT'S FIXTURE.

This House is built from the same specification as the Amateur Span-Roof, No. 2265, as above, prices as follows :—

Long.	Wide.	High.	To eaves.	Packed on rail.
10 ft.	7 ft.	7 ft. 6 in.	4 ft. 6 in.	£10 0 0 each.
12 ft.	8 ft.	8 ft. 0 in.	5 ft. 0 in.	12 0 0 ,,
15 ft.	9 ft.	8 ft. 6 in.	5 ft. 6 in.	13 8 9 ,,
20 ft.	10 ft.	8 ft. 6 in.	5 ft. 6 in.	19 17 6 ,,
25 ft.	10 ft.	9 ft. 0 in.	5 ft. 6 in.	26 17 6 ,,

Deduct 10 per cent. if required for brickwork.

When ordering it should be stated at which end the door is required (when facing front of House from outside) ; if desired it can be inserted in front.

No. T2267. THREE-QUARTER SPAN-ROOF GREENHOUSE.
TENANT'S FIXTURE.

This form is useful where the wall is not high enough for a Lean-to. The framework consists of good red deal, the lower part with tongued and grooved match-boards, roof in complete sashes. The House is supplied with 21-oz. glass throughout, half-glass door, rim lock, key, and brass fittings for same, two plant stages the length of both sides, and footpath for centre. Ventilators given according to size, and necessary ironwork for opening same, also gutters and downpipes. Woodwork is painted two coats good oil colour, marked for erection.

Long.	Wide.	High.	To eaves.	Packed on rail.
10 ft.	7 ft.	8 ft. 0 in.	5 ft. 0 in.	£14 7 6 each.
12 ft.	8 ft.	8 ft. 6 in.	5 ft. 6 in.	17 0 9 ,,
15 ft.	9 ft.	9 ft. 0 in.	6 ft. 0 in.	19 13 9 ,,
20 ft.	10 ft.	9 ft. 0 in.	6 ft. 0 in.	26 17 6 ,,
25 ft.	10 ft.	9 ft. 0 in.	6 ft. 0 in.	36 5 0 ,,

Deduct 10 per cent. if required for brickwork.

When ordering, it should be stated at which end the door is to be inserted (when facing front of House from outside ; if required, it can be placed in front.

STRATFORD, Walthamstow and Leytonstone. [279

YOUNG & MARTEN, Ltd., Merchants and Manufacturers,

IMPROVED STABLE FITTINGS.

HAY RACKS, STALL AND LOOSE BOX DIVISIONS.

No. C1052. **FLAT HAY RACK** (Cast Iron).

Painted	..	..	..	30	33	36 inches across.
Painted	..	..	..	7/6	9/-	10/6
Galvanized	..	..	..	13/6	16/6	19/6

No. C1053. **CORNER HAY RACK** (Cast Iron).

Painted	..	..	..	30	33	36 inches across.
Painted	..	..	..	7/6	9/-	10/6
Galvanized	..	..	..	13/6	16/6	19/6

Set No. C4863. **STALL DIVISION.**

FOR 1½ in. WOOD.

	£	s.	d.
1 No. C1054 Stall Post, 4 in. diameter, with Halter Ring and 18 in. Root ..	1		6
1 No. C1087 Stall Ramp, 9 ft. 6 in. long	0	12	0
1 No. C1090 Sill (with shifting piece), 9 ft. 6 in. long	0	8	3
Fitting Stall Post to Ramp	0	5	0
	£2	8	9

FOR 1¾ in. WOOD.

	£	s.	d.
1 No. C1054 Stall Post, 4 in. diameter, with Halter Ring and 18 in. Root ..	1	2	6
1 No. C1087 Stall Ramp, 9 ft. 6 in. long	0	13	6
1 No. C1090 Sill (with shifting piece) 9 ft. 6 in. long	0	9	0
Fitting Stall Post to Ramp	0	6	0
	£2	11	0

FOR 2 in. WOOD

	£	s.	d.
1 No. C1054 Stall Post, 4½ in. diameter, with Halter Ring and 18 in. Root ..	1	5	6
1 No. C1087 Stall Ramp, 9 ft. 6 in. long	0	13	6
1 No. C1090 Sill (with shifting piece), 9 ft. 6 in. long	0	10	6
Fitting Stall Post to Ramp	0	6	0
	£2	15	6

Set No. C4867. **LOOSE BOX DIVISION.**

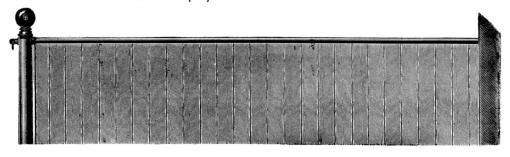

FOR 1½ in. WOOD.

	£	s.	d.
1 No. C1055 Loose Box Post, 4 in. diam., with 18 in. Root	1	7	0
1 No. C1088 Top Capping, 9 ft. 6 in. long	0	9	0
1 No. C1090 Sill (with shifting piece), 9 ft. 6 in. long	0	8	3
Fitting Post to Division and Door ..	0	9	0
	£2	13	3

FOR 1¾ in. WOOD.

	£	s.	d.
1 No. C1055 Loose Box Post, 4 in. diam., with 18 in. Root	1	7	0
1 No. C1088 Top Capping, 9 ft. 6 in. long	0	10	6
1 No. C1090 Sill (with shifting piece), 9 ft. 6 in. long	0	9	0
Fitting Post to Division and Door ..	0	9	0
	£2	15	6

FOR 2 in. WOOD.

	£	s.	d.
1 No. C1055 Loose Box Post, 4½ in. diam., with 18 in. Root	1	11	6
1 No. C1088 Top Capping, 9 ft. 6 in. long,	0	12	0
1 No. C1090 Sill (with shifting piece), 9 ft. 6 in. long	0	10	6
Fitting Post to Division and Door ..	0	9	0
	£3	3	0

STRATFORD, Walthamstow and Leytonstone.

YOUNG & MARTEN, Ltd., Merchants and Manufacturers,

IMPROVED STABLE FITTINGS.

FITTINGS FOR LOOSE BOX, 10 ft. 6 in. Square, for Corner and Stall.

LOOSE BOX, 10 ft. 6 in. Square, adapted for Corner, with Door on bevel, and Stall Division.

Loose Box Doors, 7 ft. high.

Wrought Iron Frame with Ventilating Panel to match No. 1057 Division.

	Width	3 ft.	3 ft. 6 in.	4 ft.
For 1½ in. wood	..	57/-	60/-	64/6
For 1¾ in. wood	..	58/6	61/6	67/6
For 2 in. wood	..	61/6	64/6	69/-

Brass Flush Latches, 10/5 each.

For prices of Loose Box Posts see Loose Box Divisions on this and preceding page.

Loose Box Doors, 7 ft. high.

Wrought Iron Frames with Ventilating Panel with Wrought Bars and Collars to match No. 1084 Division.

	Width	3 ft.	3 ft. 6 in.	4 ft
For 1½ in. wood	..	60/-	63/-	67/6
For 1¾ in. wood	..	61/6	64/6	69/-

Brass Flush Latch, 10/6 each.

For prices of Loose Box Posts see Loose Box Divisions on this and preceding page.

WITH WROUGHT BARS.

	For 1½ in. wood. £ s. d.	1¾ in. wood. £ s. d.	2 in. wood. £ s. d.
*2 No. C4876 Loose Box Posts, 4 in. diameter with 18 in. root	2 14 0	2 14 0	3 3 0
2 No. C1057 Loose Box Divisions, 8 ft. 6 in. long, 24 in. high	3 15 0	4 5 6	4 11 6
2 No. C1090 Sills (with shifting piece) ..	0 15 9	0 17 3	1 0 3
1 Loose Box Door, 3 ft. 6 in. wide × 7 ft. high, with Wrought Frame and Ventilating Panel to match Division	3 0 0	3 1 6	3 7 6
Fitting 2 Posts to Division and Door..	1 1 0	1 1 0	1 1 0
Brass Flush Latch..	0 10 6	0 10 6	0 10 6
	£11 16 3	£12 9 9	£13 13 9

If Divisions 30 in. high instead of 24 in. add 12/-, 15/- and 16/6 respectively.
* For 2 in. wood 4½ in. diameter posts are supplied and are included in above prices.

WITH WROUGHT BARS AND COLLARS.

	For 1½ in. wood. £ s. d	1¾ in. wood. £ s. d.
2 No. C4876 Loose Box Posts, 4½ in. diameter with 18 in. root	3 3 0	3 3 0
2 No. C1084 Loose Box Divisions, 8 ft. 6 in. long, with Wrought Bars and Collars, 24 in. high..	4 10 0	4 16 0
2 No. C1090 Sills (with shifting piece) ..	0 15 9	0 17 3
1 Loose Box Door, 3 ft. 6 in. wide × 7 ft. high, with Wrought Frame and Ventilating Panel to match Division ..	3 3 0	3 4 6
Fitting 2 Posts to Division and Door	1 1 0	1 1 0
Brass Flush Latch ..	0 10 6	0 10 6
	£13 3 3	£13 12 3

If Divisions 30 in. high instead of 24 in. add 15/- and 18/- respectively.

Set No. 4871. **STALL DIVISION, 8 ft. 6 in. long** .. For 1½ in. wood £3 14 3. For 1¾ in. wood £4 1 0. For 2 in. wood £4 8 6. Details given on preceding page.

—— EXTRAS. ——

No. C1045 Corner Manger Set for Loose Box ..	.. painted £2 5 0 per set.	
	.. galvanized £3 12 0 "	
No. C1041 Straight Set for Stall ."	.. painted £2 2 9 per set.	
	.. galvanized £3 9 0 "	
No. C1039 Ventilating Window, for 4 panes, 3 ft. 3 in. × 2 ft. 10 in. .. for wood £1 11 6 each.		
	for brickwork £1 17 6 "	
No. C1038 Ventilating Window, for 2 panes, 3 ft. 3 in. × 1 ft. 5 in. .. for wood £1 0 0 each.		

No. C1038 Ventilating Window, for 2 panes, 3 ft. 3 in. × 1 ft. 5 in., for brickwork £1 2 6 each.
No. C4930 Stable Name Plate, with sliding panel and brass horseshoe ornament { black japanned 6/9 each.
colored 7/6 each.
No. C4931 " " horseshoe pattern, 8½ in. × 9½ in. ." black japanned 2/6 each.
colored 3/- "
No. C1517, C1518 and C1585 Stable Bricks, as shewn" on page 261.

No. C1064. HORSE POT.

No. C1066 MARE POT.

No. C1071. STABLE GUTTER, with Loose Cover.

Size, 4½ ins. wide.

In 3, 4, and 6-ft. lengths .. .. .. 2/3 per foot.

Sizes	..	..	..	8	9	10	11	12 ins.
No. C1064 Horse Pot ..	..	..	..	4/-	5/-	6/-	7/-	9/- each.
" C1066 Mare..	..	..	..	4/-	5/-	6/-	7/-	9/- "

Gutter Inlets cast on, 1/6 each.

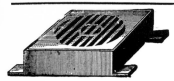

No. C1065.
STABLE GRATE AND FRAME.

Sizes	..	8	9	10	12 ins.
Prices	..	3/-	4/-	5/-	6/9 each.

No. C1069. ANGLE PIECE.

Price, 4/6 each.

No. C1070. TEE PIECE.

Price, 7/6 each.

STRATFORD, Walthamstow and Leytonstone.

YOUNG & MARTEN, Ltd., Merchants and Manufacturers,

CRESTINGS AND FINIALS.

These CRESTINGS and FINIALS can be supplied with Batts for leading into stone, or with snugs for screwing to wood. When ordering please state which is required. Various other patterns can be supplied from 3 in. to 26 in. high. Prices and Illustrations on application.

No. C1977   CRESTING, 3 inches high.

In pattern lengths, 9d. per foot run.

No. C1978.   CRESTING. 3 inches high.

In pattern lengths, 10½d. per foot run.

No. C1979.   CRESTING, 5 inches high

In pattern lengths, 10½d. per foot run.

No. C1980.   CRESTING, 5½ inches high.

In pattern lengths, 1/- per foot run.

No. C1981.   CRESTING, 6 inches high.

In pattern lengths, 1/1½ per foot run.

No. C1982.   CRESTING, 6 inches high.

In pattern lengths, 1/1½ per foot run.

No. C1983.   CRESTING, 8 inches high.

In pattern lengths, 1/3 per foot run.

No. C1984.   CRESTING, 8½ inches high.

In pattern lengths 1/- per foot run.

No. C1985.   CRESTING, 8¾ inches high.

In pattern lengths, 1/6 per foot run.

No. C1986.   CRESTING, 7½ inches high.

In pattern lengths, 1/3 per foot run.

No. C1136.   CRESTING, 10¼ inches high.

In pattern lengths, 1/6 per foot run.

No. C1987.   CRESTING, 13 inches high.

In pattern lengths, 2/- per foot run.

FINIALS.

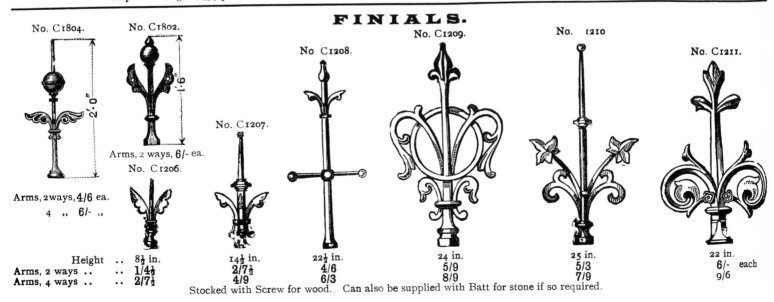

	No. C1804.	No. C1802.	No. C1206. No. C1207.	No. C1208.	No. C1209.	No. C1210	No. C1211.
Height	8½ in.		14½ in.	22½ in.	24 in.	25 in.	22 in.
Arms, 2 ways	1/4½		2/7½	4/6	5/9	5/3	6/- each
Arms, 4 ways	2/7½		4/9	6/3	8/9	7/9	9/6

No. C1804. Arms, 2 ways, 4/6 ea. 4 „ 6/- „

No. C1802. Arms, 2 ways, 6/- ea.

Stocked with Screw for wood. Can also be supplied with Batt for stone if so required.

STRATFORD, Walthamstow, Leytonstone, Millwall, & Brentford.

193

No. C4821.

PORCH AND BALCONY FRONT.

12 ft. to 15 ft. long.

Complete as shown with Iron Beam,

£11 5 0

No. C4822.

PORCH AND BALCONY FRONT

12 ft. to 15 ft. long.

Without Iron Beam, but prepared for Wood Beam,

£9 7 6

GARDEN AND PARK REQUISITES.

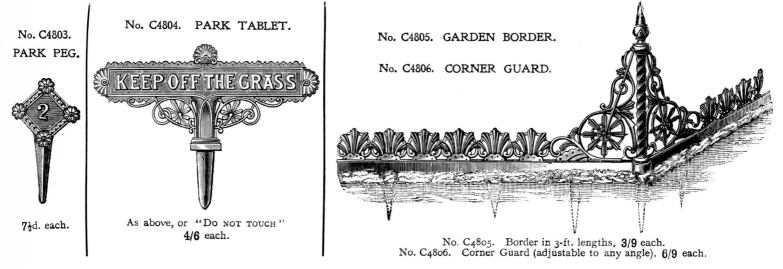

No. C4803.
PARK PEG.

7½d. each.

No. C4804. PARK TABLET.

KEEP OFF THE GRASS

As above, or "Do not touch"
4/6 each.

No. C4805. GARDEN BORDER.

No. C4806. CORNER GUARD.

No. C4805. Border in 3-ft. lengths, 3/9 each.
No. C4806. Corner Guard (adjustable to any angle), 6/9 each.

STRATFORD, Walthamstow, Leytonstone, Millwall, & Brentford.

YOUNG & MARTEN, Ltd., Merchants and Manufacturers,
ARTISTIC WROUGHT IRONWORK.

No AW4940.
GRILLE.

1 ft. 9 in. × 1 ft. 3 in.
22/6 each.

No. AW4942.
BRACKET.

1 ft. × 1 ft. 6 in.
7/6 each.

No. AW4943.
BRACKET.

1 ft × 1 ft. 6 in.
15/- each.

No. AW4944.
BRACKET.

1 ft. × 1 ft. 6 in.
15/- each.

No. AW4945.
BRACKET.

1 ft. × 1 ft. 6 in.
11/3 each.

No. AW4941.
GRILLE.

Hammered Leaves
1 ft. 9 in × 1 ft. 3 in.
£3 15/-

No. AW4936.
GRILLE.

1 ft. 9 in. × 1 ft. 3 in.
22/6 each

No. AW4946. **BALCONY RAILING.**

1 ft. 6 in. high.
22/6 per ft. run

No. AW4947. **BALCONY RAILING.**

1 ft. 6 in. high.
11/3 per ft. run.

No. AW4938.
GRILLE.

Hollow Leaves.
1 ft. 9 in. × 1 ft. 3 in
£2 5/- each

No. AW4937.
GRILLE.

1 ft. 9 in. × 1 ft. 3 in.
£1 17/6 each.

No. AW4948.
SWINGING SIGN.

Including Iron Frame
(but not board)
£4 10/- each.

No. AW4950. **FINIAL.**

30 to 40 inches high.
£1 19/- each.

No. AW4949.
SWINGING SIGN

Including Iron Frames
(but not board).
£6 15/- each.

No. AW4939.
GRILLE.

Hammered Leaves
1 ft. 9 in. × 1 ft. 3 in.
£3 each.

No. AW4951. **PANEL.**

2 ft. 6 in. × 1 ft. 6 in.
£3 each.

No. AW4952. **PANEL.**

3 ft. 6 in. × 1 ft. 6 in.
£4 10/-

No. AW4953. **PANEL.**

3 ft. 6 in. × 1 ft. 6 in.
£4 13/-

No. AW4954. **PANEL.**

3 ft. 6 in. × 1 ft. 6 in.
£11 5/-

No AW4955. **PANEL**

2 ft. 6 in. × 1 ft. 6 in.
£1 10/-

No. AW4959.
STAIR BALUSTER.

22/6 each Baluster.

No. AW4957.
STAIR BALUSTER.

7/6 each Baluster.

No AW4960. **GRILLE.**

2 ft. × 5 ft. 6 in.
£7 10/- each

No. AW4958.
STAIR BALUSTER.

30/- per ft. run.

No. AW4959.
STAIR BALUSTER.

15/- each Baluster.

No AW4961. **BORDER**

9 in. high. **7/6 per ft. run.**

No AW4962. **BORDER.**

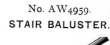

1 ft. high **9/- per ft. run.**

STRATFORD, Walthamstow and Leytonstone.

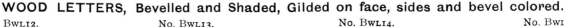 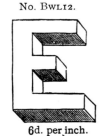

YOUNG & MARTEN, Ltd., Merchants and Manufacturers,

RIDGE TILES, ORNAMENTS, AND FINIALS.

No. W1512.
Plain Ridge Tile.

18 in. long, 6-in. wings.
Red or Blue.
4¾d. each, or **37/6** per 100.

No. W1513.
Roll Ridge Tile.

18 in. long, 6-in. wings.
Red or Blue.
6½d. each, or **50/-** per 100.

No. W1571.
Plain Capped Ridge Tile.

18 in. long, 6-in. wings.
Red or Blue.
5¼d. each, or **40/-** per 100.

No. W1572.
Grooved Ridge Tile.

18 in. long, 7-in. wings.
Red or Blue.
8d. each, or **60/-** per 100.

No. W1574.
Ornamental.

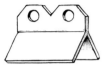

12 in. long, 6-in. wings. Red.
8d. each.

No. W4261.
Half Crest

12 in. long, 6-in. wings. Red.
6½d. each.

No. W4262.
Ornamental.

12 in. long, 6-in. wings. Red.
9d. each.

No. W4263.
Ornamental.

12 in. long, 6-in. wings. Red.
8d. each.

ORNAMENTS FOR FITTING INTO GROOVED RIDGE TILES.

No. W1575.

Blue or Red.
18 in. long, i.e., 2 9-in. Blocks.
6d. each.

No. W1576.

Blue or Red.
18 in. long, i.e., 2 9-in. Blocks.
6d. each.

No. W1577.

Blue or Red.
18 in. long, i.e., 2 9-in. Blocks.
6d. each.

No. W1578.

Blue or Red.
18 in. long, i.e., 2 9-in. Blocks.
6d. each.

No. W4267.
Red Hip Finial.

4/9 each.

No. W4268.
Red Hip Finial.

4/6 each

No. W5230.
Red Gable Finial.

4/6 each.

No. W5232.
Red Gable Finial.

4/9 each

No. W5231.
Red Hip Finial.

4/6 each.

No. W5234.
Red Griffin Finial
(hip).

27/6 each.

No. W4269.

8/6 each.

No. W5233.
Red Octagon Finial.

5/6 each.

No. W5235.
Red Griffin Finial
(gable).

27/6 each.

The above are all drawn to scale ¾ in. = 1 foot.

NOTE.—We can quote specially LOW PRICES for any of the Goods shown above for Full Truck Loads Delivered Free to any Railway Station.

STRATFORD, Walthamstow, Leytonstone, Millwall, & Brentford.

YOUNG & MARTEN, Ltd., Merchants and Manufacturers,

CHIMNEY POTS, INTERCEPTORS, TRAPS, ROOFING, AND DAMP-COURSE FELT.

CHIMNEY POTS.

No. W1430.	No. W1421.	No. W1422.	No. W1424.	No. W1425.	No. W1426.	No. W1427.	No. W1428.	No. W1429.

| 12 in. Buft Height 24 in., Buff 1/4½ each. | 10 in. Buft. Heights { 1 ft. 9 in., 1/3 { 2 ft. 2 in., 1/8 each. | 10 in. 2 ft. 3 in., Buff 2/1 each. | 14 in. 2 ft. 6 in., Buff 3/6 each. | 11 × 11 in. 2 ft. 6 in., Buff 3/9 each. | 13 in. Red. Buff. 2 ft. 6 in. 4/9 4/6 3 ft. 0 in. 5/9 5/6 4 ft. 0 in. 8/4 8/4 each. | 11 × 9 in. 2 ft. 4 in., Buff 3/4 each. | Octagon. 12 in. Buff { 2 ft 6 in. .. 3/9 each { 3 ft. 0 „ .. 4/9 „ Hexagon. 2 ft. high, 2/11 | 12 in. 1 ft. 9in., Buff 2/1 each. |

NOTE.—For the convenience of our customers not requiring a full load of **Drain Pipes alone**, we can arrange to deliver a 3-Ton lot (to some stations 2 Tons), *i.e.*, a mixed consignment of **Drain Pipes, Sinks,** or **Chimney Pots** as above, assorted, to suit requirements, free to any railway goods station where the rate from our Potteries does not exceed that to **London**, and to other stations the excess rate can be added to **invoice**.

SEWER TRAPS AND INTERCEPTORS.

No. W1631. WEAVER'S TRAP.

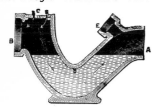

4 in. at **8/4** each.
6 „ „ **11/3** „

A—Outlet to sewer; B—Inlet from house;
C—Fresh air inlet; D—Dip of tray 3½in.;
E—Junction connecting with upright pipe
to ventilate sewer.

No. W1745. WINSER'S PATENT INTERCEPTOR.

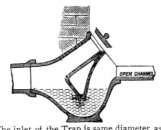

The inlet of the Trap is same diameter as the outlet, and has a cascade of 3 inches. The throat is contracted from 6 in. to 4½ in. This ensures the Trap being cleansed with a small quantity of water.

Price, in Brown Ware .. **12/-** each.

No. W1633. CHANNEL INTERCEPTOR.

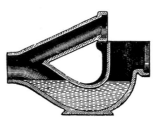

4 in. with 4 in. arm at **8/4** each.
6 „ „ 4 „ „ „ **10/-** „
9 „ „ 4 or 6 in. „ **18/9** „

No. W1634. KENON'S TRAP.

6 in. with 4 in. arm, **12/6** each.
9 „ „ 4 „ „ **25/-** „

No. W3970. MUD INTERCEPTOR.

9 in. inside at top
4 „ outlet.

Complete .. **10/-** each

If with inlet as shown by dotted lines, **1/3** each extra.

The sediment is accumulated in dish **A**, which can be readily removed and emptied.

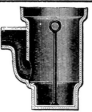

6 in. top, with 4 in. outlet at **10/-** ea.
9 „ „ „ 4 „ „ **15/-** „
Back inlet, **1/3** each extra.

DEAN'S GREASE TRAP,
With Bucket, Radiating Bricks and Iron Grating, complete.

No. W3164.

12 in. top with 4 in. outlet at **30/-** ea.

ROOFING FELT, in 30-yard Rolls, 32 in. wide

Best Asphalted Roofing Felt	**4d.** per yard
Best Inodorous Felt	**4d.** „
Asphalted Sarking Felt	**3d.** „

Original Crates containing 6 Rolls, carriage paid to any Railway Station in England.

NON-CONDUCTING DRY HAIR BOILER FELT

For clothing Boilers and Steam Pipes to preserve the Heat—covering Water Pipes and Cisterns to exclude the frost—and lining under Roofs, &c., to equalise the temperature. It is also very effective in deadening sound in partitions and ceilings.

In sheets, size 32 × 20 in.

		Weight per Sheet	
No. 1.	For Roofs, &c.	about 1 lb.	**5d.** per sheet
„ 2.	do.	„ 1½ „	**6½d.** „
„ 3.	For Water Cisterns, Pipes, &c. ..	„ 2 „	**8d.** „
„ 4.	For Steam Boilers and Pipes ..	„ 2½ „	**10d.** „
„ 5.	For Large Boilers, &c. ..	„ 3 „	**1/-** „

ANTI-DAMP COURSE FOUNDATION FELT.

In Slabs.

32 × 4½	32 × 9	32 × 13½	32 × 18 inches
1/6	**2/6**	**4/-**	**5/6** per dozen slabs

Mastic Damp-Course in Rolls 33 ft. long.

4½ in. wide.	9 in. wide.	14 in. wide.
1/6	**2/6**	**4/-** per Roll.

Carriage paid on 20 Rolls and upwards.

Patent Hair Fabric, for Covering Steam and other Pipes.

In 8 yd. lengths, 4 in. wide, about 1 in. thick, at **4½d.** per yd. run.

Prices on this page include Delivery within Five Miles of our Wharf; beyond that distance a reasonable charge will be made.

NOTE.—We can quote specially LOW PRICES for any of the Goods shown above for Full Truck Loads delivered Free to any Railway Station.

STRATFORD, Walthamstow and Leytonstone.

YOUNG & MARTEN, Ltd., Merchants and Manufacturers,

GARDEN AND RIDGE TILES, RIDGE ORNAMENTS, AND FINIALS.

QUALITY GUARANTEED.

No. W1510. Pan Tile.

Red.

6/9 per 100
65/- per 1000

No. W1511. Blue Wall Tile.

18 in. long, 6 in. wings .. 4½d. each
18 in. ,, 7 in. ,, .. 5d. ,,

No. W1512. Plain Ridge Tile.

Red or Blue
18 in. long, 6 in. wings .. 4½d. each
35/- per 100

No. W1513. Roll Ridge Tile.

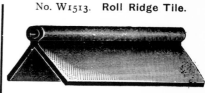

Red or Blue.
18 in. long, 6 in. wings .. .. 6½d. each
18 ,, ,, 5 ,, ,, (Blue only) 6d. ,,
50/- per 100

No. W1571.
Plain Capped Ridge Tile.

Red or Blue.
18 in. long, 6 in. wings .. 5d. each.
40/- per 100.

No. W1572. Grooved Ridge Tiles.

Red or Blue.
18 in. long, 7 in. wings .. 8d. each.
60/- per 100.

Fixed Ornamental Ridge Tiles. 12 in. long, 5 in. top. Red.
No. W1573.

8d. each.

No. W1574.

8d. each.

Red Ridge Tiles.

No. W4261. Half Crest Red
12 in. long, 6½d. each

No. W4262. Ornamental
12 in. long, 9d. each

No. W4263. Ornamental.
12 in. long, 8d. each

Ornament for Fitting into Grooved Ridge.
No. W1575.

No. 13 c. Blue.
18 in. long (i.e., 2 9-in Blocks),
5d. each.

Ornaments for Fitting into Grooved Ridges.

No. W1576.

No. 35 c. Blue.
18 in. long (i.e., 2 9-in. Blocks),
6d. each.

No. W1577.

No. 9 c. Blue.
18 in, long (i.e., 2 9-in Blocks),
5d. each.

No. W1578.

No. 12 c. Blue.
18 in. long (i.e., 2 9-in. Blocks),
5d. each.

Red Finials for Hipped Roofs.
No. W4269

2 ft. 6 in. high
8/6 each

Red Finials for Gable Roofs.

No W4264

1 ft. 6 in. high
4/6 each

No W4265

2 ft. high
5/9 each

No. W4266

2 ft. high
7/6 each

No. W4267

1 ft. 6 in. high
4/9 each

No. W4268

2 ft. high
4/6 each

The tops of Finials Nos. W4267 and W4268 are interchangeable, i.e., No. W4267 fits No. W4268 Finial, and vice versa.

In ordering Finials please state pitch of roof for which they are required—a diagram is given on following page.

NOTE.—We can quote specially LOW PRICES for any of the Goods shown above for Full Truck Loads Delivered Free to any Railway Station.

STRATFORD, Walthamstow and Leytonstone.

YOUNG & MARTEN, Ltd., Merchants and Manufacturers,

Roofing and other Tiles, Ridges, and Wall Coping.

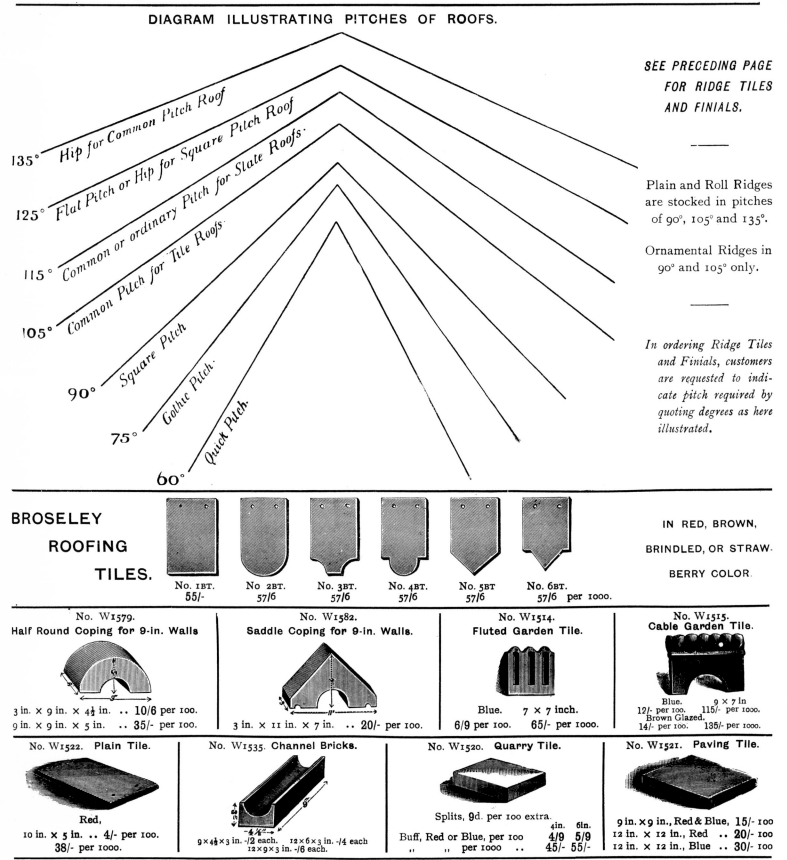

DIAGRAM ILLUSTRATING PITCHES OF ROOFS.

135° Hip for Common Pitch Roof

125° Flat Pitch or Hip for Square Pitch Roof

115° Common or ordinary Pitch for Slate Roofs.

105° Common Pitch for Tile Roofs.

90° Square Pitch

75° Gothic Pitch.

60° Quick Pitch.

SEE PRECEDING PAGE FOR RIDGE TILES AND FINIALS.

Plain and Roll Ridges are stocked in pitches of 90°, 105° and 135°.

Ornamental Ridges in 90° and 105° only.

In ordering Ridge Tiles and Finials, customers are requested to indicate pitch required by quoting degrees as here illustrated.

BROSELEY ROOFING TILES.

IN RED, BROWN, BRINDLED, OR STRAWBERRY COLOR.

| No. 1BT. 55/- | No 2BT. 57/6 | No. 3BT. 57/6 | No. 4BT. 57/6 | No. 5BT. 57/6 | No. 6BT. 57/6 per 1000. |

No. W1579.
Half Round Coping for 9-in. Walls

3 in. × 9 in. × 4½ in. .. 10/6 per 100.
9 in. × 9 in. × 5 in. .. 35/- per 100.

No. W1582.
Saddle Coping for 9-in. Walls.

3 in. × 11 in. × 7 in. .. 20/- per 100.

No. W1514.
Fluted Garden Tile.

Blue. 7 × 7 inch.
6/9 per 100. 65/- per 1000.

No. W1515.
Cable Garden Tile.

Blue. 9 × 7 in
12/- per 100. 115/- per 1000.
Brown Glazed.
14/- per 100. 135/- per 1000.

No. W1522. Plain Tile.

Red,
10 in. × 5 in. .. 4/- per 100.
38/- per 1000.

No. W1535. Channel Bricks.

9×4½×3 in. -/2 each. 12×6×3 in. -/4 each
12×9×3 in. -/6 each.

No. W1520. Quarry Tile.

Splits, 9d. per 100 extra.

	4in.	6in.
Buff, Red or Blue, per 100	4/9	5/9
,, ,, per 1000 ..	45/-	55/-

No. W1521. Paving Tile.

9 in. × 9 in., Red & Blue, 15/- 100
12 in. × 12 in., Red .. 20/- 100
12 in. × 12 in., Blue .. 30/- 100

Prices on this Page include Delivery within Five Miles of our Wharf; beyond that distance a reasonable charge will be made.

NOTE.—We can quote specially LOW PRICES for any of the Goods shown above for Full Truck Loads Delivered Free to any Railway Station.

STRATFORD, Walthamstow and Leytonstone.

INDEX

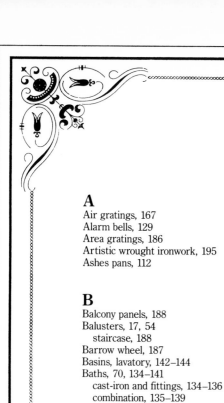

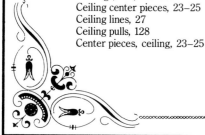

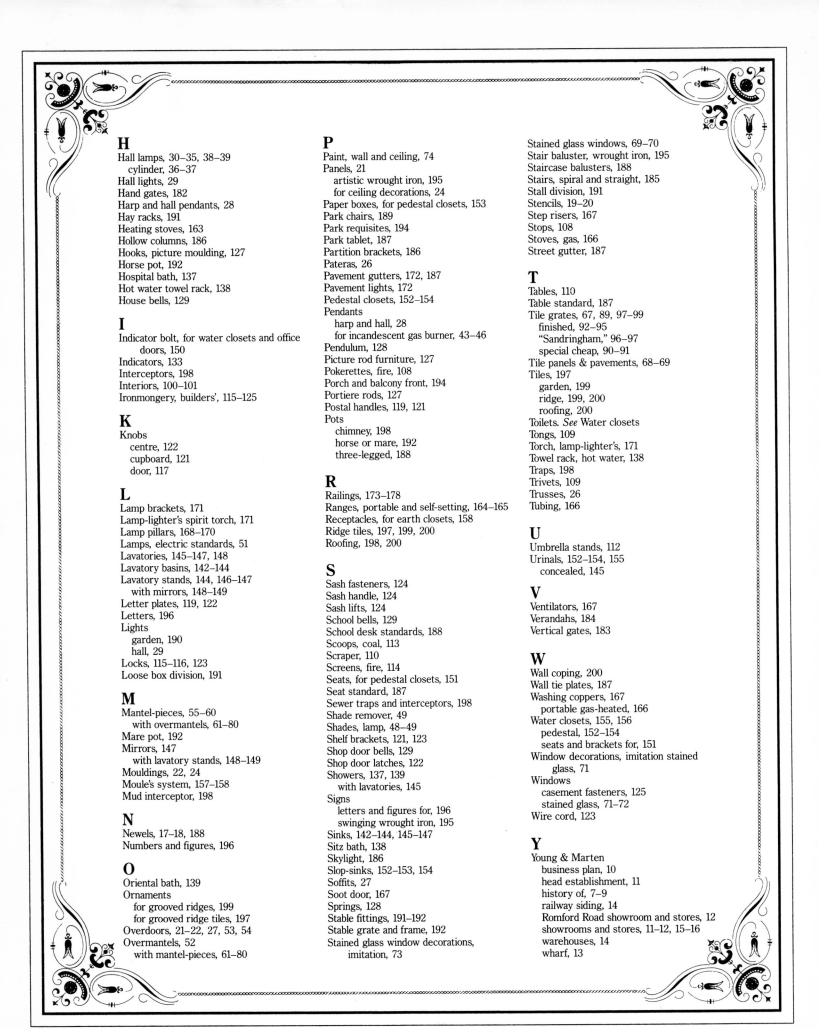